★ ★

TANKER PILOT

LESSONS FROM THE COCKPIT

Mark Hasara

FOREWORD BY
Rush Limbaugh

THRESHOLD EDITIONS
New York   London   Toronto   Sydney   New Delhi

★ ★

Threshold Editions
An Imprint of Simon & Schuster, Inc.
1230 Avenue of the Americas
New York, NY 10020

First Threshold Editions hardcover edition November 2017

THRESHOLD EDITIONS and colophon are
trademarks of Simon & Schuster, Inc.

For information about special discounts for bulk purchases,
please contact Simon & Schuster Special Sales at
1-866-506-1949 or business@simonandschuster.com.

The Simon & Schuster Speakers Bureau can bring authors to your live event. For more information, or to book an event, contact the Simon & Schuster Speakers Bureau at 1-866-248-3049 or visit our website at www.simonspeakers.com.

Interior design by Renato Stanisic

Manufactured in the United States of America

10 9 8 7 6 5 4 3

Library of Congress Cataloging-in-Publication Data is available.

ISBN 978-1-5011-8166-5
ISBN 978-1-5011-8168-9 (ebook)

To the memory of Captain John "Hoss" Kindred,
husband, father, and fighter pilot in the world-famous
Fighting Cocks, killed in a midair collision during a Korean
War Day Large Force Exercise on May 6, 1994

Contents

Foreword

I often speak of "the people who make America work." These people are largely unknown, anonymous except to their family and friends. And that's fine with them. They do not solicit fame. They're not pursuing adulation and adoration. They're happy to be noticed and even proud to be, but they don't ask for it. They're too busy doing what they do. They are not associated with glamor. *Valor* is a better word to describe their behavior. They work, and work hard. Committed to the pursuit of excellence, they do their best to live moral lives and raise their children accordingly. They are in fact often mocked and belittled for their values—not by name, but rather by our popular culture. Who are they? They come from all walks of life. They're all around us, in our towns, cities, and communities. Many of them do jobs most Americans would not do, and they are rarely jobs with public acclaim attached. America would not survive without them—in some cases literally.

It's an honor of mine to know that many people like this comprise my radio audience. I know they're there, and knowing that sustains me each day. I will never come close to meeting them all, but I know they're there, and I tell them so in many ways every day. My appreciation is not passive; I am cognizant of them each day, and these people are why I remain positive and confident about our country's future.

Let me tell you about one of them. His name is Mark Hasara, a retired Air Force lieutenant colonel whose battlefield or tactical call sign is "Sluggo."

In May 2003, a FedEx package arrived at my New York office. The package was forwarded to my home in Florida. One of my security people called me and said, "You are not going to believe what you just received." I asked what it was. "No, just get home and see for yourself," he said. When I opened it, I was in awe of what it contained. I was speechless, just stunned. The box held an American flag, properly folded, in a Ziploc bag, and five certificates signed by the aircrews who flew that flag in Iraqi Freedom's opening shock and awe campaign over Baghdad. I did not know that this was done; I had never heard of it nor thought about it. But it is a long-standing tradition: military service members carry these correctly folded battle flags into battle. After the battle ends, they mail the flags home to their families and loved ones. There was also a handwritten note on yellow legal paper explaining everything from Mark. Sluggo. The battle flag flew on two fighter jets, a Marine Corps electronic jamming plane, and two air refueling tankers, on five flights all over Iraq.

You cannot imagine what an honor this was for me. I just stood there in my kitchen staring at everything. I was overcome with pride and emotion. I could not grasp that these pilots and crew would be thinking of me in this circumstance. This was day one of the invasion of Iraq in 2003! You talk about being humbled. I still am not able to fully express every thought and emotion racing through me at the time. That battle flag is now framed and hanging in my library, with Mark's letter in the center and the certificates around the corner. I treasure this battle flag because it represents American exceptionalism and, more important, the men and women in military service who write a blank check to our country defending the values each of us holds dear.

So, let me tell you a little about Sluggo. We got to know him and his family in the years after all of this. Oh . . . you want to hear something illuminating? Mark was surprised when I eventually tracked him down. You see, that was not why he and his crew did what they did. They expected nothing in return.

Mark didn't fly glamorous fighter jets, high-flying reconnaissance spy planes, or even the mighty B-52 Stratofortress bomber. Sluggo flew the Boeing KC-135 Stratotanker, an airplane he wanted to pilot ever since he was a kid watching 707 jetliners land at Los Angeles International Airport. Mark was an instructor pilot in a plane carrying gobs of gas, 180,000 pounds of jet fuel he transferred to other aircraft in midair. There isn't an aircraft today going into combat against ISIS, moving humanitarian relief supplies to some disaster location, or performing surveillance and reconnaissance that doesn't take on fuel from Air Force refueling tankers.

Mark's book is about this KC-135 and KC-10 air refueling tanker fleet and the men and women who fly and maintain them. Tankers are the only Air Force airplanes involved in every US military activity. The Air Force tanker fleet also enables our allies' and Coalition partners' military aircraft to carry out their assigned missions across the globe.

Sluggo is one of our nation's experts in this area of air operations. He spent half his adult life flying KC-135s, planning refueling missions for multinational exercises, and creating massive air campaign plans for the tanker force supporting fighters, bombers, and reconnaissance aircraft over Afghanistan and Iraq.

While he and his family were having dinner with my wife, Kathryn, and me at the house, Mark told a story of how I helped hunt Osama bin Laden in the Shah-i-Kot Valley of Afghanistan. One of the three pieces of sky used by tankers to refuel other airplanes he named RUSH.

Now Mark has written a book taking us behind the scenes and revealing just how vital these unsung Air Force tanker warriors and heroes are in today's military air activities. The stories breathe life into an unknown corner of military operations, ranging from edge-of-your-seat exciting combat sorties to funny episodes in military command centers to heart-wrenching missions to save people's lives.

The stories in *Tanker Pilot* are more than tales of air refueling: they reveal the life of a man and an American hero, an Air Force officer managing hundreds of millions of pounds of jet fuel so other aircraft can complete their missions. These stories are Mark's personal history as much as the KC-135's history in four wars. This book gives terrific insight into the life and mentality of the men and women who serve in a sixty-year-old Boeing airplane. What makes *Tanker Pilot* so unique is that Mark took his camera with him. You will see pictures of the events he describes and of aircraft loaded with live bombs and missiles, something very rare in a memoir.

So drop your headset into the flight bag, and let's walk out to the jet. You're about to enter the air refueling world few have been fortunate enough to experience, and you're going to do it from a seat in the KC-135 cockpit!

—Rush Limbaugh

Author's Note

Marine Corps Base Camp Pendleton
Oceanside, California

Nobody Kicks Ass Without Tanker Gas . . . Nobody!

Modern military operations are no longer possible without airborne tankers. Quite simply, fuel is a weapon. Aerial refueling lengthens aircraft range, increases payload, and stretches the endurance of modern aircraft. KC-135 Stratotankers and KC-10 Extenders have one unique quality no other US military aircraft possesses: when it's time to kick some adversary's ass or save lives, tankers touch *everything*. Since 9/11, Air Force tankers have transferred twenty billion pounds of fuel. Air Mobility Command refueling tankers connect with a receiver aircraft every four minutes. Yet tanker aircrews remain airpower's forgotten heroes, the anonymous enablers of US foreign and military policy.

Consider a recent event.

Two B-2s, call signs CLIP 11 and 12, left Whiteman Air Force Base east of Kansas City, Missouri, on the night of 18 January 2017 for ISIS targets near Sirte, Libya. The bombers refueled from fifteen tankers during their thirty-plus-hour missions. Averaging 63,600 pounds from each tanker, this single bombing mission required approximately

955,000 pounds, or 146,923 gallons, of jet fuel. Your family can operate for 133 years on that amount of gas.

Tanker Pilot: Lessons from the Cockpit is the story of an exceptionally talented group of men and women I had the honor of working with for over twenty-four years. It's also the story of two amazing Boeing aircraft and decades of hard use. My objective is to give readers a behind-the-scenes look into refueling operations from the Reagan era of the Cold War with Soviet Russia to hunting bin Laden in the Shah-i-Kot Valley of Afghanistan and Saddam Hussein in the Al Mansour district of Baghdad.

Stories are written in air refueling and military language. Explanations are included in the text when feasible, but most terms can easily be found on Google. Errors in the text are strictly mine. I take ownership of all opinions and editorial comments, none of which reflect the views of the Department of Defense or any branch of US military service. A Minolta Maxxum camera and rolls of film accompanied me on almost every flight; pictures shown were taken during events as they happened. *Tanker Pilot* relates flying combat missions to elements of success used on the battlefield, in the company boardroom, or in daily life. Elements included compassion, initiative, vision, courage, culture, leadership, education, opportunity, humor, teamwork, flexibility, and, yes, even failure.

I use only tactical call signs (nicknames) or the first names of people I worked with. Only those senior Air Force leaders whose names have been in the public sphere for many years are called by their full names. Aircraft call signs, flying units, and the names of people I've worked with come from personal journals, notebooks, and logbooks carried with me. I'm greatly indebted to all those who spent time on the phone with me or e-mailed me with manuscript input. All took the time to fine-tune the stories and help dispel my temporary fog of war.

Drinks for PooBah's Party

0115 Thursday 17 January 1991
King Abdulaziz International Airport
Jeddah, Kingdom of Saudi Arabia

True courage is being afraid, and going ahead and doing your job anyhow; that's what courage is.
—GENERAL H. NORMAN SCHWARZKOPF, COMMANDER OF DESERT STORM FORCES

Courage is fear holding on a minute longer.
—GENERAL GEORGE S. PATTON

I have full confidence in your courage and devotion to duty and skill in battle. We will accept nothing less than full victory!
—GENERAL DWIGHT D. EISENHOWER TO TROOPS ON D-DAY, 6 JUNE 1944

On 17 January 2017, Desert Storm vets celebrated the twenty-sixth anniversary of the beginning of air operations over Iraq. Many of you watched Wolf Blitzer announce the opening of Desert Storm's air campaign from the Al Rasheed Hotel on that day in 1991. Earlier that morning, my KC-135 crew had launched from the massive King Abdulaziz International Airport in Jeddah, Saudi Arabia, leading a group of three KC-135s named after a delicious sushi fish. Twelve vermin fighter planes using popular beer call signs met with our three tankers over central Saudi Arabia. Three electronic jamming attack aircraft, named after household tools, joined us as we orbited out of Saddam's radar's prying eyes. This formation of tankers provided critical airborne refueling to the big Baghdad bash named after its creator: PooBah's Party. But expectations for losses on the opening night were high. *Ten percent* of the force may not come home. Maybe higher, like *15 percent*!

Strategic Air Command's 99th Strategic Weapons Wing visited every tanker base across Saudi Arabia in December 1990 with this opening line in their briefing: "Look to your right . . . and now to your left. One of you may not be here at the end of this war."

An odd motivational technique.

Iraq's air defense system would destroy 10 percent of the force, according to SAC and Air Force analysts. That day, 17 January 1991, eighty-seven US Air Force tankers called King Abdulaziz International Airport home. The 1709th Air Refueling Wing (Provisional), the largest tanker wing assembled in Desert Storm, launched 130 tanker missions or sorties over the next twenty-four hours, including twenty-six in the first hour. According to the analysts, thirteen tankers and fifty-two people would not be coming back to Jeddah. Today.

Iraqi radar detected my tanker cell formation penetrating their transparent early warning electron screen halfway through that night's mission. Two weeks earlier, three Iraqi Air Force MiG-29 Fulcrums had landed at Mudaysis Air Base and began air defense alert, one hundred miles north of our assigned refueling track's endpoint. For the first time in history, US Air Force tankers planned on being in harm's way, providing Coalition aircraft with enough gas to reach targets throughout Iraq and Kuwait and return home—except for the unfortunate 10 percent. SAC's refueling aircrews picked up the nickname "Tanker TOADs" in the 1960s during the Cold War era. TOAD has nothing to do with frogs; it's the acronym for Take Off And Die.

No one in the tanker community had trained for combat sorties like that night's. From the start of the Cold War, SAC's focus was nuclear war with Soviet Russia, period. All of our training had centered on launching at a moment's notice and flying to some point over the Atlantic Ocean or Canada to transfer gas into bombers armed with nuclear weapons. No device on the KC-135 tells pilots that enemy aircraft or missiles lurk nearby. Aircrew must rely on the E-3A Airborne Warning and Control System, or AWACS, flying high above the force to give them threat information. One additional problem: no tanker crew had ever practiced defensive maneuvers in the air or on the ground. All 1709th aircrews sat through lengthy briefings I helped create on how to perform defensive maneuvers, but none of us had accomplished the maneuvers in training. If Iraqi Fulcrums leaked through the F-15 Eagles' fighter screen and attacked, the tanker force would perform descending turns toward flat desert terrain on a moonless night for the first time in their careers. After I hit the ground loaded fat with fuel, everyone would see the fireball from Tel Aviv to Tehran.

One thing I wasn't worried about was the aircraft. I stepped off the bus to see KC-135A, tail number 63-8019, sitting in front of my crew. Vonnie, 8019's maintenance crew chief, had the aircraft forms under her right arm, her two assistant crew chiefs standing next to the crew entry ladder.

"Good evening, Captain Hasara. How are y'all doing tonight?" Vonnie asked, handing me the aircraft's 781 maintenance forms.

My copilot Kenny, Kevin the navigator, and Rick, an instructor boom operator, passed our gear up the crew entry chute and went upstairs for preflight inspection. Kenny and I fly the plane, but Kevin runs the mission. During refueling, Rick is the most important person on the crew, flying the refueling boom.

I asked Vonnie one question. "Is this jet ready to go?"

"Captain Hasara, 8019 is ready to go. We've been here for three hours preparing the aircraft for tonight's mission. My crew came out yesterday during the maintenance stand-down and fixed most small maintenance discrepancies. The jet is ready to go to war, sir!"

That was all I needed to hear. 8019 was one of seven KC-135s in the 909th Air Refueling Squadron, the Young Tiger Tanker Squadron, from Okinawa, Japan. A six-foot-tall Indian squaw under the left cockpit window, partially painted over at the request of the Saudi government, and the words *Rolling Thunder* written under her right foot adorned 8019's nose. Every pilot feels great flying his or her first combat sortie in a home-unit jet maintained by the best crew chiefs on the ramp.

Walking around the jet doing the exterior preflight check, Vonnie asked, "Captain Hasara, what are you guys doing tonight?"

Poking my head up inside the forward nose compartment, I inspected the high-pressure air bottle that would cut off the entry door if we had to bail out of the aircraft. "Vonnie," I said, "your jet is going to make Air Force history tonight."

She just beamed. "What's it going to do, sir?"

"Desert Storm's air campaign began this morning when B-52s left US bases for targets in Iraq. Eight will land here later this morning. Tonight, 8019 leads a three-ship cell, call sign TUNA 64. Our two cell mates are them"—I pointed to a plane parked behind us, then to another—"and them.

"It's a party, Vonnie—PooBah's Party, named after the brigadier general who developed it. F-4G Advanced Wild Weasels and EF-111A Spark Vark jamming aircraft approach Baghdad from the south. Navy A-7E Corsairs, F/A-18 Hornets, and EA-6B Prowlers from aircraft carriers USS *John F. Kennedy* and USS *Saratoga* in the Red Sea defend a large Navy strike package closing from the west against surface-to-air missiles, or SAMs, while attacking Al-Taqaddum Air Base. At 0350 Baghdad time, Weasels fire twenty-four high-speed anti-radiation missiles, or HARMs, at Baghdad's air defense radar stations. Tonight, the Weasel mission commander named all his flights after beers: COORS, LONESTAR, and MICHELOB. We're refueling COORS."

Standing under the refueling boom attached under the jet's tail, I illuminated the nozzle with my flashlight and inspected it. Two black wings called ruddervators move the refueling boom up and down and side to side while airborne. Inside the boom, a rigid telescoping pipe extends toward the receiver's refueling receptacle. A ball-jointed nozzle at the end of the pipe mates to the receiver's receptacle. Toggles in the receiver's receptacles lock us together after contact, and a valve opens for fuel to flow from plane to plane. Continuing my walkaround inspection of the aircraft, I asked, "Is the nozzle greased, Vonnie?"

"Yes, sir, we greased it again tonight."

The Weasel's receptacle pops up in the middle of the aircraft's spine and is very small. Extra grease is a technique learned over the past thirty years for better nozzle and receptacle mating. I moved to inspect the left wheel well and said, "Three other receivers are EF-111A jammers coming out of Taif, south of us. Their jamming equipment fills radar screens with snow at the flip of a switch. Their call signs are DRILL 71, 72, and 73. DRILL 71 is our fifth receiver. Each tanker will transfer eighty-five thousand pounds tonight. We'll land around five in the morning."

Standing halfway up the crew ladder, Vonnie handed me each red landing gear down lock, which I passed up to Rick above me. Fifteen minutes later the preflight checklist was finished. Big windows surrounded me, but it was too dark for photos at 0130 in the morning, so my Minolta camera stayed in a helmet bag hanging behind my seat. Waiting for engine start, I had some time to discuss our mission with Kenny and Kevin. Three days earlier my crew was chosen to lead this particular mission, giving fuel to the first Wild Weasel package penetrating Baghdad's missile engagement zone, or MEZ. If our receivers didn't get their gas, Baghdad's MEZ would remain alive, and people would die. I was confident but nervous.

Aircraft moved on Jeddah's ramp according to an exhaustive timing sheet found inside our red mission binders. Twenty aircraft launched over the next fifteen minutes with no radio communications, a "comm-out launch." Intelligence analysts told us Iraqis were in Jeddah listening to airport radio calls. Scribbled neatly in boxes on my lineup card, an eight-and-a-half-by-eleven sheet of paper folded in half and strapped to my left thigh, was all mission-essential information, like call signs, secure communications frequencies, code words, and modes and codes for radar identification. On the back, a map depicted all key navigation points, compass headings, mission timing, and fuel off-loads. I marked three important points in Iraq on the lineup card, called bull's-eyes: H-2 Air Base in western Iraq, called "Manny"; "Ike," an island in Lake Tharthar, west of Baghdad; and "Jack," Jalibah Southwest Airfield in eastern Iraq. Threat calls from our AWACS radar controller, call sign CHOCTAW, used those three geographical reference points to broadcast enemy aircraft movements by compass bearing, range from the point, and altitude.

"Pilot, Nav, it's time for engine start." Holding down the intercom switch under my right forefinger, I asked Vonnie if she was ready.

"Sir, chocks are in, fire bottle and fire guards are posted. . . . You are clear fore and aft on all four engines."

Eight minutes later, all four engines were running smoothly at idle. We waited for our assigned taxi time, gulping fuel. Starting engines, taxi to the runway, and takeoff to flap-retraction altitude of five hundred feet consumed twenty-five hundred pounds of fuel. I opened my cockpit window for some fresh air while we waited. Looking down at Vonnie, I patted *Rolling Thunder*'s Indian squaw on the head and gave her a thumbs-up sign.

"Pilot, Nav, it's taxi time."

"Crew, taxi check."

Reaching up to the instrument panel, Kenny flashed the landing lights, signaling to Vonnie that it was time. Across the ramp in front of us, Vonnie looked both ways and then held two lighted wands straight up over her head, waving them forward and backward. Pushing the throttles up to get us moving, I tapped the brakes. *Rolling Thunder* moved forward a few inches as the nose dipped slightly with brake pressure and continued rolling. As we turned left out of parking, Vonnie snapped to attention and rendered a perfect salute. Maintenance crew salutes are a long military tradition. They mean "Don't you guys be part of that 10 percent, and bring my jet back!" Talk to any crew chief whose plane did not return and see how critical their last salute was. Crew chiefs die inside when their jets don't return, hoping and praying it wasn't a preventive maintenance problem that brought the plane down. Kenny and I both raised our right hands and returned her salute in a military bond with Vonnie's excellent maintenance crew.

As I looked south down the ramp, I saw that TUNA 65's and 66's positions were in exact unison with mine, moving toward the main taxiway out ramp 6. Their bright top-and-bottom anticollision beacons splashed red light off the concrete and across their glossy light-gray undersides. The supervisor of flying gave me a thumbs-up after inspecting my aircraft as it taxied by his truck, meaning we were ready for takeoff with no leaks or problems he could see . . . at 1:10 a.m. on a moonless night. Chuck, another 909th Young Tiger Tanker pilot, and his crew were two hundred feet ahead of us, the very first 1709th tanker taking off that night. We stopped behind Chuck short of runway 34 right, two spare aircraft beside us on a large concrete ramp. Spare KC-135s are insurance policies. If a primary tanker breaks, a spare fills in immediately. The red anticollision lights on both spare aircraft flashed bright and steady, their engines running.

All this activity, and no one said a word on the radio.

East of Saudi Arabia in the island country of Bahrain, floodlights shone down on gray fighters in tall corrugated-metal revetments. Two dark-gray letters decorated each aircraft tail. Everyone in the Middle East respected the "WW" tail code: it meant Wild Weasel. Weasels are an air campaign no-go item, like an armed pass into another country. If the Weasels cannot get their gas to accomplish their mission in Iraq, the air campaign stops. Weasels kill surface-to-air missiles, or SAMs, and site tracking radar installations. Without Weasels, no Coalition aircraft can enter Iraq. A tall Texan, call sign John Boy, and his electronic warfare officer, or EWO, call sign Bud, stepped off their bus, bags in both hands. John Boy's commander told him he would be interviewed by the media. He just didn't expect it here, before the mission. CNN was waiting for them, anxious to know if that night was *the* night, a big scoop for ratings if they found out first. At this point, an aircrew mentally rehearses flight-critical items and wants to be alone. Anything not mission-related is like a mosquito you can't swat. On the first night of a big air campaign, CNN's correspondent asked a very irrelevant question: "Colonel, are you a religious man?"

The question deserved a good answer. CNN's camera recorded the bright-yellow patch on John Boy's helmet bag as he walked past the correspondent: it featured a black Spartan helmet laid over a vertical black sword. Two words—*Wild Weasel*—were written across the patch's top banner. A smaller silver shield on John Boy's helmet bag read "Graduate" across the top, above a red bullet hitting dead center on a yellow target. It meant the bearer of that patch was an expert at killing SAM sites. A somewhat curt answer was his perfect Weapons-School-Graduate answer to such an inquiry: "I am tonight, lady!" Airmen, soldiers, and sailors have mistrusted the media since the Vietnam War. Truth sometimes is sacrificed for the big news scoop and better ratings.

Your high school science teacher lied to you—water does burn. KC-135A Pratt & Whitney model J57 engines produce thirteen thousand pounds of thrust by injecting water into inlets and combustion chambers. Six hundred and seventy gallons of demineralized water burns in about 125 seconds during a "wet thrust" takeoff. Aircrews can tell water injection is working by the quick swings of the engine pressure ratio gauge needle and a very noticeable increase in noise and airframe vibration. Wet thrust takeoffs and 1950s-era jet engines are the reasons KC-135As are called "Water Wagons." Water Wagons are too heavy for takeoff without water, too heavy for takeoff with 165,000 pounds of fuel. If our aircraft does not get water injection, my crew stays home, becoming the new Spare Crew watching everyone else go to war. No one wants to stay home. The US Air Force fought a 1990s war with 1950s engine technology, my aircraft paid for by the Dwight D. Eisenhower administration.

Chuck's KC-135 rolled onto the runway. Two long puffs of steam from bleed valves under the cowlings indicated water injection was in operation on all engines. With the release of the brakes, Chuck's jet began rolling slowly forward. We watched as Chuck accelerated down the runway, taking off and climbing eastward. Jeddah's war started at 0112 Thursday 17 January Baghdad time.

Kevin turned in his chair. "Pilot, three minutes to takeoff."

Kenny called the before-takeoff checklist while I taxied onto runway 34 right and stopped. Holding the brakes, Kenny and I guided the throttles up to the takeoff thrust setting. Needles swung on all four Engine Pressure Ratio (EPR) gauges, which indicate thrust, and *Rolling Thunder* began shaking, water on all four engines. I released the brakes, and the jet started rolling forward, speed building slowly, the 272,000-pound aircraft pushed by only fifty-two thousand pounds of thrust. It was dead nuts at 0115 in the morning, 17 January 1991.

I pulled the yoke back 1,500 feet from the runway's end, and *Rolling Thunder* was airborne. The runway-end-identifier lights passed under us, and the radio altimeter indicated climbing through 135 feet. Kenny raised the gear handle and held it till the light went out: all three wheels up and locked. *Rolling Thunder* accelerated to flaps-up speed once it had leveled off at 525 feet, roaring right over our Lockheed Compound apartment.

As we banked right and climbed again, Kenny turned in his seat to see if TUNA 65 and 66 were airborne. TUNA 65 was level and accelerating to flaps-up speed as TUNA 66 lifted off the runway, silhouetted against hundreds of bright airfield lights. All heavy wet launches are dangerous, but one of the most exhilarating experiences of tanker life.

Clearing the PEACH and NIGHTHAWK F-117 stealth fighter refueling tracks above us, TUNA 64 climbed to altitude, turning off nonessential equipment that emitted radio waves the Iraqis could use to pinpoint our location. Reaching over his head, Kenny tuned the comm 2 radio to Cherry 4, UHF frequency 360.7, the channel used by the airborne battle manager controlling tankers in our E-3A AWACS aircraft, CHOCTAW. Kevin radioed in, "CHOCTAW, TUNA 64 flight of three tankers, mission number 5764, checking in, climbing to two one zero block two three zero, authenticate Whiskey Golf. Any updates for TUNA?"

"TUNA 64 flight, CHOCTAW authenticates November Echo. Picture clear to the north; continue as fragged" (meaning proceed as previously planned).

"Roger, CHOCTAW, TUNA 64 flight continuing as fragged. Pilot, Nav—no mission updates; continue as fragged."

"Roger. Nav, how's our timing?"

"Pilot, we're right on time. Did you hear picture clear north?"

"Yeah; you'd think they would know we're coming."

Rick, our refueling boom operator, said from the back, "Pilot, Boom checks good. Coming forward with oxygen."

"Roger, Boom."

Entering the cockpit, Rick took the red cushion out of his chair, walked back toward the galley, and laid it on the floor. With the pillow under his head, Rick stretched out, folded his arms over his chest, and closed his eyes. He did this on every flight until it was time to refuel.

Tankers use two types of refueling patterns: a left-hand oval (like a NASCAR circuit) called an anchor, or a straight-line track. The LIME PRE refueling track was an imaginary airspace tunnel five miles wide and four thousand feet thick. Located over central Saudi Arabia's An Nafud desert, LIME PRE pointed directly north at Baghdad, ending thirty miles south of Iraq's border. It was easy for the F-4G Wild Weasels to join with the formation: they simply locked our tankers up on their air-to-air radar and flew to us, a "fighter turn on." Our KC-135s used air-to-air range and timing over a geographical point called the aerial refueling control point, or ARCP, to bring us together.

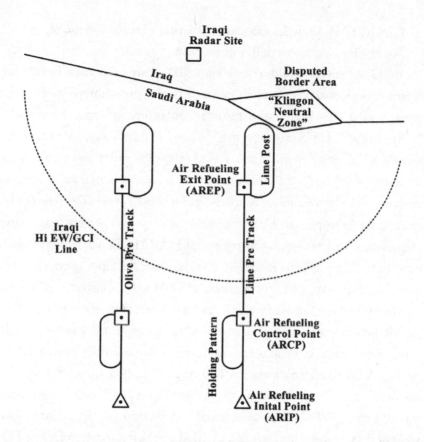

As we turned north at LIME PRE's entry point, the instrument panel clock read 0215 local. Task Force Normandy, a combined Army and Air Force helicopter strike team, would attack two Iraqi early warning radar sites in thirty-eight minutes. Desert Storm would officially begin in forty-five minutes, when F-117s dropped laser-guided bombs on three air operations centers and Baghdad's telephone exchange, nicknamed the "AT&T Building." While we orbited at the ARCP, Kenny called for the preparation for contact checklist. I could feel the boom come down and move, causing the aircraft's nose to swing from side to side with its movements.

"Pilot, Nav, there's an aircraft train coming from the east, probably our receivers. Looks about twenty miles out."

CHOCTAW again broadcasted, "Picture clear to the north."

No enemy aircraft were flying over Iraq . . . yet.

F-4G Advanced Wild Weasels are like your car's fuzz buster but on massive steroids. A Weasel's job is critically important but often the most hazardous: destroy the radar installations guiding the missiles being shot at them. Sensors all over Weasel's airframe pick up the radar signals SAMs use for guidance. EWOs monitor radar signals on large displays, sifting through electrons. Each electronic signal has a distinct beep, squeak, or tone identifying the radar mode. If EWOs hear rattle-snakes, for example, SAMs are coming after you. Weasels have faster missiles than SAMs—two fourteen-foot HARMs. When a radar instal-lation emits a signal, the HARM seeks the antenna, ripping apart metal, control equipment, and anyone near the SAM with tungsten steel cubes.

Kenny saw the Weasels' lights in the distance. "Here they come, crew!"

Two Weasels joined on the left wing outside my window. Light shone on the big WW and tail numbers 288 and 265 out my window. Rick called one approaching the boom, and the blue contact light illu-minated on the instrument panel. Kenny flipped two refueling pumps on, and the off-load totalizer showed gas leaving our fuel tanks. Two rows of lights on the tanker's belly, called pilot director indicator or PDI lights, illuminated on contact with receivers, the left row telling the re-ceiver pilot to move up or down, the right to move backward or forward. Bright neon stripes painted on the boom telescoping pipe indicate the same. When the pipe's bright yellow ball appears near the boom's ice shield, receivers are at proper extension, or "on the apple."

"Pilot, Boom. He's rock steady in the envelope."

A convoy three miles long and a thousand feet tall composed of eigh-teen aircraft—three tankers and fifteen fighters—moved effortlessly through a moonless night at 317 knots, or 8 miles per minute. DRILL 71's refueling system checked good also, and he moved up on the right wing. Now we waited for the time to push north.

John Boy's fighters calculated mission timing on ground speed, while

SAC's nuclear missions used true airspeed for timing. Slight differences in the two speeds created large timing mismatches during long sorties. John Boy had talked to Kevin two nights ago on a secure phone, passing along his ground-speed timing toward Baghdad: the time to cross the imaginary line of the Iraqi early warning and ground control intercept radar, or EW/GCI, and finally the time to drop them off at the end-point full of gas. John Boy was very specific about his timing. He could not accept ten seconds early or twenty seconds late across the EW/GCI line. His last instructions were that the entire package must arrive at the endpoint full of gas, sixteen thousand pounds or better in their tanks.

"Pilot, Nav, time to push north."

Rolling left at 0257 on the cockpit clock, I heard a voice over the radio just say "Turn."

Kevin gave me a thumbs-up as he recognized John Boy's voice on the radio. Eight minutes later, our formation passed over the high EW/GCI line. TUNA 64's cell appeared on the top of Iraqi radar screens at exactly 03:04:55, five seconds earlier than John Boy had asked.

And all hell broke loose on the radio.

"CHOCTAW has multiple threats north, Manny three three zero for thirty, medium altitude, turning south!"

RC-135 Rivet Joint airframe intelligence sensors and CHOCTAW's big air search radar had picked up enemy fighter activity near H-2 Air Base. My biggest concern was Mudaysis Air Base and the detachment of three MiG-29 Fulcrums launching off alert 125 miles in front of us. The MiG-25 Foxbats launching out of Baghdad's Al Asad Air Base were the next threat priority, with their 1,200-knot speeds, or twenty-three miles a minute.

"CHOCTAW has multiple groups of Fulcrums and Mirage F1s airborne. Fulcrums, Manny one two five for eighty-five, medium altitude, turning south!"

I looked over my right shoulder at Kevin, who moved his plotter across his navigation chart, measuring bearing and distance off the

Manny bull's-eye. Dropping his dividers on the table, he looked up, wide-eyed.

"Pilot! Nav! That's Mudaysis airfield! Those Fulcrums are coming out of Mudaysis!"

"CHOCTAW has multiple groups now—Manny one three zero for ninety-five, medium altitude, heading south!"

"Pilot! Nav! Fulcrums are off our nose inside 120 miles and coming right at us!"

Tankers were bait for Iraqi MiGs that night—just like Jimmie Doolittle used B-17 bombers over Berlin—having switched radio call signs with the F-15C Eagles community two days ago. Orbiting near the border west of us at thirty thousand feet, the F-15 air-to-air mission commander, call sign Kluso, and his four Eagles held next to a big thunderstorm, listening to CHOCTAW's threat calls. Fulcrums and Mirages were attacking the strike force earlier than planned. My crew and I did our job: we kept heading north toward the Fulcrums till John Boy's COORS flight was full, as CHOCTAW continued calling out MiGs. Moments later, Kluso did his job. I heard one of the greatest radio calls of my flying career from underneath Kluso's oxygen mask:

"PENNZOIL Check! Two! Three! Four!"

"CITGO Check! Two! Three! Four!"

"QUAKER Check! Two! Three! Four!"

"ZEREX Check! Two! Three! Four!"

Kluso then instructed his Eagles to "Push Purple One now!"

All the Eagles tuned to a separate AWACS air-to-air fight frequency. The Fulcrums at Mudaysis took off just as Scud-hunting F-15E Strike Eagles, or Dark Grays, passed east of Mudaysis's runway at five hundred feet in altitude. PENNZOIL 63 launched a missile at one Mudaysis Fulcrum on our nose and killed it at 0310. After what seemed like seconds but was actually several minutes, AWACS broadcast, "CHOCTAW, picture clear to the north." All the MiGs were dead. I cannot describe the sense of relief. Kevin raised both arms into the air and shouted, "Hallelujah!"

When we reached LIME PRE's endpoint right on time at 0315, John Boy's Weasels were not full. COORS 34 was still on the boom, taking fuel and knowing that when John Boy's flight was ready, they would just drop down and leave. My crew pushed north toward Baghdad, still pumping gas. Kevin knelt on the jump seat next to Kenny and watched the Weasels, so I didn't know how close we were to Iraq. Minutes later, Rick excitedly said over the interphone, "The last guy just got a pressure disconnect and is moving left!"

I immediately turned and looked over my left shoulder. John Boy waved as he and his wingman dropped below us. Kenny confirmed that his two Weasels and the Spark Vark were dropping down also. We had transferred eighty-two thousand pounds of jet fuel.

Were TUNA 65 and 66 still refueling?

How close were we to Iraqi airspace?

Moments later, the COORS flight appeared in front of us. Their position and green formation lights made them easy to follow as they headed north, silhouetted against an eleven-thousand-foot white cotton cloud deck near Iraq's border. John Boy's Weasels turned their lights off about half a mile in front of us. We were close to Iraq's border if John Boy's Weasels were turning their lights off. Kevin watched the COORS flight move out in front of us. DRILL 71 appeared out from under our nose, passing from right to left; it was much easier to follow, thanks to the Spark Vark's light-gray paint scheme. DRILL 71 disappeared behind John Boy's Weasels when his lights went off as he passed above the overcast. Outside Kenny's window, LONESTAR 41 passed five hundred feet below us, with MICHELOB 51 a quarter of a mile behind and catching up.

Our mission was done.

Kevin motioned with a sweep of his right hand to turn south. I pushed all four throttles up to 340 knots, ten knots below maximum airframe speed. That night was going to be an epic news night.

"Guys, let's get home. This is going to be on CNN!"

Kenny pointed west out his window to the next wave of strike aircraft passing north beside us. Hundreds of rotating, flashing red beacons moved past us.

Hundreds.

★ ★

LESSONS FROM THE COCKPIT: COURAGE

The very first lesson from the cockpit while providing fuel for PooBah's Party is that you never forget your first combat mission. The first time you "see the elephant," as the first combat sortie is called after the fear of the unknown in combat, you're scared, but you somehow find the courage to complete your mission. SAC's day-to-day training did not prepare us for a conventional war, which was no fault of SAC's in the Cold War era. The tanker force went into a major-theater air war unprepared, and if it hadn't been for the five months of buildup prior to the night of 17 January, I think outcomes may have been different. Few of us in Strategic Air Command understood how to operate in a conventional war environment, controlled by AWACS instead of SAC headquarters at Offutt Air Force Base. My crew was lucky to have some experience from flying F-15 and AWACS refueling missions out of Kadena Air Base. It didn't help that the 99th Strategic Weapons Wing briefed us that 10 percent of us were not coming home. If we weren't coming back, it would have been because none of us had performed defensive maneuvers in the airplane. In spite of these obstacles, no aircrew members at Jeddah refused to fly missions, to my knowledge.

The opening night of Desert Storm is an excellent illustration of the courage of the many people flying their first combat sortie and the maintainers launching their aircraft. Every aircrew member knew that MiGs would scramble to intercept us. Maintainers on the ramp knew that Scud missiles could rain down on them at any time. I know a number of people who were very emotional that first night. Many of us faced the fear of possible impending death as we forged ahead to accomplish our assigned tasks. Courage is facing your fears by preparing for events that will take place in your life. It takes courage to operate outside of your comfort zone and to continue functioning in the face of tremendous odds. My takeaway lesson from the morning of 17 January is that my crew displayed the courage to lead three tankers on a very critical mission supporting the Weasels. It took courage to continue well past our refueling endpoint and fly closer to Iraq with CHOCTAW calling bandits airborne and heading south so that John Boy's Weasels had the gas to kill SAMs in downtown Baghdad. Have the courage to face your fears and operate outside your comfort zones, even when the masses tell you the odds are against everything you are doing.

★ ★

2

Klaxon! Klaxon! Klaxon!

1620 Wednesday, 23 September 1987
509th Bomb Wing Nuclear Alert Facility
Pease Air Force Base, Portsmouth, New Hampshire

Confidence comes from discipline and training.
—ROBERT KIYOSAKI, AMERICAN BUSINESSMAN AND AUTHOR

*It's absolutely true that unless you can instill discipline upon yourself,
you will never be able to lead others.*
—ZIG ZIGLAR, AUTHOR AND MOTIVATIONAL SPEAKER

Pease Air Force Base's Durham Street ended with a large, fenced-in concrete apron. Signs stating "Use of deadly force is authorized" hung on the fence every thirty feet. In an underground concrete bunker, the crew lounge looked west through two large picture windows. Nine drive-through shelters covered six FB-111 bombers we called "FBs." Like their F-111 fighter-bomber siblings, the wings could move forward and backward during flight. FBs were designed for one thing: flying low and fast with nukes. FBs carried AGM-69 short-range attack missiles, or SRAMs, giving them the ability to launch nuclear warheads one hundred miles away from Soviet targets. B61 nuclear bombs are easily recognizable by their silver finish and maroon nose cones. Aircrews call

B61s "dial a yields," as they can crank up the power of the nuclear blast from the cockpit. A handful of alert FBs carried only SRAMs. KC-135s and FBs sat side by side in a large area called the Alert Facility. These aircraft of Armageddon go from sitting asleep to airborne in minutes, cold-starting their engines with explosive cartridges that belched thick black smoke as they spun the turbine blades to life.

None of us ever forgets the whooshing sound of a cart start and the smell of gunpowder in the air. Starting the engines is the easy part. Getting airborne concerned us all. Tanker pilots wondered whether the aircraft could get off the ground carrying 173,000 pounds of fuel and 5,561 pounds of water. Taxiing tankers creak and groan at emergency war order (EWO) maximum takeoff weights of nearly 288,500 pounds. If the klaxon went off, twelve heavy aircraft made a left turn, passed through a wide hole in the chain-link security fence called "the Throat," and moved onto the active runway. Two weeks in September 1987 were different, however: four additional bombers and five supporting KC-135s were generated one morning. Each Alert Facility parking space was full, so six aircraft parked in the runway 16 hammerhead, a large concrete parking area at the airfield's north end.

On Friday 18 September, the 509th Bomb Wing command post received a coded message from SAC headquarters implementing runway alert. Six aircrews drove dark-blue Air Force six-pack trucks to their aircraft, started their engines, and taxied out through the Throat to the runway 16 hammerhead. Once positioned in the hammerhead, the aircrews shut down their engines, and the explosive start cartridges were reinstalled. The entire end of runway 16 became a temporary Nuclear Alert Facility, with the same use-of-deadly-force authorization. People behind the perimeter fence looked down at us from Arboretum Drive. What a spectacle: nuclear weapons out in the open.

Each morning maintenance crews made sure all the jets were ready to respond should execution messages for SAC's Single Integrated Operational Plan (SIOP) arrive. Planners briefed us before we went out to the jets on what characters each coded launch message should contain. On Saturday morning, another message from Offutt restricted all alert aircrews inside the facility and all six runway alert sorties to cockpit alert, one crewmember on a headset at all times. My crew took turns listening every three hours for additional messages. Spike, my aircraft commander, Nav Gorney, our navigator, and Tommy, our boom operator, lay on the troop seats in the cargo compartment trying to sleep. I was in the copilot seat, headset over one ear, listening to the command radio. I clipped my grease pencil to the open sliding window's whiteboard. Looking down at TC, the pilot of FB-111 sortie 03 and its two and a half megatons of thermonuclear attitude adjustment, I could see that he was bored too. His raised left hand and extended middle digit signaled his silent protest: "Cockpit alert sucks!" Our terrible experience was caused by one thing: Soviet submarines armed with nuclear missiles on patrol in the Atlantic Ocean.

Soviet Yankee Notch class submarine K-423 left the Kola Peninsula in June armed with SS-N-21 Sampson cruise missiles capable of hitting any target east of the Mississippi River. Two other Soviet Delta III class subs carried sixteen intercontinental ballistic missiles, each armed with three to seven nuclear reentry warheads capable of hitting targets east of the Rockies. Seventy-two nuclear weapons in three subs were aimed at military and commercial targets across America—fifteen- to thirty-minute missile flight times were all that separated survival from frying in a nuclear blast.

At 1609 Sunday afternoon, K-423 opened its cruise missile doors. Fifteen miles southwest of K-423, Trident 924, a Navy P-3 Orion sub hunter, picked up the sound of launch tubes flooding. The Navy's Sound Surveillance System (SOSUS) line stretching across the Atlantic Ocean confirmed Trident 924's worst fears—a Soviet nuclear boomer boat was opening its doors. The USNS *Invincible*'s surveillance towed-array sensor system (SURTASS) also heard the Yankee Notch missile doors open and the tubes flood. Shortly after K-423 opened its doors, Navy surveillance heard the sound of both the Delta III subs' missile hatches begin systematically unlocking and flooding, two at a time. The northeastern United States had just received its fifteen-minute warning: missiles would impact the US in a quarter of an hour.

"For Alert Force! For Alert Force! Klaxon! Klaxon! Klaxon!"

BRIMSTONE, Pease's command post, was still decoding the message but wanted the force to be ready for takeoff. Spike jumped into his seat and called for the starting-engines and before-taxi checklists. Nav Gorney sat behind me, waiting for the entire emergency action message from BRIMSTONE. I wrote the message on my sliding window as Spike buckled his seat belts. My finger flicked a tab open to the start-engines checklist page.

"Battery-power switch emergency."

Spike replied, "Battery power switch is emergency!"

I continued, "Parking brakes set!"

"Brakes are set, Pilot!"

"Reserve brake pressure check!"

"On . . . Set . . . pressure checked, Pilot!"

"Check with ground, ready to start engines!"

"Ground, Pilot—clear me fore and aft on all four engines."

Hurry . . . we had to hurry. Nuclear weapons would impact in the next fifteen minutes. It takes a third of that time to start engines and take off. Sergeant Baldock, our airplane crew chief, stood in front of us, a long black cable attaching him to the jet. The six crew chiefs stood in front of their six aircraft, waiting to see smoke.

"Chocks are in; fireguard is posted. You are cleared fore and aft on all four engines!"

"Start engines, Copilot."

"Starting engines, Pilot!"

Spike pushed all four starter switches down into ground start. He then pulled out the start selector switch and pushed it down to cart start, and all of us immediately heard the loud whooshing sound of four explosive cartridges igniting like matches to a big gas can.

"Ground, Pilot—good carts on all four!"

Leaning out my window, I saw black smoke pour out from underneath the two right engines as the cartridges cooked off. I glanced at TC, whose head was down as he watched his engines spool up. Black smoke near the FB's main wheels drifted behind the aircraft in the wind. I momentarily fixated on the maroon nose cone of the B61 bomb under TC's left wing. Nuclear war was not supposed to happen. We weren't meant to do this. What had just happened, and how long did we have before Soviet nukes killed us all? A big cloud of black smoke rolled across the south end of the airfield as the aircraft in the Alert Facility fired their carts. Our starter cartridge smoke cloud passed over the people watching from the fence line on Arboretum Drive. Did they know what was happening?

Whatever was happening would be epic.

Within seconds, the RPM gauges climbed past 12 percent. Spike and I grabbed two throttles out of cutoff and put them in start. Exhaust gas temperature rose on all four engines, and as they passed 30 percent RPM, all four throttles went over the stops into idle. All engines stabilized between 58 and 60 percent RPM.

"Engines started, Copilot!"

"Engines started, Pilot!"

"Pilot, Ground—chocks are pulled. Aircraft is in taxi configuration except for the door. You're cleared to taxi!"

"Come on up, chief . . ."

BRIMSTONE rebroadcast the message. The checklist said to go to the end of the runway and hold. Nav Gorney authenticated the message, flipping plastic pages back and forth in the red EWO binder. Sergeant Baldock ran toward the airplane, taking up the ground cord and disappearing under the nose. I heard him coming up the ladder a few seconds later. Sortie one stopped to the right of the high-speed taxi line. Sortie two stopped behind sortie one's left side. TC stayed put; the hold line was full. Finishing the starting-engines checklist, I reached up, grabbed the alarm bell switch, and pulled it momentarily to the right. After a long buzzer sounded, I said over the interphone, "Taxi report."

"Boom ready to taxi!"

"Nav ready to taxi!"

"Door warning light is out; CO's ready to taxi! Starting-engines-before-taxi check complete!"

All five of us sat strapped in our seats, not saying a word. We were stunned that the Soviets would even think of nuking the US. Russian satellites could see the nuclear-armed aircraft at the runway's end, ready for takeoff in minutes. What were they thinking? The remaining alert force aircraft rolled down the main taxiway from the south side of the airfield: nine nuclear-armed FBs and eight KC-135s. BRIMSTONE called: "BRIMSTONE with a poll of the alert force. Sortie one?"

"Sortie one is checklist complete."

"Sortie two?"

"Sortie two is complete."

They continued through all twelve bombers. "Complete" meant that every aircraft and EWO checklist item for taking off to nuclear war was done. BRIMSTONE asked the same of the tanker sorties: "Polling the tanker sorties. Sortie one zero one?"

"Sortie one zero one is complete."

"Sortie one zero two?"

"Sortie one zero two is complete."

All tanker sorties were checklist complete, engines running at the end of runway 16, ready for takeoff.

I put my finger on the before-takeoff checklist while sitting in the hammerhead. Spike quickly briefed us on the takeoff procedures during the radio silence, making sure both of us understood what he and I would do if the Armageddon scenario continued. When Spike finished his brief, the cockpit was dead silent except for the sound of the running engines. None of us could talk. All of us were thinking the same thing: Did the Soviets launch an attack? What was going to happen to our families? Were they being told what was going on so they could survive? The next action message would confirm what was happening to all of us.

"For Alert Force, For Alert Force—Message follows . . ."

Nav Gorney had memorized the launch message preambles during our morning preflight and told us what the characters were. Spike turned around in his seat to see him writing with a black grease pencil on another plastic-covered page in the red mission binder. Nav Gorney thumbed through the pages and looked up at us, his eyes wide. He read the first line of the message. He still needed to validate it, but he said, "It's a launch message. . . . It says take off, Spike!"

Sortie one pulled forward onto runway 16, sorties two and three moving up behind him in an accordion motion. Sortie one's engine exhaust nozzles opened, going into full afterburner. Two long orange tongues of flame spewed twenty feet from the open nozzles. Sortie two rolled across the high-speed taxi line, with sortie three seconds behind. I remained fixated on TC's B61 bomb. I called out the before-takeoff check, and Spike hacked the small clock on the instrument panel. The procedure was that tankers launched seconds behind the FBs in minimum interval takeoffs, or MITOs—twelve-second spacing between each jet for survival: launch the most aircraft with the least amount of spacing between them in the shortest amount of time. We were launching five tankers in the same time that two commercial airliners take off, three airplanes on the runway at once. Reaching down near my left knee, I moved the water injection switch up, and two water pumps whined under the jet's belly. We crossed the hold line seconds behind sortie three. When we passed 70 percent RPM, the sound and vibration of the aircraft changed, signaling that all four engines were receiving water injection. A reading of 2.8 EPR on the RPM gauges confirmed what we all heard—water on all four. We wouldn't be able to take off if it wasn't. The jet would struggle to accelerate under this heavy weight on a runway sloping downhill.

At 181 knots, I called "Rotate!" over the interphone. Spike pulled the yoke back, the nose rose up, and the airplane left the ground. Lots of turbulence caused by the three FBs in front of us, still in burner, made for a bumpy ride. After two positive climbing indications the gear came up, and Spike leveled off at 520 feet above the ground, indicating 193 knots but accelerating. Nav Gorney called 110 seconds of water. Flap gauges showed all up just eleven seconds before water injection ran out.

People on Rye Beach heard the deafening sound of approaching airplanes. Fighter-bombers in afterburner passed overhead low, loud, and fast. Heads looked up as sortie one appeared from behind the trees lining the beach. The first FB was followed very closely by another . . . and another . . . and then a tanker, all very close together. People noticed the large external fuel tanks toed inward under each FB's wing. One aircraft carried skinny silver shapes, another long white ones. Many New Hampshirites had seen FBs and tankers taking off and landing at Pease before, but few New Englanders had seen these shapes. Car alarms began screaming from the parking lot. Several people were running from the beach toward the parking lot, hollering at people up and down the seashore. A father heard one young man screaming, "GET OFF THE BEACH! GET OFF THE BEACH!" and saw him pointing toward the parking lot.

A second tanker passed over Rye Beach low and loud. The third tanker appeared above the trees very close behind. What did this young man know that everyone else didn't? Why were these three young men running toward the parking lot, screaming for people to get off the beach? Drivers on I-95 were startled by the sight of low-flying planes and the sounds of jets flying so close together. Phone lines to the base operator lit up. People wanted to complain that their Sunday naps were being rudely interrupted by jet noise, not realizing it was the sound of their imminent deaths.

Spike rolled into a left turn, following the bombers on our assigned fan heading. I could see Star Island passing beneath us through Spike's window. Spike leaned back, his right hand pushing against the instrument panel glareshield for some leverage, to see who was following us. Sortie one zero two was 1,500 feet behind us in a turn. Sortie one zero three was 1,300 feet behind one zero two, just beginning its turn. The rest of the bombers were flying or rolling down the runway. Spike and I donned helmets and attached PLZT goggles to protect our eyes from any nuclear blast. PLZT goggles turn black within nanoseconds of a nuclear flash. I grabbed formfitting aluminized cockpit window curtains for additional protection. The world was now officially shut out of our cockpit.

The Pease Air Force Base nuclear attack stream continued climbing to the east. Radar returns on the scope next to my left knee displayed aircraft strung out in front of us abeam Kennebunkport, Maine. Vice President Bush and his family hopefully were moving away from Walker's Point. The Russians had to know that the Northeast Alert Force had launched and was heading toward them. The launch message directed all aircraft to fly to a holding point. Our instructions were to stay at least twenty miles away from SAC bases and large populated areas—in other words, targets. At the ten-minute mark after the klaxon, none of us had seen a bright flash or felt turbulence from any nuclear blasts.

Nav Gorney began running the grid checklist as we passed St. John's, Newfoundland. Grid navigation was used to fly across the higher latitudes in the era before global positioning satellites. Due to the unreliability of magnetic compasses above 60 degrees north latitude and the quick convergence of longitude lines, a false north is determined in order to fly in a straight line. Grid navigation reorients the aircraft's heading to this false North Pole by creating a more square latitude and longitude layout, similar to that near the equator. Once in grid, the gyrocompass was put in a free-running mode to maintain the new heading reference. Message traffic continued to broadcast from several agencies with names like Abalone, Gentry, and Sky King. None of the decoded messages applied to us.

My crew's mated FB-111, now called CUTLASS 01, contacted us on the air refueling primary frequency two hours out of the control point. The two navigators talked through mission specifics—mainly updating the time of the crossing of the rendezvous initial point, or RZIP. At the RZIP, each aircraft would descend to twenty-one thousand feet, the FB refueling altitude. Twenty-one thousand feet is smack-dab in the heart of any Russian surface ship's missile or gun envelope. The stream was too far away from the European coast to worry about Russian fighters. Things stayed busy in the cockpit as we flew northeast. It helped keep our minds off the pending war and our families.

CUTLASS 01 required sixty-five thousand pounds of fuel, with seventy-two thousand pounds available in our tanks on contact. If more fuel was needed, the bombers would say a code word and a number. That code word meant to transfer all the tanker fuel down to empty fuel system pipes. That one code word was a death sentence for tankers. FBs did not hold enough in their tanks to need to use the code word, so I did not expect to hear it. That wasn't true for KC-135s mated to B-52s, however; Stratofortresses held over three hundred thousand pounds of gas and could drain two tankers easily, burning fuel at twenty-two thousand pounds per hour. Remember, I flew the TOAD aircraft: Take Off and Die!

All of us were talking over the interphone about the rapid launch out of Pease and what Russia must have been thinking when Nav Gorney keyed his mic and told us all to shut up. After scribbling another coded message on the plastic front page, he flipped backward through the red binder. Navigators flipping deeper into the pages is a good thing; it meant the situation was changing.

"This is RAILCAR . . . I say again . . ."

Who was RAILCAR? Running his right hand down the checklist page, Nav Gorney marked off each item. His facial expressions were intense but showed some relief.

"Oh, dudes!"

Nav Gorney continued running through the pages, occasionally flipping back to the message characters on the front leaf. Spike pressed him about what was going on.

"They're talking. . . . Russia did not like seeing the Northeast Force launch. . . . Hang on."

CUTLASS 01 radioed us on refueling primary frequency. They had relevant information. "Pilot, Nav—go to the hold point and wait with your mated bomber. Do not go beyond the hold point. It is now a wait-and-see game. The talking heads in DC and Moscow are discussing the situation."

"Trend one zero one, CUTLASS 01. Do you have the latest message traffic?"

Nav Gorney answered, "CUTLASS 01, roger. Trend no changes to timing."

Both aircraft arrived at the hold point and waited for one of two outcomes. The first was that we would all go home; Moscow had observed this large nuclear attack force coming, and everyone backed down. Option two—the very scary version—was that discussions would break down. All Trend tankers would off-load fuel, and CUTLASS 01 and friends would continue east to their targets.

Spike wanted to take a look outside, so we removed the thermal radiation curtains. The North Atlantic below us had high whitecaps and low, broken clouds at about five thousand feet. Orbiting at the hold point, I pumped 46,700 pounds of fuel into CUTLASS 01. And we waited for instructions.

Twenty-five minutes passed before RAILCAR sent another message recalling the force back to Pease. CUTLASS 01 needed fifteen thousand pounds to make it back to home plate, leaving us with extra gas for the three-hour return trip. During the flight home, we all discussed how launching had felt. All of us were sick—sick that the Russians would even think of attacking. But none of us could describe our emotions on seeing Pease Air Force Base laid in out front of us. Everything looked as though we were coming back from a typical training mission. Nav Gorney called BRIMSTONE to pass on our maintenance code: code one, with no discrepancies. Spike landed with an instrument landing system (ILS) approach and moved uphill on the parallel taxiway back toward the runway 16 hammerhead. Several staff cars followed us in the dark. I felt it was odd that they were waving at us while we taxied. The Northeast was still in runway alert. The Security Police tech sergeant flashed two fingers at us as we rolled up to the hammerhead entry point. Spike held up two fingers, and the Security Police cleared us to enter the hammerhead alert area. Everyone in our cockpit was pissed that the Russians would do such a thing, but we were all glad to be home.

THE EVENTS DESCRIBED above became a scenario used during Wednesday Alert Changeover training in late autumn of 1987. It did not happen quite like that on that Sunday afternoon. The alert force did not launch, but planes parked at the end of the runway. A Russian Yankee Notch submarine had, in fact, crossed the fifteen-minute warning line, meaning nuclear warheads could impact Pease within fifteen minutes. The Soviet captain was smart enough not to open his doors, however. All four bases in the Northeast United States—Pease, Plattsburgh, Loring, and Griffiss—received runway alert implementation, and six Pease jets, three FBs and three KC-135s, left Alert Facility parking for runway 16's big concrete parking area in the hammerhead. All six jets stayed in runway alert for two weeks. On the last day of September, the Yankee Notch turned south and went back across the fifteen-minute line toward Bermuda. Shortly after crossing the line, SAC sent another message removing the Northeast Alert Force from cockpit alert. All aircraft taxied back into their alert cages and resumed a normal alert posture—if being in a cage with nuclear-armed aircraft is normal.

Strategic Air Command accomplished everything by a checklist, either flying the airplanes or performing nuclear missions. We trained relentlessly on checklist procedures and discipline. SAC leadership wanted to make sure that when it came time to launch and execute a nuclear mission, all of us would follow the checklist procedures cold, with few variations. During operational readiness inspections, we were tested on all EWO procedures, particularly command and control of decoded messages.

★ ★

LESSONS FROM THE COCKPIT: DISCIPLINE

The lesson I learned from flying in Strategic Air Command was checklist discipline, habitually following every step. When nuclear weapons were inbound, we acted—not reacted—because of the discipline to the procedures in our checklists. Any small break in the checklist discipline chain could have catastrophic results. Many aircraft accidents are a result of poor checklist discipline or a break in flying habits, like forgetting to put the gear down—an obvious checklist item. Having the discipline to create patterns in our lives has been a theme used by many motivational speakers. Disciplining ourselves through creating

habits leads to healthier and happier lives, increased productivity, and greater effectiveness in our work. I recently read a
terrific article on the fifty things wealthy people do habitually.
They had disciplined themselves by creating habit patterns and
doing certain things in their lives that made them successful.
Discipline your life by building habit patterns just like those we
exercised in the airplane to create a more prosperous environment for you and your family.

★ ★

3

European Liaison Force (ELF) One

0900 Friday 24 July 1987
Riyadh Air Base
Riyadh, Kingdom of Saudi Arabia

Preservation of one's own culture does not require contempt or disrespect for other cultures.

—Cesar Chavez, American labor leader and civil rights activist

We still have the most creative, diverse, innovative culture and open society—in a world where the ability to imagine and generate new ideas with speed and to implement them through global collaboration is the most important competitive advantage.

—Thomas Friedman, American journalist and Pulitzer Prize winner

Saudi Arabia and the Gulf Coast countries were terrified that the Iran-Iraq conflict in the 1980s would spill over into other countries. The Saudi government was the first to ask for American help, and in the last week of September 1981, two hundred 552nd Airborne Early Warning and Control Wing folks left Tinker Air Force Base near Oklahoma City for Saudi Arabia. Four E-3A Sentry AWACS aircraft departed on 1 October for a military airfield in downtown Riyadh. Few of us called the Sentry by its name; most called it "the Wacker." The US force became known as European Liaison Force One (ELF One), because US Air Forces Europe ran the program until US Central Command's establishment in 1983. Objectives for AWACS missions focused on expanding Saudi radar coverage of their eastern coast. The AWACS radar footprint gave the Saudis and ELF One plenty of warning for air attacks, or so it was hoped. The Wacker's APY-1 radar has over two-hundred-mile coverage, detecting air and surface targets, like ships. Each day two AWACS flew fourteen-hour sorties near the Saudi-Kuwaiti border, providing electronic detection over Iraq's Al Faw Peninsula and the Northern Arabian Gulf, or NAG. E-3A Sentries are powered by older Pratt & Whitney TF33 turbofan engines, which required refueling every five hours. ELF One refueling support came from European Tanker Task Force KC-135s rotated in and out of Riyadh Air Base every forty-five days.

AWACS support scheduled a primary KC-135 and manned spare for each mission. Sorties were not very long—about two and a half hours in duration, transferring sixty thousand pounds with each hookup. During summer months, heavy KC-135A models rotated between 1,500 and 2,000 feet from the end of the runway because of the blistering 107-degree heat. I wondered how many car alarms went off after our 2:00 a.m. takeoffs. Tanker crew chiefs supercooled the cockpits with hoses suspended in crew entry chutes running from an air-conditioning cart. Daytime temperatures in the cockpit rose to 130 degrees during the forty minutes from preflight and starting engines to takeoff. Each night I put two one-liter water bottles spiked with Gatorade lemon-lime powder in the freezer, one for each calf pocket of my flight suit. By the time we were airborne, our internal body temperatures were so hot that we felt the Gatorade go all the way down.

Shortly after 1000 in the morning of 17 May 1987, the AWACS detected a fast-moving Iraqi Mirage F1 two hundred miles and closing on the frigate USS *Stark*. Thinking the *Stark* was an oil tanker, the F1 launched Exocet antiship missiles at the radar returns. The first Exocet went through the bridge and exploded in the Combat Information Center. The second hit just forward of the first. Thirty-seven American sailors lost their lives during the Iran-Iraq conflict "Tanker War." Tensions in the Gulf were at an all-time high when my crew arrived at Riyadh Air Base a month after the *Stark* incident. ELF One intel analysts briefed us on air threats—Iran, to the west, first, and Iraq last. Iranian F-14s had shot down some Iraqi aircraft using early production AIM-54 Phoenix air-to-air missiles with a range of over one hundred miles. Phoenix missiles were not comforting news for tanker crews; an IRIAF Tomcat over the Persian Gulf could fire at the AWACS or tankers in RAINBOW's (the AWACS controlling the rendezvous on most missions) orbit and hightail it back to its base near Bushehr.

Each crew flew ELF One sorties every other day. Sorties were pretty easy; take off, fly out to RAINBOW's orbit, off-load sixty thousand pounds of gas, and recover back to Riyadh Air Base. But the Tanker War was intensifying. In the early months of 1987, Kuwait asked the US and Russia to do something about the ongoing conflict. Iran began attacking Kuwaiti tanker ships carrying Iraqi crude oil through the Persian Gulf, and the world economy reacted accordingly. The attack on the USS *Stark* had been an unfortunate by-product of this ongoing war. Kuwait wanted superpower protection for its oil shipments, but more important, it wanted intervention to stop the war. The largest naval maritime protection effort since World War II, Operation Earnest Will, began shortly thereafter. Kuwait's tankers would set sail reflagged under US registration to circumvent international law in an effort to keep safe. The very first reflagged Kuwaiti tanker, the MV *Bridgeton*, outbound from Kuwait City toward the mouth of the Persian Gulf, hit an underwater mine laid by Iran the night before. No one had thought to remove the mines from the Persian Gulf with all the fighter planes flying around. Up to this point, the US AWACS covered only the NAG. Coverage of the Persian Gulf near the Strait of Hormuz now became necessary.

Much to their credit, the Royal Saudi Air Force (RSAF) stepped up with their shiny new E-3A AWACS and offered a solution. The RSAF would cover the Strait of Hormuz, orbiting near the border with the United Arab Emirates. Orbiting a new AWACS near the strait was a very gutsy call, as the Iranian airfield at Bandar Abbas housed Tomcats carrying Phoenix missiles and F-4E Phantoms armed with the same missiles our F-15s used. Intel assessed that IRIAF Tomcats could refuel in Iranian airspace and race across the Persian Gulf to shoot Phoenix missiles into RSAF AWACS orbit from international waters. And the RSAF AWACS would need gas every five hours, just like its US counterpart. The ELF One staff did not ask for volunteers. Colonel Davis, the ELF One commander, chose our crew to refuel the RSAF AWACS on their very first operational mission. Besides the Iranian air threat, a few issues needed to be settled by picking our crew for such a prestigious RSAF operational first. Leone, my female aircraft commander, topped the list.

All of us understood the Muslim laws and culture of Saudi Arabia, in which we were guests. ELF One leaders picked their best crew, I would like to think, for this historic RSAF event. RSAF leaders made it obvious to even the most casual observer that Leone would not be allowed in *any* planning meetings for this sortie. The RSAF was a little miffed about taking gas from a tanker commanded by a woman. Pete, our navigator, attended coordination meetings, and, using his notes, mission planning went well—as long as Leone was not around while the RSAF crew was in the room. The sortie was really straightforward; just like refueling any AWACS RAINBOW mission. Pete made sure the AWACS mission crew commander, call sign SHARP ECHO, would tell us of any Iranian threats approaching our refueling formation. Any Tomcat passing Sirri or Abu Musa Island in the Persian Gulf was cause to retrograde. A Tomcat within 150 miles was our trip wire for scramming home.

A second instruction came during the last meeting. Pete found out that the RSAF AWACS wing commander, a full-bird colonel, would fly in the left seat. ELF One leadership told Pete to *not*, under any circumstances, let the colonel fall off or disconnect from the boom. If he fell off, the colonel would lose face in front of his troops, which would reflect poorly on us because a woman was flying the American tanker and would become the colonel's scapegoat if anything went wrong. The boom system has movement limits that when reached cause the latches to disconnect the aircraft. Mike, our boom operator, was not going to let that happen while the colonel was refueling. Of course, this was all dependent upon the colonel's flying ability. But ELF One leaders told us the same thing: do *not* let the colonel fall off. When we asked what to do if he reached a limit or was unstable, the answer was, again, do *not* let him fall off!

The summer heat was also our enemy. The KC-135's thrust dropped significantly when the temperature was above ninety degrees, even with water injection. SHARP ECHO 01 took off at 0600 to avoid a heavy-weight takeoff in the heat. We took off as RSAF 875 at 0900 on a two-hour flight to meet SHARP ECHO 01. Water Wagons were just pigs in that hundred-plus-degree heat. The takeoff roll was long, and the level-off was low and noisy. But our Wagon got airborne and headed southeast for the Emirati border. Pete contacted SHARP ECHO 01 on high-frequency radio to update our time of arrival to the refueling area. SHARP ECHO 01 called out a lot of radar contacts closing on the Strait of Hormuz, but no Iranian fighter traffic. As we rolled left over the ARCP, SHARP ECHO 01 was five miles behind us, its black-and-white-striped APY-1 radome spinning above the fuselage. Once stabilized in precontact, Mike flashed the PDI lights, and the colonel approached the nozzle. Leone reminded Mike to treat the RSAF colonel with tender care. Mike reached out, and the three of us up front felt the toggles latch. Mike said "Contact" over the interphone, and I flipped on all four pumps. The off-load totalizer wound up, and SHARP ECHO 01's fuel tanks filled with gas. Mike gave us progress reports on the colonel's position as we got lighter and he got heavier. Sitting next to the colonel in the right seat was an RSAF major, probably an instructor pilot in the E-3A. Mike could see the colonel working hard to stay in position, but for the most part, the jet was parked right where it needed to be.

But SHARP ECHO 01 was gaining weight at six thousand pounds per minute. Our pumps had forced about thirty-five thousand pounds into SHARP ECHO 01's fuel tanks when the colonel started to move backward, closer and closer to the aft boom limit. The Saudi colonel didn't increase his thrust by adjusting his throttles forward as he got heavier, causing him to fall behind. Mike blurted out the universally acknowledged phrase for a sticky international aviation situation as all of us sensed what was happening. He had the boom system in Manual Boom Latching, trying to keep the colonel hooked up. As he approached the aft limit, there was nothing left for Mike to do. He punched the colonel off, the toggles let go, and the contact light on our fuel panel extinguished. SHARP ECHO 01 moved back into the precontact position as the colonel's voice came over the radio.

"RSAF 875, WHAT HAPPENED?!"

Not only had the colonel lost face but he also did it behind a woman—literally. Mike became the strategic sergeant with his very quick reply: "Sir, I'm sorry! Our system just fired through, and it's *all* our fault. I'm resetting the system, so give me a minute to find out what's wrong."

Mike then moved his right thumb up from mic to the interphone on the boom's ruddervator control stick and said, "Was *that* diplomatic enough?"

We laughed up front, but we knew that the first question ELF One would ask would be "Did the colonel fall off?"

And that was exactly the first question Colonel Davis asked as he came up the ladder after we landed. Mike was the first one to tell him that SHARP ECHO 01 went to the aft limit, moving farther back as he got heavier and not compensating with power. Colonel Davis asked, "So . . . what did you tell him?"

"He fell off after about thirty-five thousand pounds, and I said it was entirely our fault; the system had fired through for some reason, and I asked him to hold at the precontact position while I tested the system.

"He stayed for about three minutes, and then I flashed him back up to the boom. He stayed on for the rest of the off-load."

"Good answer, Boom! Good answer!"

RSAF did call ELF One leaders stating they were not happy with the refueling, but the mission went well, so everyone seemed satisfied. Mike, the strategic sergeant, saved the US Air Force and his country some embarrassment.

A week later, it was time for us to leave Riyadh for England. Because of the heat and quiet hours at RAF Fairford, our takeoff was scheduled for 0120 in the morning. The tanker had a full load of gas, requiring another water-injected takeoff. Leone and I took turns flying missions, and it was my turn to fly. Holding short of runway 19 at Riyadh, Leone and I went through the takeoff procedures one last time. Looking down the runway, I could see that our flight path took us straight over downtown Riyadh, and the hotel we all lived at! If I had to be up at 0120 in the morning, so did Riyadh. The takeoff went as planned through level-off and flap retraction. J57 wet thrust takeoffs are loud—about 165 decibels. At 0121 in the morning, I pushed the yoke forward and leveled off at five hundred feet, very wet and noisy over downtown. I tapped the left rudder pedal, bringing our flight path right over the Al-Yamamah hotel. When we were directly overhead, I hollered, "Wake up, suckers!" as Leone, Pete, and Mike laughed. Colonel Davis came over comm one, chuckling and thanking us for the flyby. Our wheels touched down at RAF Fairford just after 0800. When I sat down in the ops building to finish paperwork, one of the Tanker Task Force staff asked Leone who did the takeoff. I raised my hand. He told us alarms had gone off all over Riyadh.

★ ★

LESSONS FROM THE COCKPIT: CULTURE

The lesson of flying ELF One missions was that my crew had to deal with cultural mannerisms different from those in the US while flying support missions for the Saudis. We had to understand the cultural differences and learn how to work with them, not against them. A German F-4 fighter pilot once told me Americans cook their own soup, meaning we tend to do things our own way and toss our international allies' cultural norms aside. One tremendous experience of my flying career was visiting many nations and experiencing their cultures. An important lesson learned from traveling to many countries was how to say "Hello" and "Thank you" in their languages. Working in the defense industry gave me an opportunity to observe the corporate cultures of Fortune 500 companies. During a meeting with a Jordanian avionics firm, I greeted executives in Arabic, using phrases I'd learned from spending so much time in the Middle East, and their faces lit up. It's an easy way to quickly break down cultural barriers when you can say a few words to customers and partners in their own tongue. The next time you are traveling to another country or visiting a foreign client for the first time, exert some effort and learn something about their culture.

★ ★

4

★

Brute-Force Disconnect

1430 Sunday 4 November 1990
GOPHER Aerial Refueling Anchor Point
Over the Al Jawf Region of Saudi Arabia

Everything is funny, as long as it's happening to somebody else.

—WILL ROGERS, AMERICAN COWBOY, ACTOR, AND HUMORIST

Celebrate your successes. Find some humor in your failures.

—SAM WALTON, AMERICAN BUSINESSMAN AND ENTREPRENEUR

If anything can go wrong, it will.

—MURPHY'S LAWS OF COMBAT

Local checkout for combat missions is a threefold educational process. New pilots and navigators fly with a seasoned crew the first time, watching them from the jump seats as observers. New boom operators get contacts with an instructor watching over them. The new crew flies in the seats on a second sortie a day or two later with an experienced crew watching over us. The experienced crew debriefs mistakes and things to watch out for. These sorties are called "over-the-shoulder" rides. The last step to becoming SAC-trained killers in theater is certification on the air campaign plan. Certifications are like difficult oral exams, as wing leadership asks crews questions on tactics, techniques, and procedures in a board of review. Once you pass, wing leadership signs a letter stating you are now mission ready and adds it to your personnel record. Most over-the-shoulder flights happen without incident. If nothing goes wrong, you and the plane come home in one piece. My first flight did not go so well. We came home early from our over-the-shoulder sortie and first in-country mission with a very broken jet, and a Saudi pilot went back with a KC-135 souvenir.

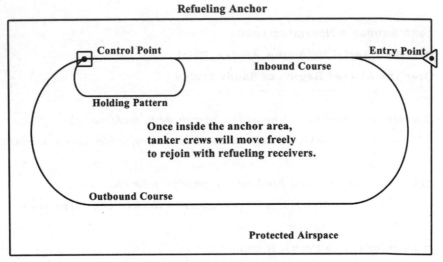

This diagram illustrates a typical seventy-miles-long by thirty-mile-wide anchor refueling area like GOPHER in Desert Storm and RUSH, O'REILLY, and HANNITY over Afghanistan's Shahikot Valley in Operation Anaconda. Anchors are controlled by a ground radar station or a controller in the E-3B AWACS like CHOCTAW, MAGIC, or BRIGHAM.

GOPHER anchor refueling area sat near the Iraqi border, close to Arar Air Base in the An Nafud desert. Since GOPHER was close to Iraq, F-4G Wild Weasels and RF-4C photo-reconnaissance Phantoms used it a lot. On our first mission as observers, SHELL 46 was scheduled to refuel two RF-4Cs from the 12th Tactical Reconnaissance Squadron from Bergstrom Air Force Base in Texas, call signs PHOTO 65 and 66.

Once the Photo-Phantoms had their gas, four RSAF F-15Cs, call signs STALLION 61 through 64, would hook up for fifteen thousand pounds each. Being only an observer on the flight, I moved all over the tanker watching the experienced crew from Plattsburg Air Force Base. After arriving at GOPHER, CHOCTAW vectored PHOTO 65 and 66 to us. I checked off the interphone and headed for the boom pod with my camera, wanting pictures of my first combat mission.

Mikey D, my temporary boom, was one of the most experienced instructor boom operators in the 909th. On this flight, he would observe during PHOTO 65's and 66's refueling, and then crawl into the boom couch as the boom operator for the next receivers. When I got back to the boom pod, Mikey D was lying next to the Plattsburg instructor boom as PHOTO 65 approached precontact position, fifty feet from the nozzle. PHOTO 65 was rock solid, taking on four thousand pounds and moving to the right wing. PHOTO 66 was also rock solid in the refueling envelope, taking on the same amount. Both Phantoms dropped below us and left to the east. CHOCTAW told us the STALLION F-15s of the Royal Saudi Air Force would arrive staggered over the next twenty minutes. CHOCTAW called back to say STALLION 61 was on his way. We could hear CHOCTAW send STALLION 61 over to the air refueling frequency. Mikey D slid over and settled into the boom couch. He moved the boom from side to side and then up and down to see how it handled. Once he was happy with the boom's maneuverability, he extended the pipe and we waited for STALLION 61.

STALLION 61 approached from about two miles back and a thousand feet below us, coming fast. The F-15 carried four AIM-7M Sparrow air-to-air missiles on the fuselage and four AIM-9M Sidewinder heat-seeking missiles under its wings. Three external tanks hold four thousand pounds of fuel each. Photographers rarely see a fighter loaded with live weapons. By the time I checked the camera's battery power and how many frames were left, STALLION 61 was a hundred feet away.

"SHELL 46, STALLION 61 requests contact," the pilot said in a thick Arab accent.

"STALLION 61, boom radio check."

"SHELL 46, STALLION 61 has you loud and clear. How about me?"

"SHELL has you loud and clear also. You are cleared to the contact position, sir."

Mikey flashed STALLION 61 the PDI lights, and he moved toward us. Once stabilized in the contact position, Mikey put the pole right in the hole. The copilot flipped on two fuel pump switches, and the off-load totalizer showed gas coming off our airplane. Four heads peered down from the boom sighting window as STALLION 61's pilot looked up at us. He reached the outer limit, and the system fired through a disconnect, releasing him from the nozzle. STALLION moved back about fifty feet to the refueling precontact position, then moved back toward us. Mikey stuck the nozzle in his receptacle again. STALLION 61 remained pretty stable this time—until he looked up and saw all of us watching and my camera pointed down at him. He waved to us, and STALLION 61 moved forward . . . and down . . .

Mikey saw what was happening and started telling STALLION 61 "Up five, back five . . . Up ten, back ten . . ." but STALLION wasn't listening. The boom was pointing almost straight down, the nozzle cocked backward at about sixty degrees. Finally, Mikey radioed the words all tanker crews never want to hear: "STALLION 61! BREAKAWAY! BREAKAWAY! BREAKAWAY!"

No movement.

Mikey said louder, "STALLION 61! BREAKAWAY! BREAK—"

STALLION 61's pilot looked down in his cockpit and pushed both throttles and stick forward. His Eagle moved instantly. All of us in the boom pod heard a loud *BANG*, and the boom extension started wobbling up and down. You could feel it through the whole airplane. SHELL 46 had just experienced a brute-force disconnect. STALLION 61 continued down and to our right. With gas still pouring out of the pipe, STALLION 61 moved back toward the boom and into precontact position. Why was he doing that?

Fuel stopped trailing when the copilot closed the air refueling line valve and cut off the boom's supply of gas. Mikey began a systems check, and the boom flew just fine—except one vital piece was missing: the nozzle. SHELL 46's nozzle had broken off in STALLION 61's receptacle. All of us could see the nozzle poking out of the F-15's refueling slipway. After looking STALLION 61 over to see what damage he had, the pilot asked, "SHELL 46, STALLION 61 requests precontact."

I was still taking pictures as Mikey looked over at me with a quizzical look on his face. "What did he just say?!"

"Mikey, he wants his gas," I said, laughing.

"SHELL 46, STALLION 61 requests precontact."

"STALLION 61, negative precontact . . . hold your position," Mikey said as he flew the boom around.

"SHELL, I need more fuel."

Exasperated, Mikey said, "STALLION 61, you just took the only means of putting gas in your airplane!"

STALLION 61's pilot turned his head left, looked over his shoulder, and saw the problem: the nozzle in his jet. The nozzle's metal flange had torn during the breakaway. But STALLION 61's pilot still had one last thing to say.

"SHELL 46, we make *AIR MESS*, no?"

Mikey, trying to keep his composure, replied, "Yes, sir! We make *AIR MESS*! SHELL 46 is done for the day and on our way home."

"Okay . . . I go home now too."

With that, STALLION 61 flipped into a ninety-degree right bank, pulled about 7 g's, and disappeared behind us.

CHOCTAW was not happy that the nozzle was gone. Three Eagles could not get gas and had to return home. I'm sure the Saudis covered their three-hour defense requirement or vulnerability period somehow. As we closed in on Riyadh's King Khalid International Airport, the nav passed to FIREHOUSE ops our maintenance code: code three, not mission capable. No one likes to hear code three. FIREHOUSE wanted to know why we were code three. The nav told them we had experienced an uncontrolled brute-force disconnect. We heard people laughing in the background as FIREHOUSE said ours was the third brute-force in two weeks. I had never seen a brute-force disconnect, so after we landed I went to the back of the jet. Nozzles connect to the boom extension with eight bolts. Six bolts had stayed with the boom. The top portion of the flange and the other two bolts had ripped off completely.

Four days later, my crew was flying again. King Khalid Provisional Air Wing's vice wing commander Colonel Ken Mills told us to visit maintenance debrief right around the corner from mission planning, a big smile on his face. In maintenance debrief, there was a table with several parts sitting on it. The most prominent piece was a tall, round metal shape: a boom nozzle. STALLION 61's hydraulic maintenance folks pulled the nozzle out, boxed it up for transportation, and put it on a C-130 for a ride back to FIREHOUSE. None of us ever forgot the sound of that nozzle ripping off, the snapping and the vibration through the airplane. I'm sure the Saudi pilot lost face with his squadron mates when they pulled the nozzle out of his receptacle. He was not the only one to write "brute-force disconnect" in his maintenance forms.

★ ★

LESSONS FROM THE COCKPIT: HUMOR

I went on my first operational combat mission in Saudi Arabia, and I came home with a broken jet! STALLION 61—the four-ship formation flight leader, no less—broke the nozzle right off our boom, but he had a good sense of humor about it, asking, "We make air mess, no?" For as long as I live, I'll never forget the loud bang of the nozzle snapping off. During the aircrew debrief we discussed how aircrews make mistakes, sometimes big ones, but we find the humor in these events and don't take ourselves too seriously. Don't dwell on the mistakes; life is too short to not find the humor in the "air messes" of our lives. Be happy you come away with the experience, but don't dwell on the brute-force disconnects. Learn to be happy and move past them. *Reader's Digest* includes a "Humor in Uniform" section in every publication. The military is often involved in some pretty funny things. As you continue to read these stories, you'll see that I've included a lot of entertaining events. There were times when we laughed hysterically in the cockpit because of a missed radio call or a mistake that most of us learned to move past. Finding the humor in the dire situations you experience helps you get through the hard times and brings greater joy to your life. Smile—you lived through it, and it wasn't that bad.

★ ★

the list to check out "the Bag," a wide black leather briefcase containing all of Jeddah's first air tasking order (ATO) missions for the first three days of the war. Only thirteen names were on the Bag's list. Lieutenant Colonel Bruce took me into a room and read me Operations Plan 1002, the war in Iraq. He explained in great detail events planned for the air campaign's first three days. I read each day's ATO package summaries, containing over 130 missions on the first day.

One of the 1709th's biggest customers was Carrier Strike Group 2 in the Red Sea, then commanded by Admiral Riley Mixson. The USS *John F. Kennedy*'s battle group contained several other ships, such as Aegis cruisers and destroyers to defend the battle group, and tankers too. Carrier Air Wing 3 was on "Big John." The USS *Saratoga* and Carrier Air Wing 17 rounded out Admiral Mixson's air wing strike force. Each week tanker MPC folks flew out to the *John F. Kennedy* to work with Air Wing 3 strike planners on the first three days' strike packages. D-Right came down the hall after one of our flights and asked if I wanted to go out to the carrier. Of course I wanted to. SAC's tanker community knew very little about how the carrier air wings operated.

On the morning of Saturday 15 December, D-Right and I donned Mickey Mouse ears and float coats for the ride out. A loadmaster briefed us on safety issues before walking us to a waiting Grumman C-2 carrier on-board delivery (COD) aircraft, wings folded and engines running, at King Faisal Naval Base on the Red Sea coast. Stepping onto the open rear ramp, D-Right and I walked to our seats for the long flight to the *Kennedy*, haze gray and under way in the northern Red Sea. I sat in a window seat on the left side, right behind all the cargo on the COD's rear deck. D-Right sat on the aisle across from me. The C-2, call sign RAWHIDE 45, taxied out to the runway, its ramp down until just before takeoff. After a short takeoff roll, the Hijaz Mountains passed by out the window, and the Red Sea was a bright turquoise blue from eighteen thousand feet. An hour into the flight, our loadmaster came over the intercom and told us what to do during the arrested landing:

5

Haze Gray and Under Way

0900 Saturday 15 December 1990
King Faisal Naval Base
Jeddah, Kingdom of Saudi Arabia

Spend a lot of time talking to customers face-to-face. You'd be amazed how many companies don't listen to their customers.

—ROSS PEROT, AMERICAN BUSINESSMAN

Today knowledge has power. It controls access to opportunity and advancement.

—PETER DRUCKER, CONSULTANT, EDUCATOR, AND AUTHOR

It is beyond a doubt that all our knowledge begins with experience.

—IMMANUEL KANT, GERMAN PHILOSOPHER

Jeddah's leadership needed volunteers to work the air campaign plan. Lieutenant Colonel Bruce from Robins Air Force Base near Macon, Georgia, led the mission planning cell (MPC). Lieutenant Colonel Wright, call sign D-Right, worked for Lieutenant Colonel Bruce and needed help on A-Model tanker plans. I jumped at the chance. Working in the MPC and also getting to fly is the best of both worlds, and a great opportunity to learn. Lieutenant Colonel Bruce put my name on sit tight, feet and knees together, cross your arms, and hold your shoulder straps with your head down, your chin on your chest. And then the loadmaster gave this ominous warning: "If we go down in the water, remember that bubbles always float up. Follow the bubbles to a hatch, and let the float coat take you to the surface. Take steady breaths from the life vest oxygen bottle. Remember to release air from your lungs as you rise." How long does it take to rise to the surface from the Red Sea's six-thousand-foot trench?

"D-Right, what's an arrested landing and cat shot like?"

"Like nothing you've ever experienced in your life—not even at Disneyland!"

As we leveled off and accelerated eight hundred feet above the water, the loadmaster told us to get into position. The C-2's wings rolled left into a 3-g carrier traffic pattern break, and we could see the deck filled with planes passing beneath us out D-Right's window. We slowed down and I heard the gear come down, and then the flap extension tubes activate. After we completed another wide left turn, the loadmaster screamed from his seat, "GET READY! GET READY! GET READY!"

Big John's wake appeared under my window, followed by the gray deck and fantail. I can describe the arrested landing only as *SCREECH—BANG—HALT.* The tires screeched on hitting the deck as the wheel struts bottomed out and the airplane came to a halt in the time it took you to read this sentence.

The COD's wings folded, covering my window as we taxied out of the arresting cable wires. The cargo ramp opened, and I saw that the ship's bow was covered with A-6 Intruder and A-7 Corsair attack planes. A Navy KA-6D tanker followed behind us. As the COD turned butt end toward the conning tower island, a big white 67 appeared behind us. As we pushed back into the parking spot, several people wearing different-colored shirts waited to transfer cargo, passengers, and baggage. D-Right leaned over and asked, "Well, how'd you like that?"

"That was outstanding!"

With a big smile, he said, "Wait till the cat shot!"

Carrier launch operations are among the most destructive sounds a human ear can experience, coming in at 160 decibels, and in some cases higher; the human eardrum ruptures at 170 decibels without protection. King Faisal's Air Transportation Office told us to use foamy earplugs under the Mickey Mouse cranial protectors, and now I knew why. Smells of burning jet fuel and greasy oil filled my nose. It was like being in a car repair shop with AC/DC turned all the way up. D-Right and I stood next to the COD's folded wings as a kneeling F-14 Tomcat's launch bar dropped over catapult number four's shuttle on the waist. A young kid waved at several people and ran out from under the nose as the launch bar contacted the big catapult shuttle. An A-7E Corsair taxied by, momentarily blocking our view. The VF-14 Tophatter Tomcat, call sign CAMELOT 110, went into afterburner and strained against the holdback bar. A Green Shirt gave the thumbs-up signal, and a Yellow Shirt tapped the deck and pointed forward. CAMELOT 110 blasted off the end of the deck and out of view.

The jet blast deflector—JBD to all on the carrier—came down, and a KA-6D unfolded its wings while taxiing over the catapult track. Another A-7E, call sign CLANSMEN 307, taxied by, its wings folded, a single AGM-88 HARM missile hanging from a pylon. Men in yellow, green, red, brown, and white long-sleeved shirts ran all over the deck. Two young sailors in purple shirts walked around the E-2 Hawkeye next to us and went downstairs. The air boss shouted over the loudspeaker at a sailor who wasn't paying attention. Everyone stood behind a red-and-yellow-striped line as the VA-75 Sunday Puncher KA-6D went under tension and spooled up its engines to max power. A few seconds later, it disappeared out of view behind the COD. The flight deck was chaos under controlled conditions.

Escorts tapped us on the shoulder and led us toward the island. We stepped off the flight deck onto a small stairway, the Red Sea passing eight stories below us under catwalks made from heavy wire mesh welded to a framework. Walking into the carrier's ATO office, D-Right shook hands with Dagwood, Carrier Air Wing 3's lead strike planner and our host. Dagwood led us through several passageways to the carrier intelligence center, or CVIC. About the size of your living and dining rooms combined, the CVIC would be our workspace for the next two days. The CVIC held most of the strike planning data and intelligence support systems, making it the natural place for large, multisquadron planning meetings. All Carrier Air Wing 3 squadron commanders gathered in the CVIC with us to review air plan changes.

An intel analyst briefed us on Iraq's air defenses from a report published by the Office of Naval Intelligence Strike Projection Evaluation and Anti-Air Research (SPEAR) Division in Suitland, Maryland. I had never heard the sort of detailed analysis of Saddam's air defense network that this report contained. The Black Hole air campaign planning cell in Riyadh had just published new strike package priorities for the first three days' air tasking order, and all the Navy refueling requirements had changed. After going over the new air wing taskings, it was our turn to ask some questions. One question D-Right had for the commanders was what the 1709th needed to do to improve our support. No one liked our Iron Maiden, the nickname for the KC-135's refueling drogue. It's a hard basket looking like a badminton shuttlecock, attached to the boom that Navy aircraft refuel from weighing more than 250 pounds. Several new air wing lieutenants had never refueled behind a KC-135 or KC-10 until operating in the Red Sea. All the comments were small things Jeddah's tanker aircrews needed to fine-tune, small and easily made adjustments to our procedures with Navy receivers. We spent the next two hours going over all the strike missions in detail, changing tanker requirements where needed and answering any questions asked; it was an incredible learning experience with our customers.

After our meetings, D-Right and I had some time off. Dagwood introduced me to my escort, a Tomcat radar intercept officer (RIO) named Dave Parsons, call sign Hey Joe. Both of us had a passion for photography. Hey Joe took his camera on every flight, and he had a great view from his Tomcat's backseat office. He showed me several of his recent pictures, which the carrier photo shop had blown up for him. He asked if I was hungry, and I told him, "You bet I am."

Hey Joe said I hadn't experienced carrier life until I had consumed a slider, a roller, and auto dawg. I thought, *What kind of Air Force initiation is this? Is it specific to KC-135 pilots, as payback for the Iron Maiden?* We headed down to the Dirty Shirt Mess, an area where all could eat while working in their dirty duds. I stuck to Hey Joe like white on rice, knowing I would never find the way back to my stateroom through this maze of passageways.

Following Hey Joe's lead, I grabbed a tray off the stack. He pointed to a cook flipping thirty burger patties on a grill.

"Those are sliders—hamburgers."

Pointing down the line, he said, "Those are rollers," and pointed at sixty hot dogs turning on a hot dog roller.

Pointing to the ice cream machine, he said, "That's auto dawg—ice cream."

"Why do you call it auto dawg?" I asked.

He laughed and said, "Because it looks like a dog with diarrhea as it comes out!"

The Dirty Shirt Mess salad bar had more items on it than my on-shore cafeteria at Jeddah. I asked Hey Joe how they got all the lettuce. He told me it came aboard while they were underway-replenishing, or UNREPing, from a stores ship that would come alongside. The ship replenished its bombs the same way. Both of us sat down at the VF-32 Swordsmen table, Hey Joe introducing me to his squadron mates as a KC-135 pilot from Jeddah. One bowed to me, saying, "We *love* tanker guys!"

I asked all of them what we were doing wrong at Jeddah, how we could improve our service to them. Each one mentioned their preference for the soft, Nerf-like drogues the KC-10 had over the KC-135

Iron Maiden. Unfortunately, SAC was not going to fix that before the war. They asked us to lock the boom when we refueled off the drogue, but there is no "lock" on the boom. A pilot with the call sign Sundance said, "Let us plug into it, don't help us." They also asked KC-135 mission planning questions: "How much gas do you hold?" "What is a KC-135's fuel burn rate?" "Do you burn the same gas you're off-loading?" The discussion lasted over an hour.

After I finished dinner, I asked Hey Joe to take me to some of the best places for pictures. I had twenty rolls of film in my helmet bag that I wanted to shoot before leaving. We walked toward the center of the ship and climbed several sets of stairs. As I stepped through a large hatch onto an island balcony, the deck spread out below me three stories down. We were standing on Vulture's Row. Hey Joe told me that this was the best and safest place to take pictures if I had never been aboard before.

A lot of people come to Vulture's Row to watch and photograph flight ops. The entire flight deck fore and aft spread out in front of me. I shot five rolls of film over the next ten minutes. Hey Joe told me there was one other place to shoot from. We stopped by the Swordsmen ready room, where Hey Joe handed me a cranial protector and a float coat. We followed VF-32's landing signal officer out onto the deck, just a short walk from the ready room. Two Tomcats came over the carrier at five hundred knots into the pattern break as we stepped onto the deck's landing area. Each Tomcat landed thirty feet in front of me. An A-6E Intruder and two A-7s came down the right side and into the overhead break pattern. I stood mesmerized by the spectacle in front of me. After all the aircraft landed, everyone cleared off the platform and went back to their ready rooms. Twelve planes had landed in seven minutes.

D-Right and I met in the CVIC the next morning to tie off a few more planning items. Dagwood then walked us to the Air Traffic Office, the passenger terminal for the carrier, for our departure back to Jeddah. Again donning Mickey Mouse cranials and float coats, we listened as the loadmaster gave us another safety brief. A Grumman C-2

Greyhound COD, call sign RAWHIDE 46, had been backed into the same spot, waiting for us to board. The first thing I noticed was that all the seats were facing aft. D-Right and I shook Dagwood's hand and stepped into the COD and sat down.

"Wait till you experience this," D-Right said, laughing.

Whatever is about to happen to me, I thought, *I'm going to remember for the rest of my life*.

RAWHIDE 46's rear cargo ramp closed as it taxied toward the bow catapults. I watched as several people standing on the deck moved by my window. The loadmaster announced that we were taxiing into the cat, so we needed to get ready; this would happen fast. Within minutes, the engines throttled up as the loadmaster screamed, "GET READY! GET READY! GET READY!" and put his head down on his chest.

I looked out the window to watch. Cat shots are a loud *BANG*, followed by a big backward jerk and another loud *BANG*. After the first bang, I came out of my seat about half an inch—remember, the seats were facing the tail! The striping on the deck was a blur. Three seconds later there was another bang, and RAWHIDE 46 was airborne. Zero to 160 knots in 307 feet.

I looked over at D-Right and screamed as loud as I could, "I GOTTA DO THAT AGAIN!"

He just laughed at me, a big smile on his face. During the long ride home, we discussed what I had learned, and I asked him a lot of questions.

The SAC tanker community knew very little about how the Navy air wings operate. Jeddah's big wing of tankers were about to refuel some of the largest carrier strike packages in combat history, but very few in the SAC's tanker plans community understood how the Navy does business. We didn't even speak their language. The carrier had a confidential communications card with their preset radio frequencies printed on it. The carrier, called "Mother," had a navigation antenna atop the main-mast that the tankers could navigate from. Mother's tactical air navigation system (TACAN) channels changed periodically, so having the carrier comm card was important. VF-32 had their own squadron radio frequency to talk to each other. I had learned about deck cycle time, going from launching aircraft to recovering aircraft and how it affected refueling operations. Most important, Hey Joe had explained how the Tomcats and Aegis cruisers defend the tankers during refueling.

One new idea the Jeddah tankers tried with the Navy was the hose multiplier concept, which was a huge success for refueling. Hose multiplier works like this: KA-6Ds, the carrier's organic tankers, fill up from Air Force KC-135s before the strike aircraft arrive at PRUNE or RAISIN refueling tracks in western Saudi Arabia. Once full, the KA-6Ds move to our wings, trailing their internal drogues as other contact points aircraft can plug into for fuel. Hose multiplier KA-6Ds gave KC-135s the ability to refuel two airplanes simultaneously. It would have been impossible for all twenty-six to thirty-four strike fighters to get their required fuel before reaching the Iraqi border if we hadn't used hose multipliers. When a KA-6D said they were on their way to my tanker's Iron Maiden, I always gave them as much gas as they wanted. The gas then spread to all the airborne Navy fighters and jammers.

On Saturday 22 December, my crew refueled the Red Sea air wings. I wrote Hey Joe's squadron's frequency on my lineup card, classified mission notes on an eight-and-a-half-by-eleven sheet of paper strapped to my right leg, hoping he might be airborne during the sortie. Kevin's mom and dad sent our crew a Christmas package containing four Santa hats and lots of chocolate. Feeling the Christmas spirit, we all took our new Santa hats on the flight. We were in a giving mood. Kevin, Rick, and I put the Santa hats on and then our headsets, while Kenny put on his hat over his headset. The wind was blowing hard out of the north at about thirty knots while we taxied out to the center runway. As we taxied out to the end of the runway, Kenny and I opened our windows at the same time. A thirty-mile-per-hour blast of wind went through the cockpit. Kenny's Santa hat went out the window in a red flash.

What could I tell the supervisor of flying? "Hey, SOF, can you pick our *Santa hat* out of the airfield fence just off the taxiway to the center runway?" We discussed what to tell the SOF as a crew. Kevin said I shouldn't tell him anything—the hat was in the fence and wouldn't hurt anybody. Good plan. We closed the windows and took off.

A controller called Red Crown in the Aegis cruiser cleared us into the carrier airspace and passed us off to Strike Control, a radar controller inside the *Kennedy*'s Carrier Information Center, their version of Jeddah's COYOTE Ops, the command post call sign at Jeddah. Kenny dialed in the Swordsmen frequency in comm two of our brand-new Rockwell Collins ARC-210 radio. I keyed the mic and said, "Hey Joe, check!"

"Hey Joe here."

"Sluggo's flying the tanker!"

"Be there in ten minutes!"

He called back minutes later to say he'd locked us up on radar.

"Where are you, Hey Joe?"

"On your nose for three miles."

I started looking for him out in front of us. I didn't see him.

"Hey Joe, where are you again?"

"Look up!"

I peered up through the eyebrow windows to see two Tomcats roll inverted on their backs and pull as hard as they could toward the boom.

"Boom, Pilot—here they come!"

"Looking for them . . ."

"OH JESUS!"

Hey Joe, in GYPSY 200, the air wing commander's brightly painted billboard jet, and his wingman, in GYPSY 201, the squadron commander's billboard jet, leveled off behind the drogue.

"How much can you give us, Sluggo?"

"How much do you want?"

"Can you give us each ten K?"

"If I can get some good pictures of you off the wing afterward, I'll top you both off."

"Deal!"

GYPSY 200 and 201 owned the bar. After getting his gas, GYPSY 201 moved down to the drogue. Hey Joe parked out my window, a camera up to his face. He was pointing at us and laughing. Hey Joe's pilot, Dawg, moved high and close to my window. Both pointed down at me.

They saw the Santa hats.

GYPSY 201 joined on Hey Joe's left side after getting his ten thousand pounds. Both Tomcats just sat there motionless in perfect fingertip formation. Hey Joe snapped several pictures and then stuffed his camera down beside him. Then I heard Dawg's voice on the radio: "Gypsies— burners . . . NOW!"

Engine exhaust nozzles opened wide. Long tongues of orange flame grew longer and longer as each stage of afterburner ignited. GYPSY 200 and 201 lurched forward and upward, gaining speed. Hey Joe called Strike passing thirty-two thousand feet. He had left us at twenty-one thousand.

My crew in EXXON 55 stayed airborne for two more hours, refueling whoever came up. Strike Control took us up to one of the MiG combat air patrol (CAP) stations near the Gulf of Aqaba. At one point we could see the Mount Sinai area, where Moses received the Ten Commandments. On our way home, we passed over the USS *John F. Kennedy*, its wake visible from twenty-three thousand feet. After landing and stopping by COYOTE Ops to drop off all our gear, we hopped a bus for the compound.

Two weeks later, D-Right found me in the hall. "Come with me, Captain."

Walking into our secret vault, he spun the safe's dial. He handed me a piece of paper from a folder marked TOP SECRET on its orange cover sheet and said one word to me: "*Read*." Only the top quarter of the page had writing. It said,

FROM: USCENTAF/CC
TO: All Units
SUBJECT: Operation Desert Storm

MSG: Implement Wolfpack. D-Day is 17 January 1991, H-Hour
is 0000Z or 0300 local Baghdad time. Good luck and good hunting! Horner

Wolfpack, the code name for the first three ATO days of the air
campaign, would commence at 3:00 a.m. Baghdad time on Thursday
17 January 1991.

★ ★

LESSONS FROM THE COCKPIT: KNOWLEDGE

One of the biggest lessons from my involvement in Desert
Storm was that tanker planners knew nothing about how the
Navy operated, but a quarter of Jeddah's wartime receivers were
Navy drogue-equipped aircraft. SAC tankers practiced very few
drogue refuelings in daily training—maybe once a year tops. I
learned a new phrase from Hey Joe while he escorted me around
the carrier: the Navy uses the term "the gouge" to mean someone has the latest and greatest insider knowledge on an event
or situation. D-Right and I needed the most recent gouge from
strike planners aboard the *John F. Kennedy* if Jeddah was to be
successful during the war.

My first time aboard an aircraft carrier at sea was quite a
shock. I knew very little about how the Navy operated, even
after reading all the documents I could find. Meeting Hey Joe
was like having a personal tutor running me all over the ship

and introducing me to the strike leads in CVIC. Face-to-face
meetings with clients are invaluable opportunities for learning
the gouge. Being aboard the *Kennedy* and meeting all those
pilots and RIOs made me a captive audience and increased my
learning curve. Never miss the chance to gain knowledge and
the latest, greatest gouge through face-to-face contact with your
clients. When it came time to execute refueling missions for
real, Jeddah tanker planners understood what our Navy customers needed. I used this gouge-learning tool during face-to-face
meetings with business customers while working in the defense
industry. Our company won a huge international contract
because I picked up the phone and called an air attaché for his
gouge on what his country's Air Force needed in an airlift/air
refueling aircraft. I had the gouge, and the company benefited
from it.

★ ★

6

Cross-Border Operations

1545 Monday 21 January 1991
King Abdulaziz International Airport
Jeddah, Kingdom of Saudi Arabia

Talent wins games, but teamwork and intelligence wins championships.
—MICHAEL JORDAN, BASKETBALL SUPERSTAR

You can talk about teamwork on a baseball team, but I'll tell you, it takes teamwork when you have 2,900 men stationed on the USS Ala-bama in the South Pacific.
—BOB FELLER, BASEBALL PITCHER

Air refueling always seems to be a planning afterthought. I've had days too numerous to count when everyone in the room believed there would always be enough tankers and more gas airborne than needed. Now tankers were at a premium, even though 324 SAC tankers were deployed around the Middle East. Fighters were being launched without aerial refueling plans nailed down. Changes were being handled ad hoc, literally by airborne battle managers in the back ends of COUGAR, BUCKEYE, and BULLDOG, the three AWACS. In-flight changes create huge ripples in refueling plans, and airborne tankers are always at the end of the planning whip. Tanker crews at Jeddah flew two missions a day in order to ensure that the air campaign had enough fuel. A double turn, as we called it, made for a very long day, twenty hours or more. Desert Storm's Combined Forces Air Commander General Horner could have used another fifty tanker airframes and one hundred more crews. They just weren't there. And this day was going to be one of those "at the end of the whip" days.

My crew hadn't been in the tanker ops building for two minutes before we saw D-Right standing at the top of the stairs pointing down at us.

"Sluggo, is your crew coming in to fly?"

"Yes, sir, we're flying this afternoon."

"Your flight is now *canceled*!" D-Right wagged his finger at the four of us. "Go to mission planning and wait for me there!"

D-Right rarely met a crew at the top of the stairs like that. Something urgent was happening. It was now stupid question time as I reached the top of the stairs and stood in front of D-Right. "What's up?" I asked.

"We're putting a four-ship together right now. You're going to refuel a bunch of Vipers who didn't get prestrike refueled."

I looked at D-Right with a straight face. "They took off not knowing where their backside mission gas was coming from? That's ballsy!"

D-Right did not have time for this.

"Sluggo, you and your crew just wait in mission planning, and I'll be there in a minute. I need to find one more crew."

Waiting in the mission planning room were D-Right's first victims, Dan and his crew from Beale Air Force Base, in California. Dan would lead the cell formation, since he got tagged first. Minutes later, Heidi's crew from Wurtsmith Air Force Base, in Michigan, walked in. Walrus's crew from the Topeka, Kansas, Guard joined us at the table six minutes later. Our formation consisted of three water-burning KC-135A models and an E model with turbofan engines as Duckbutt. Walrus's E model engine performance would become a significant mission planning element later on.

D-Right and an intelligence analyst walked up to our table and began briefing us for the emergency refueling mission. All of us sensed the urgency in D-Right's face and voice. He was in a hurry. We did not know it yet, but we were too.

"Take off for LIME PRE track and go as far north as you dare. Three eight-ships of F-16s took off on a promise that the Black Hole would find them backside mission gas. Your four-ship is the Black Hole's answer. You must be airborne in fifty—that's five-zero—minutes, ladies and gentlemen, to meet them. If you don't get there in time, all of you will be part of the largest airborne rescue effort in Air Force history!"

Rescue efforts for downed aircrews had not gone well in the last two days. The F-14 SLATE 46 got shot down the previous night, and its two-man crew were still missing. Dan asked the question all of us were thinking: "Define 'as far north as we dare,' sir?"

D-Right looked at all of us. "Yes—we know you will probably have to pick them up about forty to fifty miles north of the border. Staff Sergeant Smith from intelligence will brief you on threats in the area. I have to run and make phone calls so the Black Hole can pass your information to AWACS."

I thought, *AWACS is going to give a four-ship of fat tankers clearance across the border? Who is watching over us? The Vipers can't do it—they don't have the gas!*

Sergeant Smith briefed us that Iraqi aircraft had been very active on the first night of the war. Mudaysis would be close on our left side. She continued, "We assess that there are no mobile surface-to-air missiles under your flight path at this time. There will be two undercast decks below you, so the gunners probably will not see you."

What is the definition of "probably" in the go-to-war dictionary?

It boiled down to this: our job was to fly into Iraqi airspace sitting atop 145,000 pounds of jet fuel and in range of just about every antiaircraft gun and mobile SAM Saddam possessed. If we got hit, the Iraqis on the ground would have about two minutes to watch the fireballs drop. Pilots from the twenty-four F-16 Vipers would join us on the ground when they ran out of gas. Sergeant Smith had the audacity to ask us if there were any questions. What could we ask?

Dan told her, "No problem," and all of us just laughed.

Reviewing a map of Iraq with all the refueling tracks marked on it, Dan ran a quick cell formation briefing.

"TUNA 45 flight will fly to LIME PRE as a four-ship in standard cell formation. At the end of LIME PRE track, if we have not heard from or seen the F-16s, expect to turn north into Iraqi airspace to meet them. Weasels supporting their mission will need gas too. No idea what our receivers' call signs are. I expect each eight-ship of Vipers to be way low on gas." Dan paused to reorient the map. He continued, "Be ready to off-load as soon as we hear them on the radio. The AWACS CHOCTAW controls our mission on Cherry 4, UHF 360.7. Listen up for air threats, as Iraqi MiG bases are north, east, and west of us—and close. MiG threat calls will be from bull's-eye Jack, Jalibah Southeast Airfield. If you see any SAMs or guns shooting up, call it out and react accordingly. All other cell formation procedures are Jeddah standard." Jeddah planners had created cell formation standards that all of us were tested on. These standards were understood by everyone, the contract binding us together as a team while we flew combat missions. "Any questions?"

We all laughed again. I thought, *Semper Gumby—always flexible.*

The mission became a time-management problem as we left the building. Four tankers can carry plenty of gas for twenty-four F-16s. If we were not airborne in forty minutes, a bunch of pilots might be spending the night in the Iraqi desert—or, worse, the rest of the war in Baghdad. A normal preflight, engine start, and taxi for takeoff take about forty-five minutes. Arriving at our jet, I told Kenny, Kevin, and Rick to go upstairs and start the preflight. Our crew was lucky that the jet had already been cocked on by another crew, all the switches ready for engine start; it saved us a lot of time. Glancing through the jet maintenance forms handed to me by the crew chief, I started a very fast walkaround inspection of the jet. I was just looking for any leaks, drips, or open panels at this point. Three crew chiefs sensed I was in a real hurry and asked what was going on.

Pointing across the ramp behind our jet, I told them, "We are number three in formation with them, them, and a Kansas Guard jet on the Haj ramp. Twenty-four F-16s did not get prestrike refueling, and they will be really low on gas when we get to them. Planners told us to go as far north as we dare, so we expect to cross into Iraqi airspace. All of us must be airborne in thirty-two minutes to meet them. That is what we know right now. Engine start and taxiing will happen really fast, so keep up. We don't have time to jump to another jet if this one breaks." Their faces were priceless—big eyes and mouths hanging open.

They thought their jet might not come back that night.

At a large international airport, getting four aircraft airborne and formed up can be an exercise in patience or frustration. Dan, Heidi, and my crew were on the same ramp, within eyesight of each other. Walrus's fanjet E model was parked a mile and a half away to the north. Walrus's high-performance engines could outrun any Water Wagon KC-135. All E models took off on the west runway for this reason. The issue was that Walrus had to watch our Water Wagons take off from a mile away on the west runway and time his takeoff based on seeing Heidi in the number two jet get airborne, at which point he would know I was rolling down the runway and he should start his takeoff roll. Climbing away from the airfield, Walrus's crew would see all of us for the first time in front and to the right and visually rejoin our slower jets.

Strapping into the seat, I told the crew to start engines. We didn't have time to catch any mistakes made by the preflight crew. The engines started without issue. As we taxied out of our parking spot, the crew chief gave us a big salute. I knew what he was thinking: *Hope to see you guys again later tonight.*

As we waited at the end of our parking row for Dan and Heidi to roll by, Kevin told me we were running four minutes late. Dan and Heidi passed in front of us, and we fell in behind them. Three fat tankers were now nose to tail and heading for the runway fast. Dan knew we were late; I looked down at the INS and saw that he was taxiing at twenty-two knots. Normal speed is five to eight knots. As he approached the end of the runway, Dan sent us all to tower frequency. "TUNA 45 flight go Tower . . . Two! Three! Four!"

Then, after a ten-second pause: "TUNA 45 flight check . . . Two! Three! Four!"

"Jeddah Tower, TUNA 45 flight of four on the center and west runways, ready for immediate takeoff. We all need to go right now, Tower!"

The tower's supervisor of flying had gotten the word. Jeddah Tower cleared us for immediate takeoff.

"TUNA 45 flight is cleared for immediate departure on center and west runways. Contact departure on one twenty-three point eight."

"TUNA 45 flight, go departure comm two . . . Two! Three! Four!"

Another ten-second pause, and then: "TUNA 45 flight check . . . Two! Three! Four!"

Dan taxied into position, stopping over the painted-on 36R and the white runway stripes. Blasts of steam coming from five-inch holes on the left side of each engine indicated Dan's engine water injection was working. Dan released his brakes, and TUNA 45 started moving forward, while Heidi in TUNA 46 moved onto the runway. Her aircraft emitted the same puffs of steam, and she began rolling down the runway just as Dan got airborne at the other end. I taxied TUNA 47 up and stopped over the numbers, calling for the takeoff checklist. Kenny and I pushed the throttles up and saw four needles swing to 2.8 on the EPR gauges, indicating wet thrust, just as Heidi's plane lifted off the runway. TUNA 47 lifted off 1,500 feet from the runway's end and began a tail chase for Heidi and Dan.

Looking back, Kenny could see Walrus taking off behind us. "Four is airborne in a climbing turn, trying to catch up," he said.

Walrus would be behind us before we could catch up to Heidi and Dan.

Kevin then said, "Pilot, right now we are about three minutes late to meet the receivers."

Not a good omen.

Passing under the NIGHTHAWK corridor safely separating us from the F-117 refueling track overhead, Dan sent us all to CHOCTAW on Cherry 4 and told them the TUNA 45 flight was airborne. CHOC-TAW told us what we already knew: "TUNA 45, go to the end of LIME PRE and call us before heading north into Iraq. Go as far north as you dare. The Vipers are striking their target in a few minutes. We will tell them you are airborne and coming to them."

The "as far north" phrase sticks in my head again. *What does everyone think that means?* I kept asking myself.

Tankers had flown near Iraqi airspace since the first night of the war. Seven Riyadh KC-135s had refueled twenty-two F-15E Strike Eagles right up to the border on night one. Those Strike Eagles were chased out of Iraq by MiGs and Mirage F1s. Since then, several tankers had ventured inside Iraq, picking up low-fuel fighters, but only for short periods of time close to the border. To go across was like earning a secret badge of honor in the tanker community: you had to go into Bad Guy Territory to be part of the Cross-Border Operations club. My crew got really close to joining the club on night one. That afternoon, our four tankers might be far inside Iraq for thirty minutes or more. The Vipers could not engage MiGs when low on gas, so the Weasels might have to be our primary defenders. If the Weasels had the gas.

Reaching the end of LIME PRE, Dan made a slight left turn to parallel the border, heading northwest. He asked CHOCTAW a question all of us understood.

"CHOCTAW, TUNA 45. Where's the beer?"

He wanted to be sure before crossing the border that Weasels were close by to escort us through Iraq. CHOCTAW answered, "TUNA 45, head north now. FALSTAFF 55 flight will be refueling with COLLIE, SPANIEL, and PUG."

We kept getting little bits of very important information. Now we knew all the call signs. AWACS sent us across the border, but there was not a sense of security in my cockpit. All four of us were a little edgy.

I saw Dan's left wing rise for the turn into Iraq. Heading north, we were literally pointed straight at downtown Baghdad. Below us were two flat overcast cloud decks. Would Linus's cotton blanket hide us from people with SAMs or guns on the ground? None of us knew. The odd thought in my mind was *I still do not want to put on those big heavy parachutes in the back of the jet.* I wore a chute for two days and realized how stupid it was, sitting on all this gas. If we got hit by flak, they would see the fireball in Baghdad for sure. Kevin said over the interphone, "Gentlemen, we have entered the Klingon Neutral Zone!" He took a picture of the INS coordinates as we passed over the border.

As we continued straight north, CHOCTAW told us, "Get ready, TUNA—receivers are on your nose for ninety miles heading south at forty-seven thousand feet."

Twenty-four Vipers hung on the blades, conserving gas. Our formation was between twenty-one thousand and twenty-three thousand feet. Right after CHOCTAW told us that, COLLIE lead checked in his fighters on Amber 3, UHF 240.4, the boom radio frequency. You could hear the anxiety in their voices.

"COLLIE flight check! Two! Three! Four! Five! Six! Seven! Eight!"

SPANIEL and PUG flights checked in the same way. The last voices we heard said, "FALSTAFF 55 check . . . Two! Three! Four!"

All twenty-eight aircraft were on the same radio frequency. Dan asked the Weasel leader, "FALSTAFF, TUNA. Is there any activity around us?"

FALSTAFF 55 came back with, "TUNA, picture clear right now. Nothing on our scopes. We will let you know if something pops up."

We were standing in Saddam's desert parking lot, totally naked and not able to do anything about it. Hopefully, our first indication of trouble would not be FALSTAFF launching a HARM missile next to us. I momentarily looked down to my right at my camera on the floor next to me. The battery charge showed 85 percent, and twenty frames remained.

COLLIE lead, twenty-one miles in front of us, very excitedly said, "TUNA! COLLIE! Turn south now!" Dan sped up to refueling airspeed and started a wide left turn toward Saudi Arabia.

And it rained F-16s!

There were Vipers everywhere, falling into position on the tankers' wings and booms. The radio was garbage as all the flights were talking at once. PUG flight joined us, asking his eight chicks for their fuel states. PUG's Vipers were from the 17th TFS at Shaw Air Force Base in South Carolina; "Hooters" was written in blue across white bands at the tops of their tails. The low ball pilot of the PUG flight was PUG 6, a first lieutenant with eight hundred pounds of fuel left in his tanks. PUG 6 had about five minutes before his engine quit from fuel starvation forty-two miles north of the Saudi border.

COLLIE lead instructed, "TUNAs, give everyone one thousand pounds and then we'll cycle back through."

Mister Eight Hundred Pounds came in first. PUG 6 matter-of-factly told Rick, "Boom, we have one chance to do this, or I'm going to have to jump over the side." He meant eject, which you never say over the radio.

Rick told him, "Come straight to the boom; TUNA 47 is ready." We heard the boom pipe extending from the cockpit.

Rick asked, "You guys ready up front?"

"Prep-for-contact check is complete up front."

"Good, because I'm going to stick him when I see him. . . . Where are they?" We had seen only COLLIE and SPANIEL go by us to their tankers.

"Oh Jesus!" Rick said from the boom pod as PUG 6 descended into his view from above and parked twenty feet from our nozzle. Three PUGs joined outside my window, and three others on Kenny's side. Two PUGs were on the boom in fingertip formation so they could cycle through faster. The fingertip method is called hitchhiking and is forbidden in the States, commanders feeling it was a dangerous way to refuel.

But it wasn't forbidden in Europe or the Pacific—and certainly not here in Desert Storm, because it saved time. Kenny held his video camera in his right hand, recording in case something happened. All the Viper pilots were looking at PUG 6, with an occasional glance at our wingtips for clearance. All PUGs waited to see whether PUG 6 stayed on the boom or backed out and ejected.

Kenny and I looked at each other cross-cockpit, thinking how PUG 6 must feel. Rick said he had contact, and I started pumping gas into him. The off-load totalizer gauge hesitated and then counted up, showing gas flowing into PUG 6. Rick told us he could see the pilot's blue first lieutenant bars as he looked down from the boom pod. PUG 6 was a young guy. I pointed my camera out the window toward the left wing as Kevin hopped into the jump seat between us. He was taking pictures of the two tankers in front of us flying over two partially overcast decks. Twenty-eight airplanes inside a four-mile-wide, two-thousand-foot-tall box. In front of us, COLLIE and SPANIEL were going through the same cyclic motions we were: Vipers moved from the wings to the boom; one got on the boom, then came off the boom; the next Viper repeated. FALSTAFF 57 and 58 just hung off our wing, watching helplessly. There was nothing they could do right now . . . unless somebody shot at us.

Once all the PUGs cycled through, they began coming back for more gas. It was kind of surreal, because the radios were dead silent. All the Vipers finished refueling at about the same time and started climbing above us. COLLIE lead thanked us profusely for coming north as FALSTAFF 57 started down for our boom. The sun was setting behind the clouds below the horizon out west. As the first Weasel made contact, CHOCTAW told us, "TUNAs, turn west now."

We figured the Weasels would tell us first if something started shooting at us.

"CHOCTAW, say again for TUNA 45 flight?"

"TUNA, we need you to head west now, heading two seven zero.

There's a RESCAP west of your position for the Tomcat crew. SANDYs need the gas."

Sergeant Smith had told us that an F-14 off the USS *Saratoga*, call sign SLATE 46, had been shot down in western Iraq the night before. CHOCTAW was thinking, *Hey, since you folks are in Bad Guy Territory already, we need you to go over here now.* Rescue combat air patrol, or RESCAP, is painful. Rescuing downed aircrews is the most complex mission we do in the air. Everything stops to determine a downed crew's location and any threats near them, which takes time. Coordinating all the players and events is extremely time-consuming. Waiting for the lumbering MH-53 Pave Lows causes events to slow even further. Time and endurance become critical. Time and endurance also eat fuel, and fuel equals lots of tankers. The KC-10 is ideal for rescue missions, with both a boom and drogue, and are themselves air refuelable. But there were no KC-10s anywhere in Iraqi airspace. CHOCTAW stated two A-10s were currently covering MOCCASIN 05, a Special Forces MH-53 Pave Low helicopter picking up a downed crewmember. Good news—sort of. Tomcats have two people in them. One of the crew was being picked up, but where was the second guy?

"SANDY flight check . . . Two!"

"TUNA 45, SANDY 57 and 58 are looking to get six thousand pounds each if possible."

Those Hawgs were empty. A request for six thousand pounds up this high meant all their weapons were gone. The gun was probably empty too. Six thousand pounds is a lot of gas for an A-10, which holds only nine thousand pounds. The real issue for refueling the Hawgs was that FALSTAFF was still on the boom.

Weasels are refueled at 315 knots and twenty-eight thousand feet. A-10s refuel at 220 knots, sometimes slower, and at nine thousand to twelve thousand feet in altitude. A combat-armed Hawg will go only 210 knots even at lower altitudes. The boom gets a little mushy in its movements below 210 knots, and is uncontrollable below 190 knots. Below

190 knots, there is not enough airflow over the boom ruddervators for control, so it just dangles behind us. The only way for us to do this was for Walrus as Tail-end Charlie to slow down to 210 knots. Dan turned into a right 360-degree wagon wheel, and our formation of four spread out over a couple of miles. Now all of us were *really* naked, as if saying to Saddam, "Here we are! Come shoot at us." Walrus was trying to cut inside the wider circle of the faster tankers. As FALSTAFF 58 continued refueling in the turn, the SANDY A-10s passed under us off our right toward Walrus's ship. FALSTAFF cannot help the situation because they need the gas to get back to Baghdad. I could see out Kenny's cockpit window that Walrus was across from us, pumping the Hawgs. The SANDYs finally got all their gas and slowly climbed above us. FALSTAFF finished at the same time and headed north, off to our left. Kenny got it all on video.

SANDY 57 said, "Thanks for coming north for us."

Yeah—go home so we can.

CHOCTAW had no more receivers and released us for home. We couldn't leave until they told us we could. TUNA 45 flight landed in the evening, five hours and twenty minutes after takeoff.

All of us were exhausted walking back into the tanker ops building. Job satisfaction and the adrenaline rush are very high after missions like this. Four tankers flew naked into Iraqi airspace without seeing a shot fired. Strange. TUNA 45 flight saved twenty-four F-16s from fuel starvation. After all the Vipers landed safely back at Al Minhad Air Base, the commander of Shaw's 363rd Fighter Wing talked to our wing commander call sign Hammer on the phone, thanking him for sending tankers so far north. The SANDYs successfully covered MOCCASIN 05 as it picked up the Tomcat pilot, keeping him from becoming a POW. The lead Hawg pilot was later awarded the Air Force Cross for valor during the rescue mission, the second-highest service award behind the Congressional Medal of Honor. Unfortunately, the Tomcat RIO was picked up by the Iraqis and spent the rest of the war in Baghdad. He came home after being released with the other POWs at the end of the war.

This story came full circle in later years, when I was teaching at the Joint Forces Staff College in Norfolk, Virginia. JFSC was one of the best assignments of my career because of what I learned at the strategic and operational levels of war and the people I met in each class. One day I described this mission as part of an airpower discussion. Tazz, a good friend of mine from the F-15 community at Kadena, was in my class as a student. His four-ship of Eagles had been twelve thousand feet above us watching the RESCAP and saw us come from the east to refuel the two Hawgs. I did not even know the Eagles were there. AWACS never told us that four F-15s had orbited above us. We never heard the Light Grays on the radios, nor did CHOCTAW tell us Tazz and his Eagles had to chase away Iraqi MiGs sent to interrupt the RESCAP operation. Tazz perfectly described what we had done, the Hawgs going to the back tanker and our wagon wheel formation to let Walrus keep his position.

JFSC has a social hour for new students coming in or when a promotion list comes out. In military terms, it's called a "blender." A lot of drinks and hors d'oeuvres are consumed at a blender. It gives everyone some time to talk. One of the Navy captains going through the school was Captain Devon "Boots" Jones, the pilot of SLATE 46, the downed F-14 Tomcat. I walked up to Boots and introduced myself, telling him I was in the tanker formation refueling the Weasels and Hawgs covering his pickup. He smiled, stuck his right hand out for a shake, and told me something the tanker community hears all the time: "Drinks are on me, Sluggo!"

★ ★

LESSONS FROM THE COCKPIT: TEAMWORK

Strategic Air Command created formation standards every tanker unit was supposed to follow. The problem was that each

SAC base interpreted the regulations differently, adopting their own unique standards for flying together as a team. Jeddah's air refueling wing was a "Rainbow Wing," meaning it was a combination of active-duty, Guard, and Reserve tanker units. Many Guard and Reserve pilots came from the fighter community and understood formation contracts and standards. These former fighter pilots created Jeddah's cell formation standards, which became our team contract agreement when flying in formation. All cell lead–qualified pilots had passed a test on these procedures, and the minimum passing score was 100 percent. When Dan stated, "All cell formation procedures are Jeddah standard," everyone knew what he meant, and we followed the contract.

I learned from flying at Jeddah how formation agreements increase teamwork and effectiveness. They are also a method of reducing risk. Everyone works together as a team, using conventional procedures to achieve goals. When D-Right threw us together as an ad hoc formation, he knew we would all work together as a team because of formation contracts all of us understood. TUNA 45 flight's teamwork efforts saved twenty-four F-16s from fuel starvation and helped two SANDY Hawgs get home after saving a downed pilot. FALSTAFF's Wild Weasels executed their contractual agreement to protect the force from any ground threats. The business world understands teamwork and contracts as a means to achieve financial goals. Corporations develop policies just like formation procedures to facilitate cooperation between business units and partners. Contracts signed as agreements between partners form stronger teams when pursuing lucrative business ventures. As a leader, create and develop formation procedures to be used as contractual agreements with which your teams can increase their effectiveness and productivity.

★ ★

7

The Longest Night

Midnight Sunday 20 January 1991
King Abdulaziz International Airport
Jeddah, Kingdom of Saudi Arabia

Disciplining yourself to do what you know is right and important, although difficult, is the high road to pride, self-esteem, and personal satisfaction.

—MARGARET THATCHER, BRITISH PRIME MINISTER

Being productive gives people a sense of satisfaction and fulfillment that loafing never can.

—ZIG ZIGLAR, AMERICAN AUTHOR AND MOTIVATIONAL SPEAKER

There are some days when I think I'm going to die from an overdose of satisfaction.

—SALVADOR DALÍ, SPANISH SURREALIST PAINTER

Unscheduled receivers were becoming common on almost every tanker mission. Tankers refueled whoever showed up on the wings. COUGAR, BUCKEYE, and BULLDOG tried to keep the refueling chaos to a minimum, but tankers were given mission changes on almost every flight. AWACS was just trying to put the gas in the right place at the right time, and tanker crews were pretty accommodating to the numerous changes that happened after they were airborne. AWACS always asked us how much gas we had available and moved us to meet forces going into or coming out of Iraq. Tanker battle managers moved my tanker and crew from one refueling anchor to another on the same mission based on the battlefield situation. My crew refueled fighters in one anchor, and then AWACS told us to move across Saudi Arabia to another. This common occurrence was one reason tanker crews were so good at handling dynamic and fluid battlefield situations. Tanker Kings, refueling planners from Riyadh familiar with each day's ATO, flew on every AWACS sortie, assisting the airborne battle managers with all the refueling issues. As ATO changes happened, Tanker Kings smoothed out the rough edges of moving gas across the peninsula.

Most of the time.

The air war was in its fourth day. My crew was scheduled for spare aircraft duty. We took off only when another tanker broke. Spare crews were assigned additional duties, and that night was no different. Additional duties made for some very long nights. That spare duty shift ended Monday night, one of the longest days of my personal war. D-Right met us coming down the hall in tanker ops, a big smile on his face. If D-Right was looking for you and smiling, it wasn't a good sign most of the time. He always had changes to the schedule. That night he just had additional duties for us, usually cocking on jets or taxiing back from Kilo Row fuel bladders.

"Good evening, spare crew! Your first mission tonight, should you decide to accept it, is to get into your truck and go out to Kilo Row. There's a jet ready for taxiing back to ramp four."

"Okay, Colonel, we'll grab the keys and head out to Kilo Row. Let us get a brick."

Every spare crew carried a brick, a walkie-talkie on which command post could contact us immediately.

"There are a lot of launches you guys will cover later tonight. No rest for the wicked!" D-Right said as we stopped by our lockers. Good; at least it wouldn't be a boring night. I could maybe sleep a little in my seat during schedule breaks.

Kevin grabbed the keys for a Ford King Cab truck spare crews used for running around. The big King Cab trucks are potential hazards at night: no radio to talk with Jeddah ground, and only a single rotating yellow light on the top. Jumping into the truck, the four of us and two crew chiefs headed for Kilo Taxiway and the fuel pits. Three KC-135s stretched down Kilo Row. Tankers two and three still had hoses hooked up, so they were not full yet. The Kilo Row line chief told us the first jet was ready to go—"Just get in, start her up, and keep rolling to ramp four." As I pushed the throttles up to get moving, Kenny watched the crew chiefs following behind us in the truck out his open window. Ramp four's SOF told us to park quickly, as jets were leaving soon over the brick. Three jets had engines running and rotating beacons flashing ready to go.

After shutting down, Kenny ran through the cocking-on checklist so the next crew would just have to strap in, start up, and go. My watch said 0130 in the morning. Our boom spare jet sat on the first line of parked jets, placing it as close to the runway as possible. Spare tankers no longer sat in the runway 36 right hammerhead, because primary jets parked there when mission changes came over the radio, which happened a lot. The off-going spare crew said it had been another slow, boring shift. Coming up the ladder, Kevin was already talking to command post to see if there were any schedule changes from D-Right.

None.

Our first flight coverage started in twenty minutes; no need for engines running. Kenny tuned to BBC on the HF radio, and we settled into our seats for the night.

I was having a hard time staying awake by 0515. Kenny and Kevin engaged in idle gossip with the crew chiefs leaning against the nose tires. Both chiefs wanted to know what action we had seen and to answer their number one question: Had we been in Iraqi airspace? My crew had not at that time, but several others had. The BBC announcer spoke in the background about an RAF crew shot down on the first night of the war. I told the chiefs about my friend Rasmey, a B-52 BUFF pilot from Loring Air Force Base and a classmate at pilot training. He launched from Maine and flew across the Atlantic to bomb Mudaysis Air Base the first night. That information would have been nice to know Wednesday night, since Mudaysis was the number one threat airfield when we refueled John Boy's Weasels. As he came off target, Rasmey told me an RAF Tornado GR1 at 550 knots and three hundred feet above the runway belched out JP233 runway denial weapons. Rasmey looked back as he pulled off his bomb release and saw the Tornado get hit hard by ground fire. Rasmey did not know if the Tornado crew made it out. A lot of Tornado crews got hit dropping JP233s. Combat myth, fiction, and rumor—boredom had officially set in. We watched KC-135s taxi by us and take off. Not one broken jet.

"TUNA boom spare, COYOTE Ops."

Kevin turned around in his chair. "COYOTE Ops, TUNA boom spare, go!"

Kenny told the crew chiefs, "Heads up, ground, I think we may be launching. Get ready for start engines before taxi check."

All of us thought the same thing: *Hallelujah, the long night is over!*

"We need you guys to come back into Ops. You will be replaced by another spare crew. Don't wait for a changeover brief. You don't have time."

Kevin looked up at me quizzically. "COYOTE Ops, can you tell us what's up?"

"There's a scheduling snafu. A five-ship is on the schedule, and none of the crews are cell-lead qualified. You guys are. Come on in." That told me that all five were brand-new crews, deployed to Saudi Arabia for less than two weeks.

Kevin answered, "Roger, on our way in."

Sortie beats spare any day, and I was wide awake now.

Thirty minutes later, twenty KC-135 crewmembers gathered over a mission planning table, Kevin's chart spread out for all to see. I began a cell formation briefing to BERRY POST, a refueling airspace in western Saudi Arabia close to the Jordanian border. A package of five Viper flights, eight in each flight, all named after dogs; four FALSTAFF Weasels; and two RATCHET Spark Varks needed gas after their bombing mission for their return to three bases across the peninsula. Manny, the western bull's-eye, was 140 miles north of BERRY POST. H-3 Air Base, with MiG-21s and MiG-23s, was ninety miles away. All tankers retrograde when any MiGs were within eighty miles. COUGAR, the west AWACS, would control our mission, orbiting literally right above us. Iraqi Air Force Fishbeds, Floggers, and Foxbats were still active over western Iraq. Any calls beyond sixty miles southwest of Manny were reason to turn south.

Defensive maneuvers for five tankers would create a dangerous mid-air collision situation: my jet would head south 180 degrees. TUNA 51's cell mates would turn ten degrees off 180 degrees, so number two would go ten degrees right, three ten degrees left, four twenty degrees right, and five twenty degrees left. Three other refueling orbits bordered BERRY POST, and they might be retrograding also. Iraqi Foxbats fly at 1,200 knots, so retrograding was risking your life so you might live. Remember, none of us had ever performed these defensive maneuvers in the air, so we would have to watch outside for each other. COUGAR could vector us closer to Iraq if the F-16s' fuel situation was bad enough. I ended the briefing with "All other items are Jeddah standard," a quick way of saying follow the Jeddah formation procedures all of you were tested on. Say something if you see something. Briefing over, all twenty of us loaded onto the bus for ramp four. All five aircraft took off around 0700 without any issues and headed northeast.

After we were airborne, Kevin called, "COUGAR, TUNA 51 flight of five, mission number 5751, checking in on white four heading for BERRY POST, authenticate delta mike."

"TUNA 51, COUGAR authenticates november papa. Keep heading north and COUGAR will call your turn."

Why did COUGAR need to call our turn?

"TUNA 51 copies; continuing north. Pilot, did you hear that? They want us to keep heading north."

I did hear it. A lot of things ran through my mind: *How far north will COUGAR take us? Farther north closes the distance between us and the Iraqi threats. Are the receivers held up in the target area? All five tankers are scheduled to give forty thousand pounds each, two hundred thousand pounds total. Each tanker has sixty-five thousand pounds available, 325,000 pounds total if the receivers need it. Thunderstorms popped up along the border last night, and a high cloud deck is above us; is there good visibility in BERRY POST? Saudi F-15s are the tanker CAPs out here. Is their commit criteria for killing MiGs identical to US F-15s'? I don't know.*

Arriving at BERRY POST's refueling control point, we orbited and waited. (If you haven't noticed, tankers wait a lot.) Ten minutes later, COUGAR called with news.

"TUNA 51 flight, the package is on its way out. Turn northwest to facilitate join-up."

Kevin answered, "COUGAR, TUNA 51 flight coming northwest. Pilot, come three zero zero."

I twisted the autopilot knob under my right hand, and the jet started a gradual left turn as I pushed all four throttles up for refueling airspeed of 315 knots.

COUGAR called out, "TUNA 51 flight heading three one five for join-up," as our speed stabilized at 315 knots indicated.

"Roger, TUNA three one five heading." Switching over to the interphone, Kevin said, "Pilot, Nav—that puts us about fifteen miles south of the border."

"Roger, Nav." All of us were nervous being this close to the border.

SPANIEL 31, the package commander, radioed on boom frequency, "TUNA 51, flight SPANIEL lead on A/R primary how, copy?"

"SPANIEL, TUNA has you loud and clear; how us?"

"Loud and clear, radar contact on our nose twenty-one miles. All SPANIEL chicks check noses cold."

Noses cold check means for the eight Viper pilots to make sure their master arm switches were off, putting the safety on all forward-firing weapons—mainly the AIM-9 Sidewinder missiles on their wingtips. One Viper pilot had inadvertently fired an AIM-9 during a mission when switching between weapons modes.

Within minutes forty Vipers, four Weasels, and two Spark Varks joined the TUNA 51 flight. Fifty-one airplanes moving at 315 knots in a five-mile-long, 2,500-foot-tall group near the border. SPANIEL flight came to us, four on the left, two on the right, and two on the boom hitchhiking. FALSTAFF 43 and 44 joined wide left. The blue contact light came on, and Kenny started pumping gas. All Vipers carry ECM pods on centerline pylons because of the SAM threats, which means that they can only be filled using one refueling pump, at 1,500 pounds per minute. Their smaller fuel pipes couldn't handle more pressure; the backflow generated by using two pumps would trigger a pressure disconnect, releasing the toggles. The first Viper came off the boom, and his wingman was on twenty seconds later. Hitchhiking works; it cuts boom cycle time by two-thirds.

COUGAR's next radio call scared us all.

"COUGAR has contacts, Manny two four zero for fifty-seven, medium altitude, heading northwest."

He said it so matter-of-factly, with no increase in the pitch of his voice and no emotion. Contacts meant more than one. Kevin plotted the bull's-eye call and found that the contacts were southwest of H-3 main, seventy-three miles away. I started to turn south.

"COUGAR with contacts, now Manny two four five for sixty-three, medium altitude, now heading southwest."

Were they intercepting us? Moments later, COUGAR broadcast, "COUGAR declares friendlies off Manny near H-2." I wanted to choke whoever was in the back of COUGAR broadcasting those radio calls.

Each SPANIEL took around 4,500 pounds of gas, spending three minutes on the boom. Once full, the SPANIEL flight rose above us and headed east toward Al Minhad in the UAE. A train of F-16s followed him. SPANIEL gave one last piece of instruction to COUGAR before leaving.

"COUGAR, SPANIEL. There's a lot of work to be done up there; still a lot of targets at thirty-two fifty-five north, thirty-nine forty-four east." It was the H-3 Complex and its four airfields.

FALSTAFF 43 immediately moved toward the boom. In a few seconds, the contact light was on again. FALSTAFF wanted full tanks because they had other missions to cover, taking eight thousand pounds apiece. Looking at FALSTAFF, I thought it was ballsy to go back into Iraq with only one HARM on FALSTAFF 44. I had no idea how many HARMs FALSTAFF 41 and 42 had.

We orbited from west to east fifteen miles from the Iraqi border for over forty minutes. Scheduled fuel transfer was supposed to be forty thousand pounds from each tanker. Kenny pumped 52,500 pounds into ten fighters. COUGAR cleared us for home, and I turned for Point Bravo, Jeddah's VFR entry point for approach to the runways. Kenny and I pulled the throttles over the hump, shutting the engines down at 12:15 p.m.

I stayed in tanker ops for a while to talk with D-Right and find out how things had been going. He reported that Jeddah's tanker wing was doing very well, with few maintenance breaks.

D-Right had a BUFF update when I sat down in the Vault to help mission plan sorties. My night of spare duty would now stretch into two, my longest night. Jeddah's BUFFs had used so many bombs that the ammunition storage area was running out! 1709th leadership had a problem; within a day, Jeddah's ammo dump would be empty. The only place close by with a large weapons storage area was 2,800 miles southeast on the island of Diego Garcia, another B-52 base, but the ammo ship from Diego Garcia was not scheduled to arrive for two days. Do you think tanker guys would let an opportunity to rub the bomber guys' noses in their shortcomings pass by?

Nope.

This illustrates why KC-10s are so effective in their dual roles as refueler and airlifter. The only way to solve the problem was to send KC-10s to Diego and airlift bombs back—to reload Jeddah by airmail.

The four airlift missions bringing bombs to Jeddah were a KC-10 "Gucci Bird" combat first. D-Right showed me the paperwork planners had filled out for carrying live ammo in the Guccis' cargo compartments. Paperwork for things that go boom in a tanker is a hassle but mandatory. Two Jeddah KC-10s took off for Diego Garcia later in the evening to load twenty pallets of Rockeye cluster bombs in each jet. Each Gucci Bird returned from Diego and taxied directly to the BUFFs' parking apron on the east side of King Abdulaziz International Airport the next morning. Bombs left the Guccis' cargo compartments on K-loaders, were forklifted onto flatbed trailers, and moved less than three hundred feet to the waiting empty BUFFs. Bomb loaders prepared and hung the Rockeyes right from the flatbeds. The BUFFs took off into the night with twelve bright-white Rockeyes under each wing, just like the STINGRAY flight of F-15E Strike Eagles had a couple of nights ago during refueling, dark night . . . white bombs.

Two more Gucci Birds arrived with twenty more pallets the next afternoon, and Diego's ammo ship arrived a day late, carrying twenty thousand bombs in its holds. Bomb caskets lifted out of the ammo ship were loaded onto flatbeds, covered with canvas tarps, and trucked through the streets of Jeddah to the BUFF weapons storage area. I wondered what the citizens of Jeddah thought seeing a convoy of tarp-covered dark-blue US Air Force flatbeds driving through their city. Did they know what was under the canvas? No one seemed to care, though, as this went on for several days. The KC-10 community got a big "atta boy" from the BUFF leadership, and they continued dropping bombs on the Republican Guard throughout the rest of the war.

★ ★

LESSONS FROM THE COCKPIT:
SATISFACTION

Stepping on the bus at around 2200, I was exhausted but happy. It had been a long night, stretched into two. My crew had accomplished just about everything you could do in the KC-135 during this twenty-four-hour period. We had taxied full KC-135s from fuel pits to the parking ramp, cocked on jets so other crews could hop in and take off, spared launches of other combat missions, and finally got to fly a mission to within fifteen miles of the Iraqi border. Observing KC-10s fulfill their dual role as both refuelers and airlifters moving bombs from Diego Garcia to Jeddah was historic; it had never been done, to our knowledge. Looking across the ramp the next afternoon and watching palettes of Rockeye bombs coming off the Gucci Birds and being loaded onto the BUFFs for night missions was rewarding. Jeddah's tanker wing was doing just about every-thing tankers could do in combat operations from one airfield. Everyone's sense of job satisfaction was really high.

I have worked thirty-six-hour days during my career. Coming back to my room and slipping into bed exhausted but satisfied was one of the great things about flying tankers. I've talked to many people who have jobs they hate, and I don't understand it. They find no satisfaction in what they are doing. I've often wondered why these people don't leave those unful-filling positions to find something that will give them better job satisfaction. Working under the stress of an unfulfilling job is a terrible feeling. Fortunately, I've experienced this only once. For almost twenty-five years, I got to fly the airplane of my boyhood dreams all over the world in peacetime and in combat. I've also flown in other planes, such as the F-15 and the RAF VC-10. There were many days when I came home with an overdose of job satisfaction. If I were standing in front of you, I would tell all of you to find something that gives you tremendous job satisfaction. Don't stay in a place where you hate walking through the front door. There are too many opportunities out there now for you to find the immense job satisfaction I received from being a tanker pilot.

★ ★

8

The Kim CAPs

0907 Monday 11 July 1994
Kadena Air Base
Okinawa, Japan

You must always be able to predict what's next and then have the flexibility to evolve.

—Marc Benioff, American entrepreneur and philanthropist

Air power is indivisible. If you split it up into compartments, you merely pull it to pieces and destroy its greatest asset, its flexibility.

—Bernard Montgomery, British field marshal and Viscount of Alamein

Gentlemen, when the enemy is committed to a mistake we must not interrupt him too soon.

—Viscount Horatio Nelson, commander of the English Fleet

The first week of July 1994 was hot and humid on the island, just like every summer in the tropics. Young Tiger Tankers continued flying strategic, operational, and tactical missions throughout the Pacific Rim. All of us looked forward to the Fourth of July after a short workweek, with Kadena shutting down for the annual airshow. An 18 Wing Intel troop walked into our Sensitive Compartmented Information Facility (SCIF), the bank vault–like area we worked in Friday afternoon, Pacific Air Forces or PACAF message in hand. North Korean state radio and TV had announced that the nation's Dear Leader of fifty years had passed away in the middle of the night. North Korea's only television station showed Kim Il-sung's body lying in state. All of us knew his son Kim Jong-il, whom we called "the Chonger," was his designated successor because his dad had announced it over a year earlier. During one of the broadcasts from Pyongyang, the Chonger announced his father's funeral plans. In one of his typical rants, the Chonger stated that his father's funeral would be in Seoul. The only problem was that Kim Jong-il didn't own Seoul.

None of us knew what the Chonger meant by saying he would bury his dad in Seoul, South Korea. The second question all of us asked was what to prepare for in case he tried. All of us in Weapons and Tactics or DOT were extremely familiar with the war plans in case North Korea invaded South Korea. But what if Kim Jong-il slowly ratcheted up the pressure over time? We didn't know what to prepare for that Friday afternoon. I had been looking forward to a weekend at Kadena Marina, a local beach, with my wife, Val, and my children, Rachel, Ryan, and eight-month-old Jeffrey. But I knew a phone call might be coming, along the lines of "Time to make the doughnuts!"

It did not take long to find out what the North Koreans meant. There was a checklist of indications and warnings leaders in Hawaii used as a baseline for gauging North Korean intentions. Intelligence analysts told us North Korean military warnings increased every couple of *hours*. The North Korean military was gearing up for something big. The one item grabbing everyone's attention was the North Korean Special Operation Force dispersing.

Sometime Saturday morning, PACAF headquarters issued their warning order to prepare for operations. The order tasked the USS *Independence* battle group to begin sailing to the South Korean peninsula. *Indy*'s CAG 5 required Young Tiger tankers for support. Increasing our situational awareness, RC-135 Rivet Joint and U-2 reconnaissance aircraft missions rose. Included in this warning order was a statement instructing the 18th Wing to prepare for defensive counter air missions over South Korea. Defensive Counter-Air, or DCA, patrols over South Korea meant lots of tankers. To maintain a twenty-four-hour F-15 CAP requires eighteen KC-135R sorties. If the Eagles engaged, tanker missions would increase to twenty-two to twenty-four sorties in a twenty-four-hour period. If an F-15 engaged enemy aircraft, the first things coming off the Eagle jets would be the external fuel tanks. The ability to carry four thousand more pounds of fuel would immediately leave the airplane at the start of any air-to-air engagements. PACAF's order stated that F-15s and their support must be ready by 9:00 a.m. on Monday 11 July. My DOT boss T-Mac's phone call Saturday at lunchtime was my invitation to join the DOT planning party in the Vault. He could not tell me what was happening over the phone, but I already knew. By that afternoon we still didn't know what F-15 support would look like, so we started with an assumption of twelve-ship packages of Eagles in three CAP stations near the DMZ.

On Sunday morning Val left for church with the kids, and I walked out the door in a flight suit bound for the Vault. The solution we came up with was to fly the twelve-ship formation of F-15s with two airborne spares to the Korean peninsula, taking off at 0900 and 1600 Monday. Spitter, our DOT weapons controller, would leave in the AWACS forty-five minutes before the Eagles, and the RC-135 Rivet Joint would go thirty minutes prior. AWACS and Rivet Joint need refueling every five hours, using up four KC-135s. We devised a communications-out launch plan for all seventeen airplanes to silently leave Kadena. Everyone would take off when the control tower shined a green light at us. Four of us calculated the rejoin time, hinging on the third tanker's takeoff and climb out. Boom operators would immediately drop their booms to test all fourteen Eagles' refueling systems. Any Eagle not capable of taking on gas would return to base, and one of the airborne spares filled the hole.

Intelligence reported a Russian fishing trawler or spy ship sailing north of Okinawa. We knew the Russian trawler would send any indication of activity at Kadena straight to the Chonger in Pyongyang.

The next three-ship of Young Tiger tankers would relieve the first cell as it passed Cheju-Do Island. Eagles maintain a three-hour vulnerable time, meaning tank-fight-tank-fight-tank-fight and then come home with another three-ship cell of tankers meeting over central South Korea. Fourteen Dirty Dozen Eagles would accomplish the same sequence beginning at 1600 Monday afternoon, arriving in South Korea after sunset. Every aircraft movement had a definite time, so none of us had to talk on the radio. PACAF's order stated that Shogun Wing's air superiority packages would defend South Korea twice a day every Monday, Wednesday, and Friday, with no end date given. Nine tankers a day, three times a week for the foreseeable future would run the Young Tiger squadron out of annual flying hours.

PACAF ordered F-117 stealth fighters to deploy from the US at the same time. F-15E Strike Eagles and A-10 Warthogs based in Alaska would arrive in South Korea on Monday. Doug, my counterpart in Wing Scheduling, had the task of creating an air bridge from the States to the South Korean bases. Doug sent three KC-135s to Misawa, leaving the squadron with only twelve jets at home. Marine Air Group F/A-18 Hornets would move forward to the Korean peninsula also. All of these movements were to happen in the next seventy-two hours. PACAF's mini air campaign to keep Kim Jong-il from doing something stupid shaped up nicely through Sunday afternoon. Before leaving, Doug scheduled me on the first tanker out on Monday morning as a passenger, not a flier. The 67th Fighting Cocks were tagged with the first Monday-morning missions. The 12th Dirty Dozen Eagle Squadron filled the afternoon go at 1600. Even though I was a passenger on the first tanker, regulations require twelve hours of crew rest. I walked in the door just before 1900 Sunday night.

Monday morning's pre-mission mass brief emphasized the rules of engagement. Twenty-millimeter training rounds filled the guns, and that was all the Eagles were taking. The large Eagle fighter package was a show of force, not an in-your-face MiG sweep. WeeBee led the Eagle mission brief, and Spitter finished up on command and controlling the force. Fourteen Eagles made up the BLOWN flight: BLOWN 21 through 24, BLOWN 31 through 34, and BLOWN 41 through 44, with two additional air spares. The BLOWN call sign came right out of the Pentagon call sign book. All of us wished there were a sexier or more manly name for the event, but DoD call signs wouldn't allow it. At least it wasn't something embarrassing, like FLOWER. My good buddy Tazz was BLOWN 23, WeeBee's second element leader. Bigs, the ops group commander, had a few words to end the mass brief. His message to the force was: "Don't do anything stupid—let the Chonger do that. We don't want this to escalate."

Twenty minutes before 0900, Alan, the pilot for my flight, pushed the throttles up and we taxied out of our parking stub. As we turned right onto the taxiway, our crew could see across both runways. Fourteen F-15s taxied down the opposite taxiway toward runway 5 right, each one loaded with three external fuel tanks. To accomplish end-of-runway checks, seven Eagles taxied across the runway into another arming area. At three minutes to 0900, WeeBee taxied his four F-15s onto the runway, the second four-ship right behind them. The third four-ship waited between the runways as the two air spares moved closer to runway 5 right.

At exactly 0900 on Monday 11 July 1994, WeeBee observed a green light from Kadena Tower. I was surprised how bright the light was from over a mile away. WeeBee's exhaust nozzles opened wide as each engine went into full afterburner. The F-15s began their takeoff rolls every twelve seconds. The sights and sounds of fourteen F-15s taking off in afterburner are something you never forget. The last departing F-15 air spare brought his gear and flaps up and made an aggressive left turn out of traffic right in front of us while we sat on runway 5 left. Alan had taxied onto the runway when WeeBee blasted off. Looking northwest out Alan's window, we could see all the F-15s formed up into three groups.

And we waited.

My Wing Tactics F-15 counterpart Redeye calculated that the Eagles took approximately seven minutes to get the four-ship airborne, fly around the radar traffic pattern, and reach the five-mile initial point. As the cockpit FMS clock showed 00:07:00 Zulu time, Alan's crew began looking for the tower's green light. The light gun signal was clearly visible from the cockpit. Alan pushed the throttles up and released the brakes at 0907 on the clock. The jet strained in the heat to get 322,000 pounds airborne. On runway heading at 2,300 feet and three miles from the Kadena TACAN, I looked out the window behind Alan's seat. Tazz and his wingman were just pulling into position on the left wing. Crawling over to the right window behind Alan's copilot, I saw WeeBee and his wingman tucked in under the right wing. Alan's boom lay in the boom pod for takeoff—normally a regulation no-no, but escorting fourteen Eagles was not a Stateside training mission. I captured one Eagle refueling low over Okinawa with my camera, and the Pacific Ocean did not disappoint; it was a gorgeous turquois blue around the island. Each F-15 cycled through, receiving about two thousand pounds before getting a pressure disconnect as we passed over the smaller Ryukyu Islands north of Kadena. All four of WeeBee's F-15s plus an airborne spare checked good for refueling systems. At the predetermined point north of the island, the two airborne spare Eagles peeled off and returned to Kadena.

And Naha Air Traffic Control made a strange radio call.

"KOBE 51 flight, how many in your formation?"

Bigs had been adamant in the mass brief that none of us say how many jets were in formation. If anyone asked KOBE 51 flight how many aircraft were in our formation, the reply should be "As filed."

The copilot radioed, "Naha, KOBE 51 flight as filed."

The Japanese controller did not like the answer. Being close to the island, he must have seen more aircraft than just three tankers. He probably saw the F-15s do a lap around the radar pattern, and the fourteen F-15 radar blips merge with our tankers during climb out.

"KOBE 51 flight, Naha—say how many in formation?"

He probably thought the Americans were being sneaky again.

"Naha, KOBE 51 flight, as filed."

The copilot looked over at me. "What do you want me to do if he asks again?"

I told him what our instructions were. "You tell him KOBE 51 is as filed, and if he asks you again, stop answering."

I told them it would be okay—let the ops group figure it out after we landed. Bigs would take care of us. We had to hide from the Russian spy trawler north of the island.

Leveling off at twenty-eight thousand feet, all four F-15s remained close to our wings until we were out of Naha's radar coverage. As soon as we passed that point, all the Eagles spread out into tactical formation.

Every fighter pilot thinks tankers purposefully fly formations through clouds. Tazz has always chided me that there could be a single cloud out in front of the tankers, and we would turn to take the formation right through it. Of course, this wasn't true; I may have skirted the cloud to see if Tazz was paying attention, though. But Tazz sure gave me a hard time about it from his cockpit perch under our wing. North of the island, some high cirrus clouds stretched across our route. Alan made no attempt to alter course. I looked out the window to see Tazz and his wingman slide in close. I knew Tazz would have some words for me because he held up his left hand and wagged his index finger back and forth at me.

The boom operators left their booms down and ready to refuel all the way to Korea, and the F-15s randomly plugged in as we pressed north. Approaching the South Korean peninsula, the Eagles moved in tight again to appear as one big blob on North Korea's long-range early warning radar. As we arrived at the drop-off point, Tazz and his wingman seemed to be underneath the wings, right next to the outboard engines. WeeBee briefed us that all Eagles would explode off the tanker wings into their CAP stations when crossing a certain point in central South Korea. As we passed over the point, WeeBee made BLOWN flight's first radio call: "BLOWNS, PUSH BLACK ONE NOW!"

All twelve Eagles fanned out from under the tankers' wings and rose to their CAP locations south of the Korean DMZ. Kneeling down behind Alan's seat, I watched Tazz and his wingman select afterburner and climb to their CAP stations above the tankers. Farther behind us, two more Eagles appeared off KOBE 52, and then two more off KOBE 53, all in burner and climbing. Later, during the debrief, we learned that when all the Eagles came off our wings, every radar in southern North Korea turned on and illuminated the formation. Tazz's afterburner departure off KOBE 51's wing was the predetermined action point for all three KC-135s to return home. Right on schedule over Cheju-Do Island, our relief tankers in the KOBE 61 flight passed two thousand feet to our right and below us. The refueling plan I had created for WeeBee and his BLOWN flight of Eagles was executed perfectly. At 1235 Monday afternoon, KOBE 51's main wheels touched down on runway 5 left.

My day wasn't finished, as another air superiority package would depart at 1600. Habu Hill offers a direct line of sight to Kadena's control tower and the green light to both ends of runway 5. The afternoon launch went off just like the morning's—perfect. Even the timing was dead nuts on. Watching fourteen F-15 Eagles take off in afterburner is spectacular and deafening in the waning sunlight of the afternoon. As the F-15s turned five miles from the end of the runway, all three KC-135s launched thirty seconds apart. A lot of Eagle drivers, tanker aircrews, and weapons controllers had parked on Habu Hill to watch the afternoon go. There were a few minor things Weapons and Tactics had to refine in some of the refueling plans, but all tanker crews reported that everything went off just as planned.

The Shogun Wing flew the same schedule on Wednesday 13 July. The 44th Fighter Squadron Vampires flew the morning go, Stump leading the fourteen Eagles down from the upper fighter ramp. The Dirty Dozen flew the nighttime vulnerable period again, Jay Ray leading the formation. The Dirty Dozen had the most experience in the newly up-graded Eagles, so Skeet's squadron would always fly the night missions. After Friday's launches, Wing Scheduling noticed a problem. Kim CAPs were soaking up a lot of tanker sorties and flying hours. Nine tankers supported one three-hour vulnerable period. Three KC-135s dragged the Eagle twelve-ship to Korea, three others kept them in their CAPs, and three more tankers dragged them home from the Korean peninsula. The fuel bill was the same for the afternoon go. Each day the Shoguns flew the Kim CAP missions, eighteen KC-135s consumed 3.2 million pounds of gas a day escorting twenty-four Eagles back and forth to South Korea. BRIGHAM AWACS and the Rivet Joint required three more KC-135 sorties. F-16 Vipers from Osan and Kunsan Air Bases also needed gas on some missions. If this operational tempo continued, the 909th would exhaust its annual flying hours before August, two months short of the end of the DOD fiscal year. PACAF ordered us to keep going.

The three tankers supporting the air bridge of fighters from the States also stayed busy. F-15E Strike Eagles from Elmendorf outside Anchorage and A-10s from Eielson near Fairbanks deployed to South Korea on Wednesday 13 July. Stealth fighters arrived at Kunsan Air Base a day later. F-117 Black Jets showing up in the region sent a very clear and powerful message to Kim Jong-il: the low observable aircraft are here and flying. The Black Jets operated only after 2100. Two tankers flying in cell formation supported the F-117s by orbiting in the training areas over the Yellow Sea. The Black Jets showed back up about thirty to thirty-five minutes later for a mid-mission refueling. The Rivet Joint kept up its busy schedule, flying other high-priority missions through-out the Pacific Rim, which 909th KC-135s had to support with two air-craft, a primary and a manned spare. This mini air campaign continued for two weeks.

The Young Tigers were exhausted, running out of flight hours and then aircraft to cover the schedule. At the same time, we were doing what we all loved. Toward the end of the second week, Kim Jong-il made the decision that burying his dad, and making any other funeral arrangements, in Seoul had too high a cost. I'm sure the US government used other diplomatic, informational, and possibly economic sanctions against the North Korean government, but I think it was seeing walls of Eagles twice a day every Monday, Wednesday, and Friday over South Korea that gave Kim Jong-il reason to rethink his father's funeral plans.

PACAF headquarters sent a message bringing the Kim CAPs to an end on 25 July, two weeks after we had started the show-of-force exercise. Strike Eagles, Warthogs, and stealth fighters returned to the States behind KC-10s refilled in the air by KC-135s. Events in Korea, plus other real-world missions, ran the 909th out of annual flying hours at the end of July. 18 Wing Commander General Cliver sent a message to PACAF headquarters stating that he would lock the tanker squadron's doors on 31 July. PACAF reluctantly gave General Cliver additional flying hours to cover the added sorties. Doug took a computer product to PACAF headquarters with refueling taskings the 909th was ordered to fly without additional flight time. Taking the computer paper by the top edges, Doug tossed it across the floor. A six-foot-long exposé on over 220 additional taskings unfolded. PACAF found additional flying hours out of some bucket, but the 909th almost ran out of those before October, the end of the fiscal year. The flying tempo just did not let up that summer.

Visiting San Antonio recently for a baby christening, Doug, Shadow (a 909th boom operator), and I had breakfast at a diner near the airport. All three of us talked about how exhausted we had been at the end of those two weeks: Doug running the air bridge delivering fighters and attack aircraft, and Shadow lying in the boom pod and reaching out and touching BRIGHAM AWACS, F-15s, F-16s, F-117s, and Carrier Air Wing 5 Tomcats and Hornets. Redeye and I refined tactics and procedures used by the Shogun Wing to hide operations and coordinate mission timing, and we read all the intelligence reports generated by Eagles CAPing so close to the DMZ.

Even though all of us were tired, involvement in these critical missions gave us tremendous job satisfaction. US airpower kept a deranged enemy and his forces from invading South Korea without firing a shot. Months later, the Chonger implemented a different method to intimidate the Pacific Rim by firing ballistic missiles into the Sea of Japan. One test missile flew over Misawa Air Base, which concerned us. Additional contingency plans were created to monitor the Chonger's missile ambitions, including shooting them down if they were headed in the wrong direction. All plans required Young Tiger tanker support, exacerbating our flying-hour problem. But I was introduced to some of the Navy's capabilities, which assured me that my family would remain safe in Okinawa.

★ ★

LESSONS FROM THE COCKPIT: FLEXIBILITY

The events of July 1994 illustrated the flexibility and dominance airpower had on an adversary. 18th Wing AWACS, fighters, and tankers went from zero to five hundred knots at the speed of a newscast. Using regional plans as our baseline, T-Mac's Weapons and Tactics shop created a flexible defensive counter air plan to defend South Korea from invasion. Within a few hours of notification, Doug coordinated the construction of an air bridge with AMC's Tanker Airlift Control Center to deliver A-10s, F-15Es, and F-117 stealth fighters from the States across the planet's largest ocean. Airpower's inherent flexibility gave national and military leaders options, which we're seeing used now in the news as North Korea launches more ballistic missiles. Flexible deterrent options and our show of force kept North Korean leaders from continuing with their funeral plans and averted a catastrophic war. Kim Jong-il would just have to bury his father somewhere closer to home.

The key to airpower is its flexibility. It gives national and military leaders options to choose from as a situation develops. Recent news broadcasts have illustrated the volatility of financial markets around the world. In the business world, leaders create business and financial plans with the flexibility to adapt to changing environments. The military has a term for these flexible plans; we call them branches and sequels. Business plans developed with branches and sequels reduce risk, because leaders have flexible options for when the market takes off in different directions.

★ ★

9

Korean Air Flight 801

1045 Tuesday 5 August 1997
Tanker Airlift Control Center
Scott Air Force Base
Belleville, Illinois

America is hope. It is compassion. It is excellence. It is valor.
— SENATOR PAUL TSONGAS (D), MASSACHUSETTS

The purpose of human life is to serve, and to show compassion and the will to help others.
— DR. ALBERT SCHWEITZER, HUMANITARIAN, PHILOSOPHER, AND PHYSICIAN

We need more kindness, more compassion, more joy, more laughter. I definitely want to contribute to that.
— ELLEN DEGENERES, COMEDIAN AND TALK SHOW HOST

After four hours running missions and making sure high-priority cargo moved, the Tanker Airlift Control Center West Cell tempo slowed down on 5 August 1997. The "Breaking News" banner appeared on a flat-screen TV across from me, and CNN's videographer pointed the camera behind the reporter at a burning airplane in a driving rainstorm. They stood on Nimitz Hill, a seven-hundred-foot-high peak in the middle of Guam. I recognized the terrain immediately from flying approaches into Agana International Airport. CNN's reporter stated, "A Korean Air 747 jetliner, Flight 801 from Seoul, crashed on Nimitz Hill at approximately 1:42 a.m. this morning. You can see the fires are still burning behind me. I'm hearing rescue vehicles coming from below us now; rescue crews are having a very hard time approaching the crash site in the storm."

I reached over and grabbed Lieutenant Colonel Kay by the arm and pointed at the flat-screen.

"Sir—are you watching this?"

Lieutenant Colonel Kay turned in his swivel chair, and we watched the news report. Lieutenant Colonel Kay hollered over to Senior Controller Colonel Bailey standing at his desk. "Colonel Bailey, incoming CNN news report from Guam is on the flat-screen. It looks like a plane crash."

Colonel Bailey had his own flat-screen above his desk. His TV's volume bars increased as he pointed the remote at the screen.

CNN's videographer caught something. "Some of the survivors are walking around the crash site . . ."

Colonel Bailey quipped, "That looks like Nimitz Hill."

Nimitz Hill's radio navigation aid appeared on the right side of the screen. Korean Air Flight 801's wreckage rested in a ravine down the slope from Nimitz Hill. All of us were thinking the same thing, but Colonel Bailey was the only one who said out loud, "Did he miss the step-down altitude?"

Instrument approaches to Agana's runway 06 left have an altitude restriction keeping aircraft safely above Nimitz Hill's peak. Colonel Bailey, Lieutenant Colonel Kay, and I had flown approaches into Agana International Airport numerous times. As you passed over Nimitz Hill, it felt like you could reach down and touch it. We concluded that Flight 801 crashed into the terrain because the pilot missed the approach step-down altitude.

At the end of the news report, Colonel Bailey said what Lieutenant Colonel Kay and I already knew: "Okay, guys, come up with a plan. You know in thirty minutes my phone will ring with someone in Washington, DC, on the other end. My bet is either the State Department or the National Transportation Safety Board. Mark, you lived over there and understand the area, so come up with a plan."

Lieutenant Colonel Kay turned to me and said, "Do your magic."

The first step was finding a ride. My gut feeling told me to look at Andrews Air Force Base, outside Washington, DC, but I kept pushing the thought out of my mind, since my group controlled everything west of the Mississippi to Mumbai, TACC's geographical east-west boundaries. I finally listened to my gut when no aircraft were available on the West Coast. Pulling up the Andrews AFB schedule page, I saw that one Presidential Support C-141 Starlifter crew was scheduled to show up for their flight home to South Carolina in an hour and forty five minutes. It was perfect for this rescue mission. I told Lieutenant Colonel Kay I wanted to rip off Andrews's Presidential Support Starlifter, which required a lot of coordination. He walked over to the East Cell director and told him the West Cell needed the C-141 at Andrews. When told why, he had no problem.

The East Cell director asked if we were sure the call was coming. Of course we didn't know. Invoking the Boy Scout motto of "Be Prepared," I took the Starlifter and its crew for the mission, now called REACH 1267. My gut feeling was that the call would come from the State Department or higher because of the news reports. If no call arrived, the C-141 crew would hop into their jet and go home. Rescheduling REACH 1267's mission into the computer and coordinating with Andrews took twenty minutes.

"Man, is this crew going to be surprised when they come in to fly!"

I sat down at my desk as Colonel Bailey hollered over to Lieutenant Colonel Kay and me, "Hey, guys, it's the vice president's office. I bet it's our Guam phone call!"

Colonel Bailey picked up the phone and began talking to someone and saying "Yes, sir" a lot. The phone conversation lasted less than two minutes, ending with "West Cell already worked up a plan, Mr. Vice President."

Well, not entirely.

"There's your authorization to put your plan in motion. Eighteen members of the NTSB Go Team, their equipment, and their bags need a ride to Guam. They need to be there in eighteen to twenty-four hours. Work a plan and come see me."

"Colonel Bailey, I think we already have a partial plan. We just need to work in a gas stop."

REACH 1267's crew was augmented, meaning it had two additional pilots, navigators, and loadmasters, and so could operate for twenty-four hours. The biggest problem was range. Doing gas math in my head, I figured the crew would drop dead in Hawaii without air refueling over the West Coast. None of the KC-135 bases on the West Coast had jets available. I scanned Travis Air Force Base's KC-10 schedule to see what they had: no aircraft on alert, ready to go on a moment's notice. I was not finding anything to keep 1267 going. No refueling meant we were screwed.

I remembered a long conversation with Russ, a college classmate who flew KC-10s at Travis. Regular KC-10 training missions schedule two Gucci Birds as partners to practice refueling across northern California on Track 7 Alpha/Bravo. AR 7 Alpha was perfect for REACH 1267 to get fuel. I told Travis's command post to prepare one of the KC-10s to refuel 1267 on 7 Alpha/Bravo by putting an extra sixty thousand pounds on one KC-10. Delaying their launch by thirty-five minutes would allow them to meet 1267 and provide the gas needed to fly to Hawaii. After landing in Hawaii, the second, fresh 1267 flight crew would jump into the seats and continue on to Guam. The TACC flight plan shop computed fuel and times to every point, which I sent to Andrews's command post via e-mail. Tammy, one of West Cell's airmen, put all the changes in the schedule.

After we discussed the plan with Colonel Bailey, he gave Lieutenant Colonel Kay and me a thumbs-up. His only instructions were to watch the mission carefully, because if anything happened, bad news would travel through the State Department and possibly to the White House.

No pressure.

An hour later, caller ID showed that Andrews's command post was dialing us. Captain Riordon, the aircraft commander, had called for more information. He started the conversation with "Major Hasara, I understand my crew is not going home today. Command post told me to call you."

"Captain Riordon, have you seen the news out of Guam?"

"Yes, sir, I have. What is going on?"

All flight crews want the chance to do a mission with importance, and nothing was more important than compassionate rescue flights. Complex, high-visibility missions with changes were stressful, as was flying halfway across the world to provide support for an event that had made international news, overseen by the White House and the State Department. I always tried to make sure a good aircrew received the visibility they deserved.

Captain Riordon's crew did have a vote on my plan. I asked a little bit differently this time: "I need your crew to take this mission to Guam, Captain Riordon."

"I don't know, sir . . . Hawaii and Guam. This one's going to suck eggs!" he said, laughing over the phone.

"I am assuming by the tone of your voice that you don't mind doing this for us."

Captain Riordon answered, "Sir, we will take the mission. Anything that can be done to help the victims of Flight 801 we want to be a part of."

The NTSB Go Team pulled up just before engine start. Loadmasters strapped down their bags as the rear clamshell doors closed. REACH 1267 launched twenty minutes later, two hours after the vice president's call. Eighteen Go Team members found a warm place for the long flight to Guam. Refueling on AR 7 Alpha went without a hiccup. The second crew hopped into the seats at Hickam Air Force Base for the five-hour flight to Guam. Seventeen hours after leaving Washington, DC, 1267 touched down on Andersen Air Force Base's rain-soaked runway.

Each day I learned something new about air mobility, knowledge that helped us accomplish missions. The next morning Lieutenant Colonel Kay's team was back on moving missions. Calls to the States during the night had added a mission for survivors. One of those requirements created the most unusual request I'd received. Two hundred twenty-eight people died from Korean Air Flight 801's crash and subsequent fire. Twenty-six passengers survived but with serious injuries. Rescue efforts now focused on four of the burn victims, and TACC requested an aircraft be sent to Billings, Montana. In the two years I had worked in the West Cell, TACC had never sent an aircraft to Billings.

I couldn't figure out what was so important in Billings that a big cargo plane had to stop there before going on to Guam. Medical Evacuation Cell entered the new C-141 information into the computer, a Category 2A mission. Changes in a Cat 2A mission required coordination with and signatures from agencies in the building and the State Department. I walked to the Medical Evacuation Cell and asked one of the flight nurses what was so important in Billings.

I would never have put Korean Air Flight 801; Billings, Montana; and smokejumpers together in my mind.

Billings has a warehouse where equipment used to fight forest fires is stored, and that equipment includes portable burn treatment units. These mobile units were perfect for moving the survivors back to the US. The State Department contacted several doctors who specialized in burn treatment, notifying them that their ride was coming soon. None of us in the West Cell had known this firefighter warehouse and burn treatment equipment existed.

After one hour and thirty-five minutes in flight, REACH 1123 landed in Billings. Three hours later, 1123 flew to Hickam Air Force Base for fuel and then continued on to Guam. While 1123 was in the air, Governor Carl Gutierrez of Guam requested via the State Department that Flight 801's four most severely burned passengers come to the States. Eleven-year-old Grace Chung, the only American survivor, and three Korean nationals left Guam on 8 August in mobile burn treatment units on REACH 1123 for a twenty-hour flight to San Antonio, Texas. Unfortunately, Grace died three days after arriving in San Antonio, but her three Korean friends recovered and rejoined their families with an amazing story.

★ ★

LESSONS FROM THE COCKPIT:
COMPASSION

Rarely do American citizens see how Air Mobility Command is engaged every day in disasters around the globe. The US military is the only force that can accomplish some of these compassionate missions. I've talked to people about how relief efforts after Hurricane Katrina tore through New Orleans were accomplished from an aircraft carrier and large-deck amphibious assault ships. Large-deck amphibs have four operating rooms and a complete medical team aboard. AMC's C-5 Galaxy fleet moved helicopters from around the States to Barksdale Air Force Base Louisiana, which operated from the Navy ships. The USS *Carl Vinson* supported earthquake relief in Haiti because it was capable of producing four hundred thousand gallons of fresh water per day with its desalination systems. These compassionate missions are very gratifying for the troops involved.

Within hours of notification, Colonel Bailey's TACC team moved the National Transportation Safety Board's Go Team to Guam. When Governor Gutierrez asked for additional help for burn victims, a C-141 outfitted as an air ambulance delivered doctors and burn units from Billings, Montana, to Guam. All of us have the ability and resources to show compassion. Compassionate service increases the joy and peace in our lives. When I was a young boy, I was taught that when you are in the service of your fellow beings, you are in the service of God. Take the time to experience the peace compassion brings to someone around you who needs it.

★ ★

10

Combat Employment School

0800 Monday 12 July 1999

Fairchild Air Force Base

Spokane, Washington

I've missed more than nine thousand shots in my career. I've lost almost three hundred games. Twenty-six times I've been trusted to take the game-winning shot and missed. I've failed over and over and over again in my life. And that is why I succeed.

—MICHAEL JORDAN, BASKETBALL SUPERSTAR

Failure is simply the opportunity to begin again, this time more intelligently.

—HENRY FORD, AMERICAN INDUSTRIALIST

The function of education is to teach one to think intensively and to think critically. Intelligence plus character—that is the goal of true education.

—REVEREND DR. MARTIN LUTHER KING JR.,

AMERICAN CIVIL RIGHTS MOVEMENT LEADER

Operation Allied Force once again illustrated that nobody kicks ass without tanker gas, and that US Air Force tankers remain the world's refueling workhorse. The US deployed an active-duty and Reserve component force of KC-135 and KC-10 tankers, making up nearly 90 percent of NATO's refueling effort. One hundred seventy-five US tankers flew five thousand sorties transferring 250 million pounds of fuel. Refueling planners placed tankers close to the fight—Slobodan Milošević's fighters and SAMs were less than eighty miles away from the northern anchors. One KC-135 from RAF Mildenhall orbiting in AGIP NORTH over Bosnia-Herzegovina was about to be engaged when two F-15Cs destroyed the two approaching Yugoslav MiG-29 Fulcrums a short seventy miles away. Most of the refueling areas were less than a hundred miles from enemy airfields. Retrograde procedures were limited by the tight airspace in the Adriatic and by the participating nations. Two rescue attempts for F-117 and F-16 crews required twenty tankers to keep the RESCAP force on station. Tankers once again were the limiting factor in air operations.

Kosovo was the tanker community's wake-up call, in my opinion. In future conflicts tankers would operate closer to adversary airspace, Combined Air Operations Center (CAOC) planners would build elaborate refueling systems crossing several combatant command regions, aircrews would employ defensive maneuvers while operating inside adversary borders, and search-and-rescue operations would increase in complexity, requiring over half a million pounds of fuel. Being stationed with the Young Tiger Squadron at Kadena placed me in a select group with skills and experience in these areas.

Air Forces Europe Vice Commander Lieutenant General Bill Begert wrote after the Kosovo air campaign in the Winter 1999 edition of *Aerospace Power Journal* about refueling and its challenges in Operation Allied Force. He said,

The [Vicenza, Italy] CAOC was not properly manned initially for a rapidly expanding air campaign of uncertain duration, and it was slow in expanding a tanker staff sized for Allied Force.

When augmentees did reach Vicenza, many lacked the requisite tanker-planning skills. The team that eventually assembled was highly motivated, but it was largely a pickup team with widely varying levels of training. With its inadequate size and training in the first month of the campaign, the tanker cadre was nearly overwhelmed.

General Begert identified one problem:

Finally, Allied Force pointed out a need for a larger cadre of properly trained tanker planners prepared to plan and execute any air-refueling role. These experts will require realistic training exercises to further hone and develop their skills. As a key enabler of the Expeditionary Air Force, air refueling must be supervised and planned by well-trained tanker experts.

Tanker expertise remained in the Cold War Stone Age, geared toward stopping the Russian onslaught in Western Europe by nuclear force. Experience gained from Desert Storm was not lessons learned but lessons observed, with some attempts to correct procedure. Sadly, most experiences were not added to our employment and training manuals. Every Air Force aircraft operates based on their classified *Air Force Tactics, Techniques, and Procedures 3-1* manual, known as *AFTTP 3-1*. Defensive maneuvers in the *3-1* were still not allowed in the airplane during actual flight, only in the simulator. Most of us had never accomplished a retrograde in any training or exercise, even though many tanker crews operated near or in enemy airspace. Performing potentially lifesaving defensive maneuvers in the tanker required a waiver from the AMC director of operations, a two-star general. SAC never tested tanker defensive tactics in operational scenarios. The bomber, fighter, and attack communities used an unclassified companion for day-to-day training. All day-to-day training in tankers was based on Air Force regulation.

Graduate-level education on tanker operations had to focus on the operational level planning and execution at the Operations Center but still teach aircrews tactical maneuvers needed for survival. Everyone we talked to at the Air Force Weapons School told us our KC-135 Combat Employment School syllabus was too operational, which is where it should be, based on what the four of us learned working at the Vicenza CAOC. Becoming a part of the Weapons School, which AMC leadership kept pushing on the tanker cadre, meant we had to dive into the tactical weeds of tanker operations, though tankers make their money at the operational level.

Armed with the knowledge gained from the Vicenza CAOC, I invited the C-130 Weapons School instructors to join us in Spokane to help formulate a syllabus outline. The commandant of the Combat Aerial Delivery School (CADS), a full-bird colonel, joined him. This meeting did *not* go well, and I take credit for its failure. A discussion on tanker skill sets required to graduate from our school went on while the C-130 Weapons School instructor pilot stood writing those skills on a whiteboard. Over G, the CAD's commandant, and a C-130 Weapons School instructor pilot reminded us that our tanker syllabus taught too many operational concepts, not understanding that the operational level was where the tankers lived and breathed, because their C-130 syllabus focused on the tactical level of employment. This event, plus a few others, caused a huge rift between us and our CADS brethren in Little Rock, Arkansas.

It also caused angst among the cadre members. This friction caused all of us a great deal of stress as we tried to do what was best for our community and convince our leadership that a tanker syllabus—although great for our community—was not Weapons School–worthy because of its higher-level focus. The cadre finally made a decision to fall on our operational swords and develop the syllabus our way. A change made to our school's definition stated what we were trying to do: "The purpose of the KC-135 CES is to produce graduates possessing the knowledge and skills necessary to provide expertise in all aspects of KC-135 employment at the squadron, wing, and headquarters level." We were not going to be part of the Nellis Weapons School anytime soon with our operational focus, and this created a lot of friction with the stakeholders involved. We had to do what was best for the refueling community, and we were getting beaten down because of it.

The stress of creating this syllabus and the friction with the Little Rock folks began taking its toll on us. I was worn-out. I called Carol, our squadron commander Walt's wife, asking where he was one morning when he didn't show up for work. "Walt's home sick," she said. Then she asked me an odd question: "How are you feeling, Sluggo?"

"Terrible. My temperature is running 102 degrees right now. I'm calling to say that I'm staying home to fight this."

She screamed, "Go to the flight surgeon now, Sluggo! You're the fourth one sick with pneumonia!"

"What?"

"Go to the flight surgeon now!" she repeated.

Six cadre members had come down with bacterial pneumonia at the same time, our Intel NCO in both lungs. When I arrived at the flight surgeon's office at around 1400, the chief of flight medicine looked at me and said, "What's wrong with you?"

I just said "Building 120." He took me into a room away from everyone else. I started shaking.

One nurse wrapped me in blankets fresh out of the dryer, and another started an IV bag containing Rocephin antibiotics when the X-ray showed fluid in one lung. It took a week and a half for all of us to get better and back to work.

The cadre finally settled on a syllabus all of us agreed on. The first section contained classes on air refueling support; students then went on the road to Strategic Command in Omaha for nuclear operations, AMC and Transportation Command (TRANSCOM) headquarters at Scott Air Force Base for aerial refueling and airlift operations, and Special

Operations Command in Tampa for spec ops refueling support. The second section, Joint Air Operations, included all the operational-level planning and execution courses our students needed to plan and execute high-volume refueling operations. This instructional section was the real meat of the curriculum. Joint Air Ops began with a detailed threat overview of enemy fighters, SAMs, and antiaircraft guns. Students learned how to create an air refueling system, including crew utilization and how many aircraft were needed for an air campaign, refueling airspace construction, criteria for operating locations, and procedures for coordinating refueling into a CAOC like Vicenza's in Allied Force.

I developed the next section, Joint Tanker Operations. Visiting the Naval Strike and Air Warfare Center at Fallon Naval Air Station in Nevada, I found the Navy had a manual for naval aviation operations rivaling anything the Air Force had. The Strike and Air Warfare manual was the carrier air wing employment bible, and none of us in the Air Force had known of its existence. Every Employment School student had to experience the Navy strike planning process from the experts. After five academic classes in one day, two instructors and the students would hop on an airplane for San Diego. Students toured the USS *Coronado*, an Air Operations Center ship the Navy used as a floating operations center. Navy planners re-created the CAOC processes inside the *Coronado*'s spaces. Aegis cruisers or destroyers defend KC-135s and KC-10s with their SAMs operating inside the carrier's airspace. The captain of the USS *Princeton* then sat with students in the officers' wardroom and explained how he defended the battle group over lunch. The best part of the Joint Air Operations section came that evening; after we had all dropped our bags in our staterooms on the aircraft carrier, we went to my favorite Mexican food place in the Old Town district of San Diego.

The next two days were spent at sea observing carrier operations firsthand and digesting briefings from the different agencies on the carrier. Numerous trips to carriers at sea are why I retired with ten catapult takeoffs and arrested landings on my résumé.

The next section addressed the tanker flight regime vulnerable to enemy engagement. Tankers were most vulnerable during takeoff and landing, when they flew slowly with their gear and flaps down. Tactical arrivals and departures at airfields required waivers from the AMC's director of operations just to fly the maneuvers. After classroom instruction, students hopped into two tankers and headed for Fort Hood, Texas, and Roswell, New Mexico. The Army's Missile Intelligence Agency at Fort Hood educated students on heat-seeking man-portable air defense systems, or MANPADS—shoulder-fired missiles any caveman could operate. Each student handled shoulder-fired surface-to-air missiles in a domed simulator and found that it wasn't that hard to track a tanker. All students developed tactical arrivals and departures in a flying exercise at Roswell, New Mexico, with Missile Intelligence Agency instructors watching over them. This education was invaluable in the run-up to Operation Iraqi Freedom, when a huge speedboat kept chasing KC-10s landing at Al Udeid Air Base, aka the Deed.

Weapons School graduates from the Portland, Oregon, F-15 Eagle squadron and Western Air Defense Sector (WADS) taught students airborne defensive retrogrades. Again, the AMC director of operations had to sign waivers for us to fly these restricted maneuvers in the plane. Tanker crews flew defensive maneuvers, protected by Portland's Eagles, as the Navy's Aggressor TOPGUN squadron from Fallon attacked the tankers. The Aggressors, Eagle pilots, and WADS weapons controllers debriefed tanker crews on their performance upon landing at Fairchild after each mission.

After AMC leaders had a long discussion with the Nellis school leadership, the Weapons School allowed KC-135 CES students to manage refueling operations for the Weapons School's Mission Employment integration phase, the largest Weapons School event. Getting into ME put our foot in the door at Nellis. I guess they felt refueling was a headache we could handle for them, and our students were glad to take on the role. Our students accomplished all refueling planning and execution for Blue Air, the good guys in the two-week exercise, and Red Air, the bad guys opposing the Weapons School forces. Weapons School leadership later allowed our students to attend Weapons School core classes on Soviet air and SAM threats and Air Force aircraft capabilities and limitations. The Space Division began teaching our Global Positioning System section of instruction, some of the best courses I've sat through on how GPS works.

Mission Employment—now called Weapons School Advanced Integration Phase—scenarios grew in intensity over the two weeks, reaching their peak during the second week—at night. The night integration missions were the most intense of the curriculum. I flew one night with our C-130 brethren using night-vision goggles while performing a Non-Combatant Evacuation mission. The Predator sensor operator called out ground threats to A-10s orbiting overhead, which immediately rolled in on the enemy location for suppression while we approached the landing zone where the evacuees waited. Two nights later I flew in the AWACS, observing the airborne battle managers control the entire ME fight. The Weapons School's vice commandant call sign Flat and I discussed the KC-135 syllabus as we stood over a radar console. Flat told me something very interesting; the Weapons School was beginning to look at teaching operational-level courses also. I told Flat to come see us; we could help, and already had courseware built.

These training scenarios were difficult problems with complex solutions, and students didn't always perform as flawlessly as you see in the movies. Sometimes there was wholesale bloodletting over the Nellis Test and Training Range, and student failures were always the greatest learning opportunities, as well as being very humbling.

The Offensive Counter-Air/Strategic Attack (OCA/SA) exercise replicated a "Shock and Awe Opening Night" scenario, utilizing both stealth aircraft and their nonstealth counterparts, like F-15Es and F-16s. We called it the "Kick Down the Door" scenario. During one OCA/SA night event, the students felt they had a pretty good solution. All the first-wave jets launched and refueled from three tankers orbiting in Caliente Bravo, in the eastern portion of the Nellis Range complex. Murphy's Laws of Armed Conflict walked onto the range shortly after the Blue Force pushed off the tankers. One small breakdown in F-15C radar coverage led to the destruction of eight Blue Air aircraft during the training period's first few minutes. Coming off the Red Air tanker full of gas, MIG 03 slipped through untargeted and unafraid. The first unfortunate soul MIG 03 killed was CUJO 33, a B-52 assigned to destroy a simulated modern Russian SAM site defending the target complex with a long-range missile. MIG 03 remained alive and well behind the Blue Air strike packages and shot down two more students before being killed himself. Everyone paused when AWACS called out MIG 03's position *behind* Blue Air's line of forces. A Strike Eagle turned around for a close-range AIM-120 AMRAAM face shot that killed MIG 03, but the damage was already done.

The major problem created by CUJO 33's demise was that the SAM site lived for another few minutes and was able to launch sophisticated missiles at the incoming package, destroying five more Blue Air attackers. An F-16CJ Wild Weasel finally destroyed the SAM site, and in all the confusion, the students reset the attack. After a long pause to regroup, Blue Air achieved their training objectives, minus eight aircraft whose weapons were nullified from being killed before release.

The student mass debrief went long into the morning hours, and several students failed the ride. An Adversary Tactics Group instructor replayed the mission on the wall screen, explaining their game plan and how well it had worked. The SAM operators told students the tactics they had used to unravel their master plan. MIG 03 leaking through and killing CUJO had just made it easier for the SAM site to kill whoever came into view.

We felt that our syllabus was pretty tight when our first four students arrived in June 2000. The corollary to Murphy's decree that no plan survives its first contact in combat was no syllabus survives its first contact with students. Rewrites to the syllabus happened as we taught classes. Our first class mockingly asked us, "When can we see the syllabus?" Our first approved syllabus didn't flow correctly, and our second class loomed in weeks. We rewrote the syllabus almost end to end for the second class. One CES cadre member call sign Mojo pinned a piece of paper to his cubicle wall with the improved "Secret Syllabus" on it. Air Mobility Warfare Center and CADS leadership didn't know we had made such huge changes, and we were not about to tell them because of the potential beatings. All of us knew that disciplinary action might follow for Secret Syllabus. We taught our second class from Mojo's Secret Syllabus until we rewrote it again for the first 2001 class. After that, courses flowed better, and the students left with the skills needed to perform as subject-matter experts in any strategic, operational, or tactical refueling environment.

Our new school commander attended the second class, going through with one of the biggest groups we graduated. After several meetings with CADS leadership, my time at the KC-135 CES came to an end. Over G told me I needed to leave the CES and go somewhere else. What he meant was that my services were no longer required there and it was time to move. When Over G told me I had to leave the CES to stay competitive for a command position, I told him I didn't. My family liked it in Spokane, and both sets of grandparents lived twelve hours away in Salt Lake City. The 92nd Air Refueling Wing needed experienced pilots and expertise in planning refueling missions. If I was going to stay in the Air Force a while longer, at least I would have fun doing it. Orders officially moving me to the 92nd Air Refueling Wing came in April 2001. Little did any of us realize what September of that year would have in store.

★ ★

LESSONS FROM THE COCKPIT: FAILURE

All of us experience hard landings and failures in our lives. When I left the Combat Employment School, I felt a great sense of failure. Unfortunately, we now live in a one-mistake world. I wasn't going to command a tanker squadron, which meant I was no longer promotable. I felt I had no more left to give. I didn't know when I was going to retire, but I wanted to fly for a little while longer and get my confidence back. Being able to fly in a squadron without all the pressure of working for a promotion let me catch my breath. The hard realization that I was no longer promotable hurt and was discouraging, however. Where was I supposed to go, and what was I meant to do?

A common military term is "vector check." A vector check usually comes to soldiers, sailors, and airmen while they visit with their supervisor or commander. Failing at the Combat Employment School was a big vector check for me, although I didn't realize it at the time. If I had become a squadron commander, I would never have been able to deploy to the CAOC and be involved in the planning and execution of Operation Anaconda and the Shock and Awe campaign in Iraq. I feel sometimes our hard landings are God's way of telling us to go in a different direction, no matter how painful it might be. The course I took after leaving the CES allowed me to experience even greater job satisfaction under some of the most intense and stressful conditions an airman can go through. As you think about the hard landings in your life, you should now realize that you were vectored to a direction, which was better for you and your personal growth, as well as for your family. Don't look at your hard landings as failures that stop your progression. Realize that the hard landing is a vector check pushing you toward better things in your life.

★ ★

11

Clear and Visibility Unlimited

0550 Tuesday 11 September 2001

Fairchild Air Force Base

Spokane, Washington

Opportunity often comes disguised in the form of misfortune, or tem-porary defeat.

—NAPOLEON HILL, AUTHOR OF PERSONAL SUCCESS LITERATURE

America has stood down enemies before and we will do so this time. None of us will ever forget this day.

—PRESIDENT GEORGE W. BUSH,
IN HIS SPEECH AT THE WORLD TRADE CENTER RUBBLE

Are you guys ready? Let's roll.

—TODD BEAMER, GIVING THE SIGNAL TO TAKE
UNITED AIRLINES FLIGHT 93 BACK FROM THE AL QAEDA HIJACKERS

Sunlight was just creeping through our bedroom windows when the phone rang next to Val at 0550 Tuesday 11 September. Travis, barely a month old, slept between us. Val picked up the phone, and in a groggy state I heard a family friend, Staci, screaming, "WHERE IS MARK?! WHERE IS MARK?! WHERE IS MARK?!"

Val told her I was asleep right next to her, since it was 0550 in the morning and we had a new baby in the house, hint, hint. I overheard Staci telling Val to wake me up and turn on Fox News. I rolled over and grabbed the remote off the nightstand and pointed it at the TV. I'm a news junkie, so Fox News was already dialed in. Staci told Val a plane hit a building in New York City. Fox News commentators confirmed that an airliner hit Tower One of the World Trade Center Complex at 0846 eastern time, four minutes earlier. In the military, we call this "the CNN Effect." In less than five minutes, a big global event will show up on cable news because of how networked the world is. We even plan for the CNN Effect in many operations. I watched the building burn, but too many things didn't add up in my head. A large fire was consuming several floors near the top. It was a CAVU day in pilot language—clear and visibility unlimited.

How could an airline pilot with thousands of flight hours hit a building in broad daylight?

There were no flight routes near the Towers. The Fox News commentators just kept saying a plane had hit the World Trade Center.

My subconscious brain screamed *attack*, but I couldn't believe it. Who would be so bold?

As I sat in bed, I thin-sliced through the images on TV. Airliners could be precision-guided weapons in the right hands, delivery vehicles for explosive content. Was this an attack? Middle East terror groups like Hamas or Hezbollah must have been involved. What was that group and their leader's name again . . . something Laden? Thoughts bounced around in my head like a golf ball in a tiled bathroom. Gut feelings screamed *attack* in the six inches between my ears. But I couldn't wrap my head around it. America did not get attacked like that.

A second airliner appeared in the upper right-hand corner of the TV screen, nose pointing toward Tower Two. My cognitive functions stopped as I focused on the jetliner's flight path. It was like I was at a stoplight with the gearshift in neutral. The plane disappeared behind

Tower One, and a massive fireball exited Tower Two's north side. Val gasped, her left hand over her mouth.

The military portion of my brain shifted into gear immediately and shoved the pedal through the floorboards. I bolted from bed, waking Travis, and headed for the shower.

We are under attack!

I was watching my generation's Pearl Harbor on cable news.

THE US IS NOW A NO-FLY ZONE, JUST LIKE OVER IRAQ!

All of this went through my head as I shed my clothes in the twenty feet from bed to shower. I just wanted to shave and wash my hair, because I knew I might not be home for a couple of days. Val walked in three minutes later saying the wing command post had just called. I had been recalled, and needed to go in immediately. I stepped out of the shower and looked at the clock: 0613.

Val had laid a clean flight suit on the bed and put my boots on the floor. She then asked, "Silly question: When do you think you'll be home?"

As I stood to zip up my flight suit, Fox News showed PANTA flight, two F-15Cs from Otis Air National Guard Base in Massachusetts, zip across New York City's skyline. Eagles were on patrol over New York City; HUNTRESS controlled all East Coast airspace. Good. Nothing would get by the Eagles, so New York City was safe. What was happening on the West Coast? Light Grays burn eight thousand pounds per hour in their patrol stations, and two thousand pounds per minute fighting in afterburner. Would the Eagles punch off external wing fuel tanks to chase airliners? A four-ship of Eagles needed eighteen tanker sorties over twenty-four hours—twenty-two if they were shooting missiles, because then the external fuel tanks would be punched off. Eagles would have five to six patrol stations down the West Coast. Worst case, 132 tanker sorties every twenty-four hours. I needed to call WADS and get Soup, a WADS controller and Weapons School graduate, on a secure line. How would his BIGFOOT agency manage tankers? Would Tinker

Air Force Base send an E-3 AWACS to McChord or Mountain Home? AWACS needed gas every five hours, so five more tankers . . . 137 sorties. Most important, what were the rules of engagement for killing a US airliner over the United States? Who approved that engagement? I could not wrap my brain around killing a US airliner over the States. Wayno, the other 92nd Air Refueling Wing CES grad, was on the road. I was a one-man show. I needed to talk to Wybo, the wing scheduler, to see what we could do.

"Hon, I have no idea. Tonight, tomorrow, maybe Friday . . . Gotta go. I love you!"

In the twenty-five minutes from our driveway on the North Hill to Fairchild's front gate, I crunched tanker math in my head. Another thought came to me: many of my Air Force friends were now airline pilots. Where were Pee Wee and Slider with Delta? Where in the world were Shredder, Flounder, and Zoid with American? I hoped Shredder was on air defense alert in his Fresno, California, Guard Viper. My thirst for information was almost unbearable, and I wanted my assumptions to immediately become fact. Spokane's law enforcement roamed the highways, all kitted out as I drove along I-90 and Route 2 through Airway Heights. When I arrived at the front gate, a mile-long line of cars was waiting to pass through one lane. It took me forty minutes to get on base, and as I walked into Fairchild's command post, the second situation briefing was projected on the screen. CNN and Fox News were on mute on flat-screen TVs. A briefer said US airspace was closed, all air traffic was grounded, and airliners were landing everywhere outside the continental US. Military aircraft were the only thing flying. Good—there would be a clear field of fire for any fighters shooting missiles at airliners.

What was I saying?

Wybo was already in and working on a plan. He and I immediately started a mission analysis exercise. I told him my numbers. He said they were a good start, but nobody would move until they saw requirements from AMC. Both of us agreed that tankers and refueling were critical. A no-fly zone of this scale could not happen without a strong tanker plan. None of our grads were at NORAD. Fairchild aircrews must have been in crew rest then. If I were commander in chief of NORAD, what would we defend? The big West Coast population centers were obvious targets. Wybo pointed to the Seattle/Tacoma area on our map. BIG-FOOT was at McChord Air Force Base south of SEATAC, a very busy airport. Well, not busy anymore. Moving south to Portland, an F-15 Guard unit sat on the ramp. Passing Mount Shasta, San Francisco was the next big population center—big targets downtown and a famous Bob Marley–sized bridge. Fresno Vipers probably covered San Francisco International. I hoped Shredder was at home and not flying an American Airlines trip.

"Nuts; we need to add Hornets out of Lemoore to the mix."

Drogue sorties. Six to eight thousand pounds every twenty-five to thirty minutes for Hornets. Hornets were the critical fuel-factor aircraft, just like they were in carrier air wing operations. I needed to know how many drogues Fairchild had available. Wybo was already working the no-fly zone tanker plan. None of us had any direction and were doing a lot of this on the fly without authorization from wing leadership or the TACC. Wybo coordinated two refueling areas with Canadian Air Traffic Control, bringing CF-18 Hornets back to their home station of Canadian Forces Base Comox from an exercise at CFB Cold Lake in Alberta. STAMPEDE, just west of Calgary, moved the CF-18s westward on their first hookup for gas. ORCA, off Vancouver Island's west coast, allowed Comox Hornets to launch to the tanker in minutes. Wybo worked his planning magic on the phone through his network of people, solving complex and time-critical refueling problems with folks he had met and talked with around the water cooler. When it's crunch time in war, you always go to the guys and gals you talked with at the water cooler. Wybo's relationships saved us valuable resources and time on 9/11.

Farther down the California coast was LA—a big population center with lots of traffic. Fresno Vipers sat alert at March Air Reserve Base in San Bernardino. The last major city on the coast was San Diego. I wrote down the mileage between each airport. The biggest problem was building and coordinating refueling airspace with the FAA and BIGFOOT. I wanted a fluid refueling system, able to move anywhere whenever the tankers were asked to do so, but I also wanted to give the fighters a clear field of fire. I looked for alternate airfields. Fortunately, there were a bunch. San Diego was the only issue; Naval Air Station North Island's 7,500-foot runway was too short. KC-135s require eight thousand feet, so I told everyone to use North Island only as a last resort.

KC-135s would be on alert like in the old SAC days by this afternoon. What condition was the Fairchild Alert Facility in? Boom and drogue spares had to be part of every schedule. 9/11's tanker bill was huge—140 sorties transferring eighty thousand pounds each equals 11.2 million pounds of jet fuel, and that was just for the West Coast. I built a phantom list of specified, implied, and essential tasks to develop the West Coast refueling system. I still couldn't believe what I was doing.

The defense of the West Coast was getting off to a frustratingly slow start. Everyone waited for AMC to tell us what to do. I didn't blame wing leadership—it was an AMC cultural and institutional mind-set that caused us to ramp up so slowly. I wasn't at Kadena; over there, my commanders, Brigadier General Cliver and Bigs, would have had two tankers on Bravo Patio with 180,000-pound fuel loads and ammo folks hanging the air-to-air missiles on four F-15 Eagles fifteen minutes after the second airliner hit. Different command, different employment philosophy. TACC told us what to do only after they received requirements. I knew TACC felt the same frustration as the requirements slowly trickled in. Seattle and San Francisco must have had air patrols overhead by then. Had anyone thought to launch tankers? I realized tanking was a pickup game at that point. Wybo was leaning way forward in building a flying and alert schedule, but he and I could lean only so far without requirements. My frustration level was pretty high; some important basic things could be done then, but AMC wouldn't turn a fan blade without requirements.

Wybo already had twelve crews in crew rest at base billeting when the requirements finally came in. Fairchild's first mission was . . . Montana. A crucial FEMA team needed a ride back to Washington, DC, from Bozeman. Two days later, while I sat on alert, the aircraft commander told me it was the creepiest mission he'd ever flown. Lots of radio chatter with air traffic control typically fills our ears as aircraft talk back and forth to ATC while flying across the US. He told me there wasn't a word on the radio during his flight across the country. Chicago Center told them they were the only aircraft flying in their sector. Two F-16s from Selfridge Air National Guard Base in Michigan joined on their wings south of Chicago for some gas, but that was it. After landing at Andrews AFB, the crew waited for another assignment. They came home the next day after refueling fighters over DC.

Additional missions finally started coming in. Refueling sorties for the Seattle CAPs came first. A sortie orbiting south of Portland came next. Strip alert lines started coming in, and Wybo used crews already on the day's flying schedule to fill them. Fairchild's old Cold War–era alert facility needed cleaning, but the phones still worked. By the end of the night, seven KC-135s sat in the old SAC Nuclear Alert Facility. Twelve tankers had been on alert around the US when American Airlines Flight 11 hit Tower One; over one hundred tankers sat at alert nationwide by Tuesday evening. Tuesday afternoon started feeling more like air defense exercises at Kadena: air refueling made easy by launching fighters and tankers as packages. Keep fighters on the nipple until they committed to attack. BIGFOOT or the fighters would tell us where to relocate based on the tactical situation. My job got easier as the day grew longer. Additional fighter CAPs entered the system Wednesday morning. Hornets from Lemoore and Comox appeared on the schedule. Drogues now hung off the booms of several tankers on Fairchild's Alert Facility Christmas tree.

Some crews asked what was a good bingo, the name for a comfortable fuel reserve that indicated to pilots it was time to return to base. I told every crew to calculate three bingos: first bingo for returning to Fairchild and sleeping in your own bed. Second bingo for getting an aircrew to McChord AFB south of Seattle or Travis AFB near San Francisco. Third bingo for any eight-thousand-foot runway with a control tower and a fixed-base operator, or FBO, to fill the tanker back up with gas. Each tanker carried a fuel credit card in the crew entry door or the maintenance forms that fuel specialists used to pay the bill. Then call command post with a cell phone number after landing. I knew BIGFOOT or AWACS at some point would keep a tanker up past the Fairchild bingo.

I finally pulled up in my driveway late Wednesday morning, tired and scheduled for alert Thursday afternoon. The US no-fly zone and defense of our airspace became Operation Noble Eagle on 14 September. None of us had ever imagined having to defend US airspace from attack.

Between pulling alert and planning Noble Eagle missions, my crew prepared for our Incirlik Air Base, Turkey, deployment. The evenings at home were very emotional in the aftermath of seeing thousands of lives lost in Manhattan, Washington, DC, and Shanksville, Pennsylvania. I held month-old Travis one night in a rocking chair next to our bedroom window. I was going to miss a good portion of the first few years of his life. Rocking Travis to sleep, I pondered being deployed over the next year or more. Tears ran down my checks as I sang to him asleep. Within the week, three CES grads—Dewey, Rubber, and Staples—received orders to deploy. Dewey hopped on the rotator out of Baltimore for

Prince Sultan Air Base's CAOC. Rubber and Staples headed to Florida, assigned to AFNORTH and the 601st Air Operations Center at Tyndall AFB. Rubber and Staples' first task at Tyndall? Create Noble Eagle's air refueling system across the US, which they did with the utmost expertise and class.

★ ★

LESSONS FROM THE COCKPIT: PATRIOTISM

The events of 9/11 were my generation's Pearl Harbor. I don't say that to offend World War II veterans, because I know there was a difference. I do feel that the Greatest Generation and my generation fought for the same values, against very similar enemy ideologies. A foreign adversary was trying to destroy everything we valued in the United States and in our Constitution. It angered me. I was heartened to see people stand up to defend the values we hold dear in the United States. Numerous famous people left lucrative jobs to fight this horrific adversary—Pat Tillman being one of the most visible. Our oath of office states that the officeholder will "defend the Constitution of the United States from all enemies foreign and domestic." Notice there is no time stamp on the oath.

The United States continues to be a land of promise for the world. I understand that it is not perfect, but whenever I came home from overseas, I knew it was the best place on earth. People come here because they know they can enjoy prosperity if they will just work hard toward the goals they set for themselves. Long before 9/11, I inserted a piece of paper into my wallet, and it's still in there to this day. It is my personal Title of Liberty. I have written upon it to remember my God and religion, the freedom my family enjoys here in the US, and the peace afforded my wife and family as citizens of this great nation. Our Founding Fathers also sacrificed their time, talents, fortunes, and, in some cases, lives so there would be a place people could come and find freedom.

★ ★

12
★

"The Lick"

Slow down and enjoy life. It's not only the scenery you miss by going too fast—you also miss the sense of where you are going and why.

—EDDIE CANTOR, ACTOR AND COMEDIAN

I decided to fly through the air and live in the sunlight and enjoy life as much as I could.

—EVEL KNIEVEL, AMERICAN DAREDEVIL MOTORCYCLIST

I spend most of my time at the ranch with my family, and enjoy life—watch the sun come up, watch it go down, thank God for another day, and just be happy.

—MARCUS LUTTRELL, NAVY SEAL AND AUTHOR OF *LONE SURVIVOR*

US aircraft have conducted military actions and humanitarian relicf out of Incirlik Air Base, or "the Lick," since February 1955. Stretching across 3,320 acres, fifty-seven hardened aircraft shelters and weapons storage bunkers dot the western side of a single ten-thousand-foot runway. Incirlik houses all kinds of US weapons, including tactical nukes during the Cold War in case a strike needed to be made against Soviet Russia. The Lick's location became critical to U-2 spy plane overflights of Russia during the Cold War. After Desert Storm ended, the Kurdish insurgency rose up against Saddam Hussein's repressive regime, capturing every city in northern Iraq except Kirkuk. Iraqi Air Force helo gunships brutally put down the Kurdish revolt in April 1991. The UN High Commissioner for Refugees estimated that over 750,000 Iraqis fled to the Turkish mountains. UN humanitarian operations started after news crews showed millions of Kurds fleeing on foot to camps in the mountains. Incirlik-based C-130 Hercs air-dropped relief supplies across northern Iraq in Operation Provide Comfort. US fighter planes defended those airdrops from what remained of Saddam's air defense network. Operation Provide Comfort began in April 1991, enforcing a United Nations–mandated no-fly zone north of Iraq's 36th parallel to keep Saddam's air forces from killing the Kurdish population.

Operation Provide Comfort transformed into Operation Northern Watch (ONW) on 1 January 1997, continuing to enforce the no-fly zone above Iraq's 36th parallel. Combined Joint Task Force Northern Watch, made up of US, British, and Turkish air forces, executed aerial denial to Saddam's forces. Air policing an area as large as northern Iraq was an exercise in logistical support. No-fly zones devour a lot of airborne fuel. Tanker transfers of over 450,000 pounds were common for a three-hour ONW vulnerable period. Pre-canned mission packets streamlined tanker planning after years of routine operations above the 36th parallel. Eight KC-135s and two RAF Vickers VC-10 tankers pumped gas to thirty fighter and reconnaissance aircraft while orbiting east to west in the ONW restricted operating zone, or ROZ. The ROZ was a potentially dangerous place for tankers. Eastbound orbit legs pointed directly at Iran and the Zagros Mountains. Lake Urmia was clearly visible across the Iranian border at the east end of the tanker orbit. The eastbound leg was only a few miles north of the Iraqi border. Iraqi Foxbats could arrive within missile-firing range on the tankers in six minutes from Qayyarah

West Airfield. Foxbats routinely travel at speeds approaching those of a .30-06 bullet, about 2,800 feet per second. Foxbat high fast fliers present a tough intercept problem for F-15 Eagles. Saddam's air force often flew while the fighter force refueled in the ROZ. Cowards. I never felt nervous or worried flying in the ROZ, seeing the F-15 contrails above us.

In May 2000 the 93rd Air Refueling Squadron needed an aircraft commander for a Northern Watch rotation, so I volunteered. For thirty days, copilot Danny and boom operator Johnny crewed with me, and we made a great flying team. Deploying to Northern Watch gave us another KC-135 CES syllabus data point to test in real-world combat, a test it passed in spades. Every curriculum event was mirrored in the mission planning or flying of ONW sorties in the ROZ. These missions were just a lot of fun, and an excellent time to concentrate on my flying skills. This deployment was Danny's first trip off station after mission qualification training, or MQT, and I enjoyed teaching him advanced tanker employment on every mission. From an ONW perspective, the CES syllabus was dead nuts on. But Stateside training still did not mirror what the tanker community accomplished in combat.

Some ONW combat events the tanker community were restricted from practicing at home. We did not live up to TOPGUN's motto: "Train like you fight, and fight like you train." One cell-formation event that tankers accomplished every mission was not allowed in the States. ONW missions required additional tankers to join the first three-ship cell in the ROZ. A fourth and fifth KC-135 took off for the ROZ to join up later in the vulnerable period with the first three-ship of tankers. Using the third KC-135's Mode III IFF squawk, four numbers identifying the aircraft to radar, I performed a visual rejoin behind the third tanker. Creating a larger refueling group put more gas and more contact points to distribute the gas in the right place. Put the gas where it's needed—seems natural, right? Nope—not during a training mission in the States. Yet on every mission I flew in Desert Storm and Northern Watch, AWACS brought tankers together to create a larger formation with more contact points for gas. It was infuriating that tanker tactics remained immature in concept and deed after two major air campaigns, and the KC-135 CES battled our command and culture to change employment shortcomings. All of us on the initial cadre have scars from trying to change our employment culture.

As I sat in our crew's first mass brief, I understood what every aircraft was doing, but more important, I understood why they were doing it. Each mass brief was just like sitting in a Weapons School Mission Employment brief—only the Red Forces were shooting real missiles and antiaircraft shells at the Coalition forces. Each mission commander discussed their flight's roles and responsibilities, fielding questions about their game plan to deal with Saddam's defenses. Northern Watch leaders covered response options to Iraqi air defenses shooting at Coalition forces in detail. Assignments for potential response options were outlined, so everyone knew who would do what if Saddam fired at us. Saddam had placed a $14,000 bounty on any American pilot shot down and captured during a Northern or Southern Watch vulnerable period. The Coalition developed an elaborate rescue plan for anyone shot down inside Iraq. Rescue helos operated from a base near Batman, Turkey, close to the Iraq border. Yes, that's its real name, and Batman served as a divert runway in case any Coalition aircraft had emergencies.

Northern Watch sorties were pretty easy to plan after years of no-fly zone activity. All vulnerable periods operated off a coordinated schedule planners built a few days before each event. Coalition leadership approved the schedule after the plans shop briefed strategy and game plan. Planners published essential tasks on the timing sheet, on the front plastic page of our red mission binders. The Excel spreadsheet showed engine start, taxi, and takeoff times for every aircraft. The timing sheet highlighted each tanker's receivers, refueling times, and off-loads. My crew took this sheet out of the red binder and followed along in the mass brief, filling out lineup cards that we strapped to our kneeboards for every mission.

Northern Watch lineup cards were like all others, eight-and-a-half-by-eleven sheets of paper folded in half and strapped down on a knee-board. Lineup cards are a quick way to see critical mission information in a single place. Kneeboards are canvas "desks" worn on our thighs when flying; I always strapped mine to my right leg. Everyone, pilot or weapons system operator (WSO), who visited South Korea had a knee-board from Royal Bag, right outside Osan Air Base's main gate. Royal Bag personalized each kneeboard with your name and wings. Crews filled out lineup cards with all mission-essential information during the mass brief, most importantly the search-and-rescue code words and numbers. They also served as scratch pads for writing down changes to sortie off-loads, receivers, or timing. I wish I'd kept a few because of their historical value.

Coalition aircraft transited east for fifty-five minutes through an imaginary airspace corridor just a few miles north of the Syrian border. This corridor ended at the ROZ, our operating playground over the gorgeous Cilo-Sat Mountains. Since the ROZ was so close to Iraqi air threats, a choreographed order of events happened during each vulnerable period. No one went into the ROZ without protective F-15s and coverage from the AWACS, call sign MAGIC. The F-15s arrived first, followed minutes later by MAGIC. A Navy EP-3E intelligence and surveillance aircraft from Naval Station Rota, in Spain, arrived next. EP-3Es worked closely with the AWACS and fighters flying over Iraq. The EP-3E was an old Lockheed Electra turboprop-powered airliner converted into a signals collection plane, call sign QUASAR.

QUASAR vacuumed up all the electrons directed at the Northern Watch force, sifted through the radio waves to understand threats to the force, and passed the information on. The most important thing QUASAR gave us was Saddam's air defense network's intentions. QUASAR departed Incirlik first but traveled to the ROZ so slowly the jets passed over it. Leading the DRAKE 51 flight of three tankers, my cell passed above QUASAR low on our right, big black antennas clearly visible all over the aircraft. QUASAR was already talking to MAGIC after collecting the electrons washing over the force as it approached the ROZ. F-16 Wild Weasels followed closely behind the three tankers, providing the ability to kill SAMs. Approaching the ROZ entry point, I contacted MAGIC on the command frequency.

"MAGIC, DRAKE 51 flight in the block two five zero to two seven zero, on time, parrot india checks." The transmission had a clicking sound because HAVE QUICK secure radios hop across several frequencies, making it difficult for Iraqi listening posts to hear us.

"DRAKE 51, MAGIC radar contact, parrot india sweet sweet all three aircraft. Picture clear to the south."

Iraqi Air Force MiGs and Mirages weren't flying at the moment. Iraqi pilots would be stupid to take off with four F-15s on station in the ROZ. MAGIC confirmed that all three tankers' IFF codes appeared on their big radar displays. The LANCE 21 flight, F-15Cs flying in pairs, left contrails high at our ten o'clock.

Approaching the ROZ's eastern edge, DRAKE flight turned to the west fifteen miles short of the Iranian border. If you crossed the ten-mile Iranian buffer zone, MAGIC warned you of your encroachment. Inside five miles, Iran warned you. Tabriz Airfield, an Islamic Republic of Iran Air Force interceptor base, lay just beyond Lake Urmia. I wasn't worried about MiG-29 Fulcrums there. The Eagles could manhandle them. DRAKE flight pumped all the fighters full in twenty-five minutes before entering northern Iraq and starting another UN-mandated northern no-fly zone period. Missions would be challenging for my co-pilot Danny, recently arrived from training at Altus Air Force Base in Oklahoma. He would be like I was in HEIDI, SANDI, and ERICA flights over Germany thirteen years ago; he didn't have a lot of experience in the jet with lots of fighters waiting for gas. Johnny was an experienced boom operator and had seen it all.

Four 4th Fighter Wing F-15E Strike Eagles, call sign ROCKET 31 flight, participated in each vulnerable period for emergency defense suppression. ROCKET's purpose was to kill any SAMs or guns threatening Coalition aircraft. The correct military term is the destruction of enemy air defenses—appropriately spelled DEAD, but pronounced "*deed.*" Two Strike Eagle element leaders carried an AGM-130 two-thousand-pound TV-guided, rocket-propelled bomb, nicknamed "the Whale." Strike Eagle crews try not to use Whales, very expensive half-million-dollar weapons, unless needed to stay out of SAM range. Two GBU-12 five-hundred-pound laser-guided bombs filled out their bomb load. ROCKET wingmen carried two GBU-10 two-thousand-pound laser-guided bombs and four GBU-12s. The reason I tell you the weapon loads is because of gas. ROCKET flight's weapon loads were heavy, affecting Strike Eagle fuel consumption. Flying at tactical speeds and high power settings while carrying heavy weapon loads drives fuel consumption much higher. The heavier the jet, the more gas it uses. Strike Eagles took on fifteen thousand pounds every time they hooked up, the most of any Northern Watch receivers. This was why I paid attention to weapon loads during the mass brief. That day the ROZ was a photographer's dream, and I snapped pictures of airplanes with live missiles and bombs flying over a famous mountain range on a clear day.

Spangdahlem Air Base's 23rd Fighter Squadron Fighting Hawks Weasels armed with HARMs hunted Saddam's radar network. Strike Eagles and Weasels are a lethal combination. This pairing has an ominous name: SEAD/DEAD. Weasels kill SAM tracking radars, while the Strike Eagles destroy SAM launchers or antiaircraft guns. Pronounced "*seed/deed,*" the name means suppression of enemy air defenses or destruction of enemy air defenses—we kill you two separate ways. Shoot the radar tracking head and then all of its body parts so the site can never come back.

A RAPTOR photo-reconnaissance pod hanging from an RAF Jaguar recorded and sent photographic imagery of anything weird found on the ground or of targets destroyed. Intel used RAPTOR pod imagery for keeping track of Iraqi defenses. Marine EA-6B Prowlers orbited in northern Iraq, jamming long-range radar and communications. Jags and Prowlers refueled from RAF VC-10 drogues. The RAF's No. 101 Squadron leader offered me a seat anytime I wanted to go with them. He was very interested in hearing about the KC-135 CES and our syllabus. Coalition cross-training was one benefit of being at the Lick.

As we approached the ROZ refueling control point, I turned the formation left again, away from Iran. Minutes later, ROCKET 33 and 34 passed beneath the tanker formation in a tight turning rejoin—our first receivers.

"MAGIC, picture clear to the south. Standby AOB dump."

MAGIC sifted through the broadcasts of the current air order of battle (AOB) to the fighters. QUASAR and MAGIC's passive detection systems pinpointed air defense systems that were painting us on radar. A long-range acquisition radar north of Mosul was painting the entire force, so Saddam knew we were coming. An SA-2 Guideline Fan Song target-tracking radar near Tal Afar radiated for a few quick sweeps and then turned off. Foolishly, they'd made themselves a target. Mosul always shot at the force. Most of the attacks or response options happened because some fool at Mosul fired at the Coalition. With my right hand twisting the autopilot turn knob, I took a look outside at our receivers. MAGIC told the force what defensive systems were actively following us on radar and their locations off the bull's-eye, the georeferenced point at Mosul that all threat calls are made off of. Every ROCKET flight WSO had his head down in the cockpit, scribbling MAGIC's information on his lineup card. As MAGIC passed the AOB dump, I turned in my seat to see DRAKE 52 and 53 matching our bank angle perfectly behind us. The entire strike force was spread across three tankers, filling up before entering northern Iraq. What an incredible sight against the mountainous backdrop.

I told Danny to dial a frequency into the comm two radio above his head, the discrete radio frequency MAGIC and all aircraft listened to while the force patrolled Iraq called "strike common." Listening on strike common was a good way to know what was going on over Iraq and an indicator of when the force would be back for gas. Fighters always told MAGIC over strike common when they needed to head for the tanker. Also, it's just cool listening to the dialogue between all the aircraft. Strike common was pretty quiet through the first vul period. The first vul period is always slow, like two boxers in the ring during the first round, both sizing each other up before a few punches are thrown. ROCKET 31 and 32 rejoined on my tanker's wings as we turned back to the east on our third orbit around the ROZ. Johnny in the boom pod said over the interphone, "Pilot, Boom—I've got two Dark Grays passing underneath us; one's coming up to the boom now, and one's headed toward the right wing."

ROCKET 32 approached the precontact position in a tight high-g turn, vapor coming off his wingtips as he disappeared underneath us. ROCKET 31 rejoined steady off the right wing outside Danny's window, waiting. It was an incredible sight. The olive drab–colored AGM-130 rocket–propelled bomb hanging from the wing and the darker gunship-gray paint of the Strike Eagle was a sharp contrast to the blue sky and green mountains. MAGIC passed new coordinates and information over strike common as ROCKET 31's WSO wrote them on the canopy with a black grease pencil. The second vul period had targets.

Minutes later, ROCKET 32's toggles released with a pressure disconnect, his tanks full. Johnny got a thumbs-up from ROCKET 32's pilot as he moved to the left wing and his refueling door closed.

"Man, Pilot—he has a lot of bombs hanging off him!"

I answered, "Boom, wait till you see what the Whale ROCKET 31 is carrying!"

ROCKET 31 dropped down off Danny's wing toward the boom, and I heard Johnny stick the extension into his receptacle. ROCKET 32 passed from under our tanker's left wing and hung outside my window. I mentally stopped flying the jet, just staring at ROCKET 32's bombs and missiles listening to strike common in the background. I spent a lot of time just looking out the window this flight, enjoying the parade of fighters rotating on and off the tankers while flying over the beautiful mountains. I subconsciously recorded the scenery passing around me while maneuvering the formation in the ROZ. The pictures I took mentally and physically were spectacular.

The fighters were our most important and primary customers in combat, so tanker crews focused on their mission timing and gas. One face-to-face meeting provides a wealth of customer knowledge in the corporate environment, and it was no different in the refueling world. Customer satisfaction in air refueling meant the tankers dropped the fighters off as close to their entry or push points as possible, filled to the gills with gas—something all my F-15 bros taught me at Kadena. Cutting the anchor orbit westbound leg short dragged ROCKET flight and his teammates to within miles of their push point a few minutes early. ROCKET 32's pilot gave me a thumbs-up, happy to be close. I looked back as we turned east toward Iraq to see DRAKE 52 and 53 still had chicks in tow on the wings and boom. Good; everyone would be full right on the border.

As we headed east toward the Iranian buffer zone, the Strike Eagles, Weasels, and Prowlers moved south into Iraq, the Light Gray Eagles leaving long white contrails behind as they pushed at thirty-two thousand feet. The tanker cell was only three miles away from the Turkish/Iraqi border at spots. A few days earlier my bank angle had gotten away from me, and the shallower angle took a three-ship cell within half a mile of Iraq, MAGIC warning me of my impending border incursion. Note to self: tankers had a half-mile buffer to the south before MAGIC called to warn you. MAGIC was right—the second time into Iraq, the force was busy.

"MAGIC, ROCKET 33, being engaged by guns near Saddam Dam, bull's-eye three two zero for twenty-eight. Two fifty-sevens and an eighty-five."

"MAGIC copies, JAGUAR 51, posit?" AWACS asked the Jag for their position. Shouldn't they have seen him on radar?

"MAGIC, JAG 51 is bull's-eye three one one for fifty-six, running the pod on objectives four and five. I can be over Saddam Dam in seven mike."

"ROCKET, WARHAWK, BANSHEE, and JAG, MAGIC requests fuel status."

"MAGIC, ROCKET 33 and 34 have thirty minutes' playtime."

"MAGIC, WARHAWK 41 and 42 have twenty-five minutes' playtime."

"MAGIC, BANSHEE 45 same."

"MAGIC, JAG 51 has twenty-five minutes also."

The guns near Saddam Dam fired shortly after refueling, so all the package players were good for gas. Minutes passed as MAGIC coordinated the response option with ONW leaders in Incirlik's command post, who were watching MAGIC's radar and intelligence picture projected on their big screen. Leaders just wanted to confirm that antiaircraft guns firing met the Coalition rules of engagement. Target vetting was a process leadership went through to make sure all the international law boxes got checked. Guns firing at Coalition aircraft was always a no-brainer. ROCKET 34 attacked all three gun emplacements with his laser-guided bombs. The crew killed the biggest gun with a GBU-10 two-thousand-pound bomb, which was kind of overkill. Parts went everywhere. After three hours patrolling Iraq, the entire force joined on the tankers and headed west to recover at Incirlik. The base was always easy to find in late afternoon or evening, because the lights shining on the beautiful Adana Mosque could be seen from seventy miles away. Every vulnerable period ended with a mass debrief in which all the players discussed what happened and things we needed to change. Each mass debrief began with the Strike Eagle aircrews showing video of each target destroyed. ROCKET 34's video of the three gun emplacements blowing up was spectacular. The Joint Task Force commander ended the debrief with his guidance for the next mission. After changing into civilian clothes, most of us went out to dinner at Mujdats, a great place for Adana kebabs.

One Friday evening each month, all the aircrews gathered for a party at the dorms. We relaxed in the big courtyard between the barracks, grilling burgers, dogs, and steaks. We had a great time listening to the Strike Eagle crews who had dropped bombs on the guns. But this Friday night was different because of one visitor. A gentleman in his mid-seventies stood behind two large electric blenders, mixing strawberry and lime margaritas. All of us recognized his face. He had led us in singing the National Anthem to kick off the Saturday-night formal dinner at the twenty-fifth Vietnam POW reunion in summer 1997, a Congressional Medal of Honor hanging around his neck. Colonel George "Bud" Day tended bar and poured margaritas into any red Solo cup stuck in front of him. His son flew Weasels at Spangdahlem. Walking up to the Fighting Hawks' table, this great American war hero held up both pitchers. "What'll you have, Sluggo? Strawberry or lime?"

I was a designated driver that night, and I don't drink anyway because of my LDS faith. I introduced myself as the nephew of Bob Jeffrey, former cellmate of Colonel Day. He set both pictures down, reached over the table, and gave me a vigorous handshake. Colonel Day said a lot of great things about Robert's character while they were in the Hanoi Hilton. He kept pouring margaritas for others while we talked. The party lasted well into the evening, and we heard great stories and learned a lot from meeting the guys who flew the jets we refueled. It wasn't very often you got served drinks by a former POW and Congressional Medal of Honor winner while listening to your customers' requests for better service.

A thirty-day deployment to Operation Northern Watch was perfect for this old tanker pilot. I got to teach my young copilot a lot of techniques and make adjustments to a few things in the CES syllabus.

I was elated the CES syllabus prepared our graduates to plan and run no-fly zone tanker missions like ONW. Coalition forces had a very busy month in May 2000. Tankers transferred a lot of gas because of all the strikes on the Iraqi air defense network. Combined Joint Task Force Northern Watch executed thirteen response options during the month of May, the most bombs dropped in 2000. Twice during the month a Strike Eagle dropped all six laser-guided bombs on guns near Saddam Dam or the Orchards near Mosul. The visual pictures of these flights are something I'll never forget.

In September 2001, the 97th Air Refueling Squadron was on the hook to deploy KC-135s as part of the Air Expeditionary Force bucket leaders chose squadrons from to deploy around the world. None of us could have anticipated events after 9/11, though. After certifying at March AFB with JP, the instructor pilot guiding me through mission requalification, I volunteered for a scheduled deployment to the Lick, a place I enjoyed. My son Travis was born in mid-August, so I felt it was a safe bet to deploy back to Turkey and help plan and fly combat missions over northern Iraq. After the 9/11 attacks, many of us wondered if we would deploy to Turkey. All four tanker squadrons were so busy supporting Noble Eagle that some thought there was a good chance we wouldn't go. 92nd Air Refueling Wing commander Colonel Erv Lessel told us AMC had not called off our deployment, and I didn't think they would. He did say those deploying might stay well past the ninety-day rotation date. If I was going to get stuck somewhere, the Lick was the best place to spend several months. My crew dropped our bags in the bins and flew east for Turkey on 19 September 2001.

After an overnight stop at RAF Mildenhall, my crew flew across France, between Bern and Zurich in Switzerland, across the Italian Alps, and out over the Tyrrhenian Sea. Flying down the west side of Italy's boot was another one of those twenty-eight-thousand-foot views I'll never forget. Passing over Messina, we turned left for Adana, Turkey, and Incirlik Air Base. Special Instructions, or SPINS, and flying procedure briefings occupied the first three days at the Lick, requiring a perfect score on the rules-of-engagement test. The flight surgeon told us we would all come down with a massive case of diarrhea, what he called SMA, within the next three weeks. Most of us dined outside the Lick's main gate in the many great places to eat. Adana kebabs at Mujdats are delicious, and two pieces of flatbread and soda with the kebabs cost only six bucks. I did all my crew debriefs at Mujdats, an informal place where the three of us could relax and talk about how to improve our flying skills.

Pacific and European Air Forces fighter squadrons filled the fall 2001 Air Expeditionary Force rotation bucket. Light Gray Eagles from Kadena's famous 67th Fighter Squadron maintained protective cover over the force, commanded by Lieutenant Colonel Dude Browne. I loved seeing the Cocks' red-striped twin tails and Shogun head on each vertical fin forming up outside my tanker windows again. Destroying any guns or SAMs shooting at the Coalition were Bro's World Famous Highly Respected 555th Fighter Squadron's job. All Triple Nickel defense suppression Vipers carried a single GBU-12 on each wing, so the jets were pretty clean and didn't consume a lot of gas in this configuration. I met Bro during Operation Allied Force when he led Aviano Air Base's mission planning cell in "the Wingtip," the big bank vault–like room where all planning for the 31st Fighter Wing and its support missions took place.

Lieutenant Colonel Zot Dennis commanded the 14th Fighter Squadron from Misawa Air Force Base in northern Japan. His Samurai Wild Weasels carried two HARMs for killing Iraqi radar. Several of Zot's Vipers had fired HARMs at Iraqi radar during that deployment, and tail number 422 had HARM silhouettes on his left side, signifying three radar kills. EA-6B Prowlers of the VMAQ-1 Banshees jammed Saddam's long-range radar and communications. No. 54 Squadron RAF Jaguars carrying RAPTOR reconnaissance pods photographed anything the Coalition attacked and blew up. MAGIC in the AWACS

The General Dynamics FB-111A was designed to penetrate Soviet Russia at low altitude in any weather with nuclear weapons. The two empty wing pylons carried nuclear bombs or missiles when the FBs sat in Pease Air Force Base's Nuclear Alert Facility. KC-135s were ready to refuel them on their Strategic Air Command attack missions. *Courtesy of the author*

Proof water does burn: Two KC-135s perform a wet thrust minimum interval takeoff (MITO) with clouds of engine smoke from their water-burning Pratt & Whitney J57 engines. Being number two or three in a five-aircraft wet MITO takeoff was intense but one of my favorite memories of flying "Water Wagons." *Photo courtesy Department of Defense*

An F-16D from the 416th Flight Test Squadron approaches my crew's KC-135 during a business effort to Edwards Air Force Base in California. KC-135 business efforts provided critical refueling support for test and training activities, such as this F-16D testing the Low Altitude Navigation and Targeting Infrared for Night (LANTIRN) system, housed in the dark-gray pod on the bottom of the aircraft. LANTIRN allows F-16s to direct laser-guided bombs and to navigate through bad weather. *Courtesy of the author*

A common KC-135 business effort is providing refueling training for airlift aircrews like the one flying this Lockheed C-141B Starlifter connected to my crew's KC-135 in A/R 400 over Nebraska, Kansas, and Texas. A Starlifter transported the National Transportation Safety Board's Go Team to Guam after Korean Air Flight 801 crashed in August 1997. *Courtesy of the author*

A Boeing E-3B Sentry Airborne Warning and Control System aircraft of the 961st Airborne Air Control Squadron refuels in the MOBILE 8 anchor off the coast of Okinawa, Japan. Tanker crews deployed to Riyadh Air Base in the 1980s to refuel the AWACS during European Liaison Force (ELF) One, defending Saudi Arabia from potential attack by Iraqi or Iranian aircraft during their eight-year war. *Courtesy of the author*

Some "air messes" are more humorous than others. SHELL 46's round refueling nozzle can be clearly seen in STALLION 61's open receptacle above the engine intake. The brute-force disconnect with this Royal Saudi Air Force F-15C shook the entire airplane. *Courtesy of the author*

My Desert Shield crew flies this KC-135 during a refueling mission over the Red Sea. You can see that the boom is down and trailing the drogue, which US Navy fighters and attack and jamming aircraft plug into for fuel. The larger hose can transfer one thousand pounds per minute. *Courtesy of Lieutenant Commander Dave "Hey Joe" Parsons*

You can clearly see Lieutenant Commander Parsons in the rear seat of GYPSY 200 taking pictures of me while I take pictures of him on a MiG combat air patrol over the USS *John F. Kennedy* and USS *Saratoga* in the Red Sea, December 1990. *Courtesy of the author*

Lieutenant Commander Parsons took this picture while refueling from the "Iron Maiden," the nickname Navy aircrews gave the KC-135's drogue because of its unforgiving nature. A "basket slap" by the 250-pound Iron Maiden could destroy the canopy or remove the refueling probe from a Navy or Allied fighter plane. *Courtesy of Lieutenant Commander Dave "Hey Joe" Parsons*

The refueling community owes a debt of gratitude to the British company Flight Refueling Ltd. (FRL), now Cobham plc. FRL continued to improve air refueling technology and processes from World War II through the Korean War, and now a majority of the world's receivers refuel from a drogue. This F-14 Tomcat, call sign CAMELOT 111, is connected to the boom drogue adapter attached to the boom's nozzle, its probe plugged into the red Iron Maiden basket. *Courtesy of the author*

Air Force tankers could not refuel the large number of Navy fighters going into Iraq during Desert Storm. The "hose multiplier" concept, providing additional contact points for fuel transfer, was implemented to refuel more aircraft faster. The KA-6D flying beyond the KC-135 acts as a second tanker and contact point, refilling its own tanks by plugging into the Iron Maiden when low on gas. *Photo courtesy of Lieutenant Commander Dave "Hey Joe" Parsons*

Every 909th Young Tiger Air Refueling Squadron aircrew is trained in a number of refueling techniques, one of which supports Special Operations Forces throughout Asia. My crew is performing low-altitude air refueling (LAAR) with this Air Force Special Operations Command MC-130 Combat Talon II a few thousand feet above the Pacific Ocean. 909th aircrews supported 353rd Special Operations Group MC-130s during exercises and real-world SOF missions at low altitude; it was one of the most fun refueling missions I ever flew. *Courtesy of the author*

My crew flew Technical Sergeant Vonnie Petersen's KC-135A, tail number 63-8019, nicknamed "Rolling Thunder," on the opening night of Desert Storm in support of PooBah's Party, the destruction of Iraq's air-defense network. This picture was taken several days after the opening night; the nine Aladdin's lamps signified the number of missions Rolling Thunder had flown since Desert Storm began. *Courtesy of the author*

Two F-4G Advanced Wild Weasels from Colonel George "John Boy" Walton's 561st Tactical Fighter Squadron wait to refuel from my crew's tanker in the BERRY POST refueling area, fifteen miles south of the Iraqi border, during Desert Storm. FALSTAFF 43 and 44, pictured here, defended thirty-two F-16s from SAMs as they attacked the airfields of western Iraq. *Courtesy of the author*

Three F-16s of the PUG flight head toward Saudi Arabia on our wing with only minutes of fuel left in their tanks, anxiously waiting to hook up to my KC-135. None of the twenty-four F-16s would have made it out of Iraq without our four Jeddah-based KC-135s flying miles into Iraqi airspace to pick them up. One PUG F-16 pilot told our boom operator we had one chance to connect or he would have to eject; he had only eight minutes of gas left in his tanks. *Courtesy of the author*

While deployed to Andersen Air Force Base in Guam, my crew refueled this KC-10 Extender, or "Gucci Bird," as it dragged four F-4E Phantom IIs from a Stateside base to Australia for a joint exercise. CORONETS, movements of fighter aircraft from the States to overseas bases, require strings of tankers across thousands of miles, with many of the fighters flying fifteen-hour sorties to get to their destinations. *Courtesy of the author*

orbited at thirty-two thousand feet as airborne battle managers in the back end watched over northern Iraq and protected the force. US Navy EP-3Es from VQ-2 Sandeman still collected electronic, signals, and communications intelligence. MAGIC and Sandeman did not need refueling. The Eagles and Vipers refueled off the KC-135s, while the Prowlers and Jags refueled from the No. 101 Squadron RAF VC-10s. The tanker total off-load had not changed in a year—we still transferred half a million pounds every vulnerable period.

Military aircraft receive unique names or have artwork painted on their noses. Sadly, current directives don't allow nose art on airplanes, as seen during World War II, the Korean War, and Vietnam. Political correctness doomed this military tradition a decade ago. Zot's Samurai Squadron, however, brought along one Viper that was the perfect example of a maintenance crew chief with a sense of humor. On my crew's first ONW mission, we pumped gas into one of Zot's Weasels. Boom operators always record the tail numbers of the aircraft refueled to track who got the gas and which command would pay for it. Northern Watch paid the gas bills, but we still had to keep track of our receivers. My boom for this trip, Will, piped up over the interphone as our first receiver got a pressure disconnect and moved to the left wing.

"Pilot, Boom—he doesn't have a tail number."

"What are you talking about, Boom?"

"Sir, the aircraft tail number is a name. It's BOB!"

"Hang on, Boom, he'll be outside my window in a minute. I'll take a look when he's out there."

The numberless Weasel appeared from beneath our tanker and parked off the left wing. Chuckling over the interphone, I told Will, "Boom, Pilot—I have the first receiver's tail number."

"Okay, give it to me."

"The first receiver's tail number is eight zero eight."

"What's that again, Pilot?"

"BOB is tail number eight zero eight."

BOB's crew chief had filled in the left sides of each script numeral eight with a black grease pencil. Everyone in the squadron said BOB stood for Bombs Over Baghdad, which was stitched into BOB's black vinyl intake cover in big yellow letters. A single black HARM silhouette under the left canopy rail showed BOB had fired a HARM at an Iraqi radar and killed it. BOB had the highest utilization rate during the deployment, flying every time he was scheduled.

One unique thing about the F-16 is its boom interphone system. Once the boom nozzle locked into the Viper's receptacle, our interphone systems were connected and we could talk back and forth securely. Receiver pilots could tell us how much gas they needed or just talk to us during long flights to break the boredom. Timber, a female fighter pilot in the 14th Fighter Squadron "Samurais," had a distinct voice that was always a welcome change from the male voices. She always wanted to talk to us while getting her gas. As the blue contact light illuminated on the instrument panel, Will, my boom, welcomed our next customer.

"SAMURAI 43, TEXACO 63 boom contact over interphone. How do you read, sir?"

"Read you loud and clear, Boom. How are you guys doing today?"

"Hey, Timber, it's Sluggo flying the tanker. How's life in northern Iraq today?"

"Hey, Sluggo, do you have your camera with you?"

"I've always got my camera with me, Timber. Look at the scenery around us!"

"It's nice with all the new snow. I want some of these pictures, Sluggo."

"Everybody does, Timber . . ."

"SAMURAI, you should be taking on gas now," Carol said over the interphone.

"Yeah, my gas gauge is moving up. . . . How much is one pump worth?" Timber answered back.

Carol, my copilot, told her, "About fifteen hundred pounds a minute, ma'am."

I asked her, "Is anything happening down south?"

"Not today. It's pretty boring in northern Iraq. But things always get exciting in the second and third vul periods."

Bzzzzzzzzt! Bzzzzzzzzt! Bzzzzzzzzt!

Will heard the buzz and asked, "What's the buzzing noise in the background, ma'am?"

"Yeah, you like that? My radar homing and warning system gives me tones through the interphone. That's what you are hearing. It's the Spoon Rest radar north of Mosul looking at us. The operators know all of us are refueling and getting ready to violate their airspace again, so they're taking a quick radar look now before we come back into Iraq. He's a target now."

"Seems a little weird, listening to Saddam's radar painting us over your interphone," Will answered.

"Just long-range radar paints right now. Worry when it's a constant buzzing sound. Iraq doesn't have the SAMs to reach us here, though."

"Did not know that, ma'am."

"They always seem to shoot at us the second time we sweep through northern Iraq. It'll be interesting to see what happens when we go back in thirteen minutes from now."

"Boom, CO—she's getting close to her six-grand off-load."

"Roger, CO."

"Yep, Boom, I'm getting close to full. Sure do appreciate all this gas . . ."

I told Timber, "We have about sixty-five K available for you and the EDS Vipers today."

"Are you guys burning the same gas you give to us?"

"We burn the same gas we're giving you. Gas pumped to you comes from all the tanks which drain into fore and aft body where the pumps are."

The boom fired through a disconnect, and the interphone went silent.

"Pilot, Boom, she's coming to your side."

"Roger, Boom . . ."

Looking over my left shoulder, I saw Timber appear out from under the wing and settle in the observation position just off the wingtip. I reached down and grabbed my camera off the floor. The lead tanker started a turn to the east toward Iran, and I followed. Both tankers in front of us had chicks in tow, aircraft on the boom or wings still refueling. The force didn't fire a shot that day in Iraq, Saddam's forces never challenging Coalition aircraft. ONW forces had gone a month without firing a shot. No-fly zones are mostly boring.

My crew rolled down the runway at 0900 on 30 October, the fourth tanker to arrive in the ROZ. The Cilo-Sat Mountains were blanketed in the first snows of winter and partially obscured by low, puffy clouds, a great backdrop for pictures. I could see on the instrument panel displays the first three-ship of tankers was turning west as my crew approached the ROZ. As we turned left to fall in behind the tankers, the city of Hakkâri passed beneath us, snow covering the high mountains above the town. Four Weasels loaded down with HARMs, AMRAAMs, and Sidewinders joined on my wings for gas. Carol flew the jet this mission, and I pumped gas and took a lot of pictures. Several receivers moved closer to the jet than normal. One moved so close our wings overlapped. Someone wanted to be really close to the camera. Before the mass debrief started after the mission, Zot asked for the pictures I took.

"Zot, how did you know it was me?"

Zot's retort came immediately. "Sluggo, we can see your gray head for miles!"

Every receiver knew it was me in the cockpit. No other tanker pilot in the 97th Astros had a full head of gray hair. Even with my ball cap on, every fighter pilot could still see my gray head in the window. The second tell was my big Minolta camera. I sent Zot a few of the in-flight shots. A three-ship formation of Bro's Triple Nickel Vipers is in the gallery. That was a great day to just sort of throttle back and watch the world go by.

Tactics Review Boards held by commanders created a forum to hear ideas from the troops flying the missions for how to develop better ways to accomplish our objectives. My brief covered improvements to retrograde procedures if Iraqi Air Force MiG-25 Foxbats made a high, fast run into the ROZ and attacked the tankers. The F-15 pilots and AWACS mission crew commander gave me their input on retrograding the five-ship of KC-135s and two VC-10s away from the Foxbats, which could travel twenty-two miles per minute. I wanted the British VC-10 pilots' input on the new retrograde procedures because I knew very little about how they operated in a defensive situation. During my discussion with the VC-10 pilots, it became clear to them I didn't know how they employed. Combined Joint Task Force Northern Watch rules allowed pilots to fly with any of the Coalition partners. So I asked, "Hey, Devon, what's the probability of me hopping on a flight?"

"Anytime, Sluggo. Come on along, mate!"

"What should I bring with me?"

"I hear you take a lot of pictures. The last row of seats is a great place to watch the Jaguars and Prowlers take gas. Bring your camera."

"Okay, sounds good. Do you guys order boxed lunches for your flights?"

"You can see that all of us are gaining weight. We eat hot bacon and cheese sandwiches on the way out to the ROZ, and hot ham and cheese returning to base."

The VC-10 is an airliner converted into a tanker, with a galley oven for heating food. Loadmasters would buy several long loaves of fresh Turkish bread outside the main gate and bacon, ham, and cheese at the base commissary. During the hour-and-fifteen-minute flight out to the ROZ, a loadmaster fired up the oven and baked the bacon-and-cheese sandwiches. He made five two-foot-long sandwiches, cut 'em up, and brought them to the cockpit on paper plates. It smelled like we were flying inside a Subway sandwich shop. Surprisingly, VC-10 cockpits use old 1970s avionics with a couple of new displays thrown in for situational awareness. All VC-10s are air refuelable, and listening to Devon describe the Operation Black Buck missions to the Falklands while we ate was fascinating.

Once the VC-10 checked in with MAGIC and passed into the ROZ, we orbited in the seventeen- to twenty-thousand-foot altitude block to accommodate the slower Jags and Prowlers. When the flight engineer reeled out both baskets, I grabbed an oxygen kit from the galley and headed to the back. Each drogue dangled just behind the engine pods, and the loadmaster was right—the rear row of windows provided a great view of the refueling over the Cilo-Sat Mountains. The first thing I noticed was that the VC-10 baskets didn't jump around as much as the KC-135 drogues. They remained rock solid in one position behind the plane. Every Jag and Prowler pilot stuck right into the drogue on their first try. The other thing I noticed was the loud engine noise, with the fan blades spinning next to me. As the first Prowler plugged into the basket, the electronic countermeasures officer (ECMO) in the front seat saw my face and my camera in the window. He waved as I began snapping pictures. He must have alerted the pilot that someone was in the back window with a camera. For the next eight to nine minutes, both of them looked up at me while I snapped pictures. I got one of the Jag pilots to look up while he was concentrating on staying in the basket. Each Prowler took eight thousand pounds, the Jags about six thousand each. VC-10 tankers have one severe shortcoming, however: they have terrible gas mileage. They consume approximately sixteen thousand pounds per hour, but hold only 170,000 pounds of gas. The knowledge gained from these two flights was extremely valuable the following year during Operations Anaconda and Iraqi Freedom.

All of us knew President Bush would keep his word, given at the Twin Towers, that the people who did this would soon hear from us.

Do you want to know one way to tell America's military is about to go to war? KC-135s and KC-10s depart US bases. While I sat in my room the night of Sunday 7 October, a knock came at my door. Carol asked if I had heard the news.

"Why, what's going on?"

"The air strikes in Afghanistan have started."

I grabbed the remote and watched the BBC's David Loyn broadcast the opening strikes of Operation Enduring Freedom. An Arabian news crew showed explosions in downtown Kabul and Kandahar. I knew from my involvement in the Weapons School's Mission Employment and Integration Phase that American fighters and bombers were striking critical targets across Afghanistan. Special Forces soldiers were on the ground supporting those attacks in the main cities and probably also in the mountains. The Navy was probably leading the way, since Afghanistan is a landlocked country. Later in the broadcast, Loyn mentioned a carrier off the coast of Pakistan. All the Navy strike aircraft sent in to kick bin Laden and Al Qaeda's ass needed Air Force or British tankers to do the job.

★ ★

LESSONS FROM THE COCKPIT: JOY

We don't often take the time to throttle back and enjoy the scenery around us. We rush through life, going to fast-food places to eat so we can get back to our desks, thinking we'll be more productive. I've learned that just isn't so. When I returned to Fairchild after this deployment, I drove Val nuts. I kept asking her, "What do I gotta do next? What do I gotta do next?" She always told me the same thing: "It's time to throttle back and play with the kids for a while." It was a great relief to have some downtime with the family and enjoy the scenery in a stress-free environment. Toward the end of my Northern Watch deployment, I could concentrate on the mission and stay in formation but still enjoy looking out the window through my camera. Two of my pictures are in the gallery.

I have witnessed majestic scenery while flying in the airplane. One evening at dusk we passed over Tokyo, with its bright lights and neon signs. We closed in on the Aleutians while the aurora borealis began its nightly show. Shortly after sunrise, Denali appeared in the windscreen, so I asked Anchorage Center for permission to take a couple of laps around the mountain to burn down gas. My crew never forgot this flight; it was one of my most memorable.

Learn to throttle back and find joy in the scenery. Push away from the slides or spreadsheets and take a look out the window to see what's happening around you. It's a great stress reliever and will bring much greater joy and happiness in your life. You'll still have to fly the jet, but spend some time enjoying the ride.

★ ★

13

No Plan Survives

0800 Sunday 3 March 2002
Combined Air Operations Center
Prince Sultan Air Base
Kingdom of Saudi Arabia

No plan survives its first contact with the enemy.

—Prussian general Helmuth von Moltke

Plan early, plan twice!

—Murphy's Laws of Armed Conflict

The general who wins the battle makes many calculations in his temple before the battle is fought.

—General Sun Tzu, author of *The Art of War*

When you're out of gas, you don't have many options.

—Robby Gordon, American race car driver

Tuna, the Master Attack Plan (MAAP) cell chief, left a note on my desk saying he needed to see me. I walked out of the Guidance, Apportionment, and Targeting, or GAT, shop, hunting for him, and found him coordinating a contingency plan down on the CAOC floor.

"You looking for me, Tuna?"

"Yeah, got a few minutes, Sluggo?"

"Sure, let's go back to the GAT shop and talk there—I want the Tims to be part of this discussion."

Great refueling experts worked for me, and I kept two of them close at all times, both from the 21st Air Force at McGuire Air Force Base in New Jersey. Both happened to be named Tim, both were KC-10 boom operators, and they were the best NCO refueling planners I'd worked with. All of us called them "the Tims." "Timmay" outranked the other Tim as a senior master sergeant. He knew how to arrange an initial tanker schedule quickly, and his schedules required very few changes. "Golfing Tim" had some planning algorithm in his brain that allowed him to look at a schedule on our whiteboard and instinctively know what adjustments to make so that the plan would flow without a hitch—or at least with very few issues. No one planned for Sir Murphy to walk onto a battlefield, and the Tims helped with those off-the-cuff chaos plans in a big way. Don't get me wrong, all of my guys and gals are great—the best in the Air Force, in my opinion. The Tims were just invaluable to tanker programs in time-crunched situations. I invited the Tims to join Tuna and myself at the table. Tuna then gave the Tims and me another military "science project."

Military science projects can be intensive and are always time-consuming. Science projects create lots of numbers, graphs, and, unfortunately, PowerPoint slides that are rarely used for anything. Science projects also give military planners an opportunity to wrap their collective heads around a problem, analyzing missions and subsequently producing courses of action based on assumptions that hopefully will become facts when going into battle. Tanker folks do a *lot* of science projects, because all air operations hinge on airborne fuel, particularly when operations go bad. Worst of all, tankers are always the last people to get the air plan, instead of the first. Gramps, another CES initial cadre member, and I had just finished a Tuna science project for Somalia the week before, and some of that information would help us through Tuna's new one.

Al Qaeda and Taliban fighters fleeing Afghanistan headed for Somalia, a rest-and-recuperation location for wounded radical Islamists. Mogadishu is known as "the Dish" to every service member. Osama bin Laden lived for several years in neighboring Sudan, so the Horn of Africa was nothing new to Al Qaeda. Several terror camps located in the deserts of Somalia sheltered Al Qaeda fighters and helped them evade the Coalition forces that were hunting them in Afghanistan. Bin Laden's operatives retreated from Afghanistan to an island off the Somali coast we called "Gilligan's Island," then onto the mainland, where they dispersed into the desert camps. The camps were unique, and easy to pick out if you knew what to look for: tents and Datsun King Cab trucks in the open desert. Our best option for Somalia was an all-bomber show: Diego BUFFs and Thumrait Bones. Thumrait Air Base's Bones—B-1 bombers—hardly needed any gas due to the short distance across the Gulf of Aden to Somalia. Gramps and I placed all refueling airspace directly over each camp, since all forms of Somali air defense remained in a state of disrepair from years of civil war. We doubted anyone in Somalia knew how to operate SAMs. But every terrorist is proficient with antiaircraft guns! Twenty-three-millimeter double-barreled guns bolted to the beds of Datsun trucks, called Technicals, roamed all over Somalia. They parked at night in the desert Al Qaeda camps. Hot Technicals baking in the equatorial sun showed up really well on infrared targeting pod imagery.

Bombers refueling behind tankers at twenty-eight thousand feet created long white contrails, just like those left by airliners flying over your house. Gramps and I wanted the resting and recuperating Al Qaeda and Taliban Bad Guys to see death filling up on its energy drink right above them just before the warheads came raining down on foreheads. I named all the Somali refueling anchors after NASCAR drivers: STEW-ART, EARNHARDT, GORDON, JARRETT, and WALTRIP. I know nothing about NASCAR, but a lot of NASCAR fanatics worked for me. I placed GORDON twenty miles off the coast of Mogadishu. I wanted to make sure the bombers and Navy fighters did not have to go far for a fill-up. If the US Air Force got the call to level the Dish, the bombers would do it from GORDON, and the tankers would watch the conflagration from just offshore. The corridors stretching across Somalia to and from each anchor area I named after NASCAR tracks: BRISTOL and DAYTONA crossed the entire length of Somalia, with POCONO and TALLADEGA crossing the Gulf of Aden between the Dish and Yemen. If tasked with a science project, at least have fun doing it. Project Somalia proved to be a great learning experience—it wasn't a lot of fun, because it took a lot of time away from other things that were going on, but it gave us really good information for bomber refueling operations anywhere in the Middle East. The experience came in handy a year later over Iraq.

Tuna's MAAP cell received another Operation Enduring Freedom battle rhythm change at the beginning of February. The rhythm change created Tuna's dilemma, which spawned our newest science project. Air support was winding down because *no one* fights during Afghan winters. Every ground force since Alexander the Great's knew that fighting during Afghan winters was impossible. The Afghan humanitarian relief operation, or HUMRO, increased its C-17 and C-130 airdrops, but fighting slowed way down. Each day's Afghan ATO became pretty static, with tankers flying a canned schedule day after day with only minor adjustments. Tuna's science project had one objective: to answer the question of how big the air refueling bill would be if the air campaign used a central close air support (CAS) air patrol theory, two to four fighters or a bomber over central Afghanistan that troops could call in a firefight. I asked him the usual AMC question: what were the CAS requirements? Tuna shrugged and said, "I don't know."

"There must be CAS requirements, Tuna! I can't do this if I don't know what the receiver requirements are."

I always got this comeback on science projects: "Sluggo, just use what we're doing now."

"That's a really broad picture, Tuna—Bones from Thumrait, BUFFs from Diego, fighters from the Jab [Ahmed Al Jaber Air Base], two carrier air wings, plus throw in the Coalition at Manas Air Base and the French carrier *Charles de Gaulle* to cover all the strikers. Intelligence, Surveillance, and Reconnaissance or ISR assets like AWACS, JSTARS, and Rivet Joint need gas too. What are the requirements, Tuna?"

"Yep, sounds like you got 'em all. I need this the day after tomorrow," Tuna said with a smile.

The Tims and I just laughed. "Oh, okay, Tuna! No worries!"

Still smiling, he said, "I know you guys will come up with something I can use. I just need to know what it will cost us in gas to implement this theory of employment."

Gramps and I figured that our best approach would be to maximize the number of desired mean points of impact, or DMPIs, destroyed with the least amount of fuel consumed. This fuel-consumed-per-bombs-available exercise became another great learning experience in Sun Tzu's calculations temple. The assumptions the Tims and I started with were that all strike and ISR assets would remain on station for three-hour vulnerability periods. BUFF and Bone bombers would stay on station for four hours. Visiting with each MAAP fighter, bomber, and ISR planner, the three of us gathered fuel consumption rates for all aircraft flying over Afghanistan. I had a good idea of consumption numbers from the core classes taught at the Combat Employment School, but I wanted to make sure my team used actual rates for airplanes loaded with bombs.

Bones burned twenty thousand pounds per hour. The Bone base in Oman was close, only ninety minutes' flight to central Afghanistan. Bones carry twenty-four precision-guided weapons in the three weapons bays. BUFFs flew fifteen-hour sorties from Diego Garcia, burning twenty-four thousand pounds per hour and hooking up five times for eighty thousand pounds each time they touched a tanker. BUFF wing pylons carried six precision-guided munitions on each side. An all-bomber show was Tuna's obvious option one. Carrier-based Tomcats and Hornets burned eight thousand pounds per hour at tactical speeds, carrying three to four laser-guided bombs from an hour's flight away in the Indian Ocean. Option two became an all-Navy show. Hybrid option 2.1—a single bomber and four Navy fighters—gave forward air controllers options for big bombs or twenty-millimeter bullets.

Option three was by far the most ineffective and inefficient use of gas. Air Force F-15Es and F-16s coming from the Jab in Kuwait turned out to be the worst possible choice based on gas consumption and bombs available. Transit time from the Jab was three hours, and when added to three-hour vulnerable periods over Afghanistan and then three hours' flying back to the Jab, it consumed ridiculous amounts of gas. If the situation intensified during the ground battle, Strike Eagle and Viper sortie duration would increase to more than ten hours. An F-15E four-ship carried eight GBU-12 laser-guided bombs but required 480,000 pounds of fuel for a nine-hour mission, according to our calculations. Half a million pounds on *one* mission! Vipers were a little better, just 360,000 pounds, but they carried only four bombs each: minimal bombs on DMPIs with a high gas cost. Thumrait's Bones didn't come close to needing this amount of gas, and could carry more bombs longer. AWACS and Rivet Joint still needed their eighty-thousand-pound fill-up every five hours. Grumman E-8 Joint STARS had recently arrived at Al Udeid from Robins Air Force Base in Georgia, and they required the same fill-up as AWACS and Rivet Joint. With a PowerPoint brief my team created, I showed the new director of mobility forces (DIRMOBFOR), Brigadier General Skip Scott, options one, two, two point one, and three, with their supporting numbers. He was visibly shocked at how much fuel the Strike Eagles from the Jab required. All of us were, but the Strike Eagle planner said the numbers were correct. I went through the brief page by page with Tuna that night, and his instructions set me back.

"Sluggo, take that brief and hide it in the deepest, darkest dungeon you can find."

"Wait . . . what? What are you talking about, Tuna?"

"No self-respecting fighter pilot wants that information to see the light of day. Everyone wants to get into this war, and excluding fighters from the Jab is not going to happen. That dog don't hunt, Sluggo."

"Tuna, you wanted to know the fuel cost for an employment strategy and battle rhythm change. Here it is. You don't have to like it, but the numbers don't lie. These are the gas facts. You know what the gas bill will be, and better yet, what options you have based on consumption rates per bombs carried."

I understood what Tuna was saying. Everyone wanted to be the guy or gal whose name ended up in the newspapers behind the headline "Osama bin Laden Killed by US Airstrike."

By mid-February, many of us were hearing rumors of an impending Army operation. There wasn't a lot of information, and the CAOC thought it would be a ground fight with minimal air support. Tuna's science project looked like it might be useful after all, even though he didn't like what it told us. Even the Battlefield Coordination Detachment (BCD), the Army's planning cell in the CAOC, didn't seem to know what was going on. The Army colonel in the BCD said that the 10th Mountain Division was rumored to be planning ground operations in the Shah-i-Kot Valley, in the mountainous area of Paktia Province bordering Pakistan. Ninth Air Force commander Lieutenant General Mike Moseley had traveled to the Gulf Coast countries and was out of pocket. CAOC director Major General John Corley ran each nightly colonels' staff meeting in General Moseley's absence. During one meeting, an Air Force colonel said, "Sir, there's an operation coming. All I know is that it's big, it's Army, and it's named after a snake."

No one knew what this snakelike operation was. It seemed that no one could find out what the 10th Mountain was up to. We kept hearing that it would require minimal support, but the action itself remained a big secret. Five days before the 28 February start date, the 10th Mountain sent a 110-page operation order (OPORD) PowerPoint brief to the CAOC detailing air support requirements. It set our entire building on fire. The air support taskings were large, and airlift support might not be sustainable. Combined Joint Task Force Mountain's operation, called Anaconda, was going to root out all remaining hard-core Al Qaeda and Taliban forces in a five-kilometer-wide, nine-kilometer-long valley. Intelligence estimated two to three hundred enemy fighters were hidden in the Shah-i-Kot Valley, "the Place of Kings" in Pashto. But the 10th Mountain had not included us in the planning process. Predator UAVs (unmanned aerial vehicles) should have been staring at the objective areas last week!

Brigadier General Scott called all Air Mobility Division chiefs together to discuss the 10th Mountain's OPORD brief and their needs. Tuna's science project saved my tanker team's collective tail ends from starting the meeting with a blank sheet of paper. Tuna's central CAS science project contained most of the information my team needed to create refueling operations near the Shah-i-Kot Valley. Unfortunately, airlift planners did not have a contingency plan to fall back on. I had not included C-17 airlifters in my calculations, figuring that airlift fuel was an additional requirement we could deal with later.

General Scott needed our refueling plan the next day, Sunday 24 February. My tanker team went right to work. Based on the central CAS theory science project, I knew what Anaconda's original fuel requirement numbers were. Al Qaeda had nothing to threaten the tankers with unless a very determined terrorist hiked up a nineteen-thousand-foot mountain peak, so we placed the tankers thirty miles south of the Shah-i-Kot, with a short five-minute flight time to each anchor. A third anchor north of the Shah-i-Kot was designed for all ISR aircraft, but fighters could use it too. Since the A-10s were not players, all the anchors were above twenty-two thousand feet, but only four thousand feet above some of the taller mountain peaks. The psychological effect on Al Qaeda and the Taliban of watching fighters, bombers, and reconnaissance aircraft fill up on gas overhead was huge in my mind.

I named each refueling anchor after conservative talk radio and television hosts. A Rush Limbaugh listener since Desert Storm, I placed the RUSH anchor, the largest of the three, directly southeast of the Shah-i-Kot. The tankers would need to decrease their bank angle from thirty to fifteen degrees while increasing airspeed to turn in a wider circle as the B-1s got heavier with gas. RUSH was where the Bones would go to fill up. O'REILLY was west of RUSH by only fifteen miles, and was directly south of a prominent mountain called the Whaleback. HANNITY lay directly north, oriented northwest to southeast and wedged between commercial airway flight paths the Afghan government had opened to generate millions in revenue. All aircraft could refuel in O'REILLY and HANNITY except the Bones. As events unfolded, O'REILLY grew wider to accommodate refueling the Bones. To be bipartisan, I opened two large refueling anchors just inside the Afghan border on the far left of the country next to the Iranian border. HILLARY and KENNEDY were irrelevant to Anaconda's air battle but were crucial to other operations going on in Herat and Farah provinces. One thing Gramps and I included was fighter holding points three thousand feet below the tankers. I told the strike planners to keep all fighter aircraft below the tankers at these geographic points, something the Employment School cadre had wanted to try for a long time. When a fighter pilot needed gas, all he or she had to do was look up, and a tanker would be somewhere close. We called it "staying on the nipple." Every fighter liaison officer and planner loved our easy-to-use refueling system.

Poor weather delayed Anaconda's start date, giving us forty-eight more hours to finalize the refueling plan. My tanker team felt that the

Anaconda plan was pretty tight. Our only concern was what would happen if Anaconda unraveled in execution. Invoking the Murphy's Laws of Armed Conflict planning axiom "No plan survives its first contact with the enemy," we made sure that two KC-135 boom spares remained on strip alert at Al Udeid. Al Dhafra Air Base's KC-10 tankers held one hundred thousand pounds of reserve fuel and could handle any last-minute emergency requests from one of the Shah-i-Kot Valley refueling anchor areas. KC-135s with extra gas could transfer fuel into the Gucci Birds before leaving the refueling anchors, a practice known as consolidating. The Gucci community hates consolidating, but it saves our collective butts every time it's in the ATO. Several of us in Tanker Ops and Plans talked through potential solutions if gas became an issue. With a large chart of the Shah-i-Kot Valley spread out over a table, we talked through what could go wrong and possible solutions for those problems. I stood in Sun Tzu's calculations temple with some of the best tanker operators on the planet, feeling pretty good about the next day's schedule, the amount of gas available, and what to do if the plans changed. None of us could have imagined what was actually about to happen.

The morning of Sunday 3 March, I walked by the tanker ops desk on the CAOC floor on my way up to the GAT shop. I frequently walked through the CAOC front door at 0800 and stayed for however long I was needed. Talking with the ops desk folks gave me a good sense of what was going on. As I walked up to the desk, I noticed that two of my planners, Cardiac Bob and Struks, working at the Tanker Operations desk, were heads down and really busy with execution. I asked how things were going, and saw that Cardiac Bob's blood pressure was way up. He told me the US and Afghan forces had come under heavy fire in the mountains when they stepped off their CH-47 Chinook helos in the Shah-i-Kot. 101st Airborne and 10th Mountain forces, called Task Force Hammer, got hammered. An AC-130 gunship misidentified a Special Ops team near a place called "the Finger" and fired on them, killing one American and three Afghan militiamen. Knock-it-off calls went out over all radios, and the planned fifty-five-minute pre-assault air bombardment lasted sixty seconds and six bombs. Anaconda evolved from needing only a handful of strikers to a maximum effort in the time it took you to read this sentence.

Task Force Hammer then came under heavy mortar fire from the Whaleback. 10th Mountain troops were pinned down on the southern end of the valley floor in a hollow now called "Hell's Halfpipe." The 10th Mountain troops had only one 120-millimeter mortar with them, having expected no resistance during their insertion. 101st Airborne troops in blocking positions to the north came under similar fire. Initial air support from two of six orbiting AH-64 Apache attack helicopters stopped when they were forced to withdraw after receiving significant battle damage from precise Al Qaeda and Taliban antiaircraft fire from the mountain peaks. Every Apache took hits, and a handful could not fly again after landing. From the CAOC floor, I watched battles taking place at several key locations on Predator video feeds. That Predator video still haunts me. BOSSMAN in the AWACS's voice on AC-1 command net constantly chattered with instructions and requests for immediate CAS. All of us on the CAOC floor were in a situation none of us were trained for—crisis action and battle management in real time. All the fighters and bombers over the Shah-i-Kot Valley now became airborne artillery, gulping down hundreds of thousands of pounds of gas. Our plan did not survive the opening hours of Anaconda.

Intelligence estimates had been totally wrong. There weren't a couple hundred Al Qaeda and Taliban in the mountains surrounding the Shah-i-Kot; there were probably five times that number. If the CAOC had been involved earlier in the planning, several Air Force Predator UAVs flying over the Shah-i-Kot could have established patterns of life at all the landing zones, could have seen who was living there and what they did every day. One Predator showed up on station within an hour of troop insertion. UAVs should have been staring at the Shah-i-Kot for *days*, not an hour. VF-211 Checkmates Tomcats flew Tactical Airborne Reconnaissance Pod System (TARPS) missions over Shah-i-Kot, capturing miles of video data linked back to USS *John C. Stennis* and the CAOC. My tanker team had not known why the Tomcats flew so many TARPS sorties; now we knew. Electronic intelligence heard bin Laden's voice coming over an Inmarsat phone during the first battles. Public Enemy Number One was here, in the Shah-i-Kot Valley, just as Lieutenant Colonel Pete Blaber from Delta Force had said he would be.

Forward air controllers and Special Operations Reconnaissance Forces now called for air strikes by the bombers and ground-attack aircraft stacked overhead. Command and control relationships that had not been set up before kickoff created significant roadblocks to the effective use of air support. Many of the on-call close air support, or XCAS, sorties returned to their Gulf Coast country bases without dropping a single bomb, using thousands more pounds of gas. Tankers ran dry when ground-attack fighters stayed on station beyond their vulnerable periods to attack new targets half an hour late. One KC-10 tanker offloaded over 180,000 pounds of gas and returned to Al Dhafra, leaving us with no emergency tanker. XCAS and time-sensitive target (TST) strikers used all the reserve gas tanker planners had put overhead as an emergency supply. Good—it had done what it was designed to do, but now our one-hundred-thousand-pound reserve was gone. We launched two strip alert KC-135s to fill the void. Both jets refueled CAS receivers and dumped eighty thousand pounds of unused fuel into the next Gucci Bird before returning home. Fighters were directed to hit a target and then told by another agency to come off and wait while command elements figured out priorities. Meanwhile, BUFFs were burning twenty-four thousand pounds per hour and F-15Es ten thousand holding with unreleased weapons. That afternoon I told Vinnie, the ops director, that Anaconda was out of reserve gas.

I spent Saturday afternoon and evening upstairs in the GAT shop working on Anaconda's Sunday air plan. Numerous issues stood in our way. Anaconda's strike aircraft schedule changed every ten minutes, causing huge ripples in the refueling plans. No one could nail down what Sunday's ATO would be. XCAS sorties increased tanker requirements by half a million pounds. A six- to eight-million-pound off-load day was a real possibility. Tankers had been passing less than half that amount before Anaconda started. Millions of pounds airborne meant nothing if there were only a handful of contact points at which to pass it around. Only five of thirty-eight tankers would not fly Sunday, staying on strip alert if needed for emergencies.

All other Al Udeid, Al Dhafra, Sheik Isa, and Manas tankers were stacked two high in RUSH, O'REILLY, and HANNITY by the Tims. RAF tanker planners offered their L-1011 and VC-10 tankers from Masirah Air Base in Oman, which the Tims included in the heaviest drogue portions of the schedule. French C-135FR tankers coming down from Manas refueled French Mirage 2000Ds and some of the Tomcats and Hornets. I told the Tims a KC-10 would stay high in RUSH or O'REILLY for twenty-four hours from then until Anaconda was over. The tankers still had a drogue problem: not enough in the theater. USS *John C. Stennis* and Carrier Air Wing 9 transitioned from night to day carrier and were not flying sorties. USS *Theodore Roosevelt* and Carrier Air Wing 1 flew their last sorties before replacement by USS *John F. Kennedy* and Carrier Air Wing 7 on 11 March. Several KC-10s equipped with wingtip air refueling pods (WARPs) flowed through the daily schedule, but the tankers still did not have enough drogues for seventy refueling control times.

I sent a message to AMC headquarters that night asking how many KC-135 Iron Maidens there were in the inventory and how healthy they were. Paragraph two asked when the new Multi-Point Refueling System, or MPRS, pods would be coming into the KC-135 fleet. Distance remained the air campaign's biggest shortcoming, and gas was once again the real issue. Every airplane going into or out of landlocked Afghanistan needed refueling now. If a tanker broke, it took at least three hours for a replacement to arrive. The tanker ops desk had to think three hours ahead of the fight in the Shah-i-Kot to launch strip alerts in time to refuel aircraft waiting over a changing battlefield.

One bright spot happened on Sunday, in spite of the resulting headaches it caused. French Navy Super Étendards from the aircraft carrier *Charles de Gaulle* had to gas up every twenty minutes, and could use only the KC-10 Nerf-soft drogues. A Gucci Bird met the Étendards above the *Charles de Gaulle* and dragged them to Anaconda's op area. One forward air controller gave an Étendard permission to drop one GBU-12 near troops in contact next to an Al Qaeda cave. French rules of engagement were more restrictive than the American rules, requiring a code word from French leaders in the CAOC to release weapons. The French pilot asked K-MART, the CAOC's call sign, to pass the code word so the Étendard pilot could drop.

Only one problem: the Navy captain and director of operations call sign Moose never received the French bomb release code word. In true US Navy Hornet driver fashion, he told BOSSMAN to pass the code word "pork sausage." Not amused, the Étendard pilot called back asking for the correct code word. The French general heard the commotion and told Moose the right code word. He sent BOSSMAN the correct code word, and the Étendard dropped the first French laser-guided bombs of the war smack-dab on a group of Al Qaeda fighters in a cave complex, killing them all, according to the Predator video.

One Super Étendard developed mechanical problems over the Shah-i-Kot, and a KC-10 with a broken boom returning to Al Dhafra dragged it to *Charles de Gaulle*'s location before turning for the UAE. The French pilot recovered safely aboard the *Charles de Gaulle* and flew strike missions the next day. It was a big save by the Gucci Birds and the tanker team, for which the French three-star general thanked General Scott profusely. The Étendards continued to wreak havoc on Al Qaeda and Taliban positions over the next few days, but used a lot of Gucci Bird gas doing it. I found out later that US Air Force tankers had enabled French naval aviation history.

Moose's pork sausage Étendard was the first French aircraft to drop a laser-guided bomb in anger on an Al Qaeda position. After Anaconda ended, the French general and the *Charles de Gaulle* carrier air wing commander who worked as the CAOC liaison officer asked to see me in the general's office. The general handed me a beautiful Mirage 2000 tie tack, the plane he flew. The French Navy air wing commander gave me an ashtray from the *Charles de Gaulle* captain's quarters and a *Charles de Gaulle* ball cap. *Charles de Gaulle*'s captain had sent them up as a reward for all the Air Force tankers' hard work. They thanked my team again and again for our excellent refueling support.

There has been a lot written and spoken about French military efforts throughout history, or the lack thereof. These two outstanding officers commanded one of the most professional groups of airmen I've ever supported. Every time they were called upon to work tough battlefield issues during Anaconda, our French Coalition partners performed flawlessly.

CAOC leadership halted Operation Southern Watch, the Iraqi no-fly zone, on Sunday afternoon. Every asset then supported Shah-i-Kot Valley operations except one, which was probably needed the most. A-10 Warthogs were not playing in Anaconda. Hawgs would just tax our already stretched refueling system further. Trying to talk through the radio mess had been problematic for tankers in RUSH, O'REILLY, and HANNITY. Comm frequencies changed, and not everyone got the word. Soldiers and airmen on the ground were screaming for air support, and some fliers remained unaware of the secure communication changes. Strike aircraft continued holding over the Shah-i-Kot past their off-station times, exacerbating the fuel-shortage situation. Strike executors in ops had to come up with a new plan on the fly, creating massive ripples throughout our tanker program. A KC-10 off-loaded 180,000 pounds before returning to Al Dhafra on Saturday night. I launched a strip alert KC-135 from Al Udeid on Sunday to make up for the one-hundred-thousand-pound KC-10 tanker loss.

One stroke of good tanker luck saved us that day. AMC owned eight air-refuelable Special Ops KC-135 airframes, called "Christines" in the tanker world. One Christine finished its mission early and offered BOSSMAN its support after a thirty-thousand-pound off-load into an AC-130 gunship. I instructed my tanker ops folks at the desk to off-load all excess gas into the Christine or a KC-10. The Christine's crew stayed three hours past their off-station time taking on gas and unloading it to receivers, enough time for an Al Udeid strip alert tanker to arrive. STILLETO, the E-8 Joint STARS, began flying missions from Al Udeid also, creating a better air-to-ground command and control system for vetting CAS target requests. Strike Eagle and Viper fourships from the Jab passed each other in the Arabian Gulf carrying retained weapons home. The tankers had a razor-thin fuel reserve over the Shah-i-Kot on Sunday because the Christine's crew stayed out for so long.

Just before Anaconda had begun, I got a call from CENTCOM Engagements. Engagements is CENTCOM's group for vetting every country wanting to deploy forces in Operation Enduring Freedom. Grinch in CENTCOM Engagements called to say that Royal Netherlands Air Force KDC-10s would soon be part of the refueling forces at Manas Air Base. Grabbing NATO's ATP-56 refueling bible, I looked up the KDC-10's approved receivers. I called Engagements back and let Grinch have it right between the eyes.

"Grinch! The KDC-10 doesn't do me any good! It can only refuel five boom aircraft. According to ATP-56, the KDC-10 can only refuel F-15s, F-16s, NATO AWACS—not USAF AWACS, mind you—RC-135s, and MC-130s. It carries a lot less fuel than Air Force KC-10s, so in hot weather, it's just a big KC-135R model eating up ramp space at Manas and off-loading sixty thousand pounds. I don't need another small-off-load boom aircraft, Grinch. Disapproved; resubmit in ninety days for final disapproval!"

"Sluggo, you have to take them. These guys are players! They want to be in this fight. They want to fly out of Manas with the European Air Force Vipers—which includes Dutch Vipers—and be a part of this battle. You have to take them on."

"Grinch, you're an old Marine pilot. *The tankers need more drogues!* The kind you use—you know, that Iron Maiden thingy we dangle in front of the Hornets!"

He reminded me how much everyone hated the Iron Maiden. Complaining wasn't going to get me anywhere. Grinch won, I lost. On Sunday evening, as I worked on Monday's plan with the Tims, Gramps came to me with a big smile on his face. He had news, but I wasn't sure from the look on his face whether it was constructive or destructive.

"Hey, Sluggo, got a good news story for you today. The Dutch KDC-10 has their Joint STARS qual!"

"What do you mean?"

"We can add E-8 Joint STARS to ATP-56's matrix for the Dutch KDC-10," Gramps said, laughing.

I knew what Gramps meant, and we both laughed hysterically.

There is a long process for qualifying receivers behind US Air Force tankers. It involves ground and airborne testing of tanker and receiver refueling system compatibility. The day before, Tanker Plans had *accidentally* scheduled the KDC-10 to refuel the E-8 JSTARS, an airframe the Dutch were not approved to refuel. Remember, they were qualified for only five airframes. The STILETTO JSTARS refueling behind the KDC-10 went off without a hitch, because the JSTARS is just an AWACS without the black radar pancake spinning on the top. Still, a US Air Force aircraft refueled from an unapproved international tanker. General Scott was not going to like it, but he had to know. I related to him that we had a new receiver matrix thanks to my oversight on Sunday's schedule. He didn't know what I meant. I told him STILETTO had hooked up with an unapproved international tanker that afternoon—the Dutch KDC-10 was not an approved tanker for the STILETTO JSTARS aircraft. General Scott looked at me and smiled, saying calmly, "Fog of war, Sluggo. Keep moving."

All of us in the Air Mobility Division loved working for Skip Scott.

My air refueling control team (ARCT) folks did a great job creating a refueling plan from scratch for Monday 4 March. Snooze, a good friend and KC-10 squadron commander at Al Dhafra, called to talk ATO planning. One of his KC-10s logged a fifteen-hour sortie on Sunday, causing a huge ripple in his flying schedule. It was the Reliability tanker, off-loading around 180,000 pounds. I gave Snooze an update on the Shah-i-Kot Valley battle situation from watching Predator video. I told him Gucci Bird abuse was just beginning, since they had both booms and drogues. No plan survives its first contact with the enemy, and Anaconda's refueling plan went into the wastebasket hours after the operation started. Famous or stupid things people said during military operations were immortalized on a quote board hung in a high-traffic area for all to see. Walking out of the GAT shop at 2330 to get some sleep, I saw that someone had written "Plan early, plan twice!" in big bold letters on the quote board.

I walked into my bedroom on Sunday just before midnight. Exhausted, I sat on the edge of my bed and unlaced my boots. I went through every refueling event of the last two days. All our planning had done little to prepare us for what happened over the Shah-i-Kot Valley. Tuna's science project had saved our butts, because my team knew each aircraft's requirements and we could use that knowledge to change plans. I worried that Monday's air plan would suffer the same fate as Saturday's. My tanker team had looked at every possible ripple for Monday's ATO before leaving, and I still had doubts that it was an executable plan. I turned on the TV at a low volume, and was asleep ten minutes later.

★ ★

LESSONS FROM THE COCKPIT: RESILIENCE

Google defines resilience as the capacity to recover from difficulties or the ability of an object to spring back into its original shape. Anaconda's original plan didn't even survive its first day. Moose told me during a telephone conversation that when RAZOR 03 got shot down, all eyes turned to him as the director on the floor. He frankly said that he started pulling things out of his ass. His gut instincts were based on decades of operational and tactical experience, though. It took about forty-eight hours to recover from the difficulties encountered atop Takur Ghar, requiring a maximum effort by a lot of agencies to bring Operation Anaconda back to its original objectives.

Anaconda is an excellent example of operational resilience. Tuna's science project gave my team valuable knowledge they could use to overcome the difficulties of maintaining stacks of airborne fighters and bombers over the Shah-i-Kot Valley. Airpower dropped a lot of bombs on the Al Qaeda and Taliban fighters hiding in the Shah-i-Kot. The maximum airpower effort allowed the Coalition to get back on its feet and back into its original form. British, French, and American strike aircraft hurt bin Laden and the Taliban once we regained our battle rhythm. When we experience difficulties in our lives, we have opportunities to practice resilience. Your resilience to hard times and the reshaping of your life builds the kind of character and expertise you can gain only from passing through the Refiner's Fire.

★ ★

14

Hawg Drag

0115 Monday 4 March 2002
Combined Air Operations Center
Prince Sultan Air Base
Kingdom of Saudi Arabia

The Chinese use two brush strokes to write the word "crisis." One brush stroke stands for danger; the other for opportunity. In a crisis, be aware of the danger—but recognize the opportunity.

—PRESIDENT JOHN F. KENNEDY

The most important thing is to try to inspire people so that they can be great in whatever they do.

—KOBE BRYANT, BASKETBALL SUPERSTAR

No phone call at 0115 brings good news. In an odd twist, Fox News's *The O'Reilly Factor* was playing on TV, which I never turned off when falling asleep.

"This is Lieutenant Colonel Hasara. May I help you, sir or ma'am?"

You never knew whether the person on the other end of the line outranked you. This time it was Golfing Tim. He did not have good news.

"Sir, we need you back here pronto."

"Tim, I've only been in bed since midnight. What's going on?"

"Cannot tell you over this line. Just get dressed, hop on the bus, and get back here ASAP."

"Roger, see you in twenty minutes. Can you give me a hint?"

"Remember the receivers conversation we had yesterday? Our worst fears are realized. Rumor is it's political too."

"Okay, Tim, thanks for the call. I'll see you in about twenty minutes."

Boots on and zipped into a clean flight suit, I splashed cold water on my face in the bathroom. Survival School teaches you the body works better with a clean face, so that was the only preparation I made before walking out the door. During the entire bus ride, my mind ran through every possible scenario, unconcerned with having to come back in but wondering what the emergency was. I walked through the doors by the 9/11 banners and hurried upstairs to the GAT cell. Gramps and the Tims were leaning over a map on the table, planning something.

I asked them, "Okay, guys, what's going on?"

At approximately 0245 on Monday 4 March, a Navy SEAL fire team called MAKO 31 riding in a 160th Special Operations Aviation Regiment (SOAR) MH-47 Chinook known as RAZOR 03 had approached a mountaintop called Takur Ghar. Skimming low over the landing zone, the pilots and SEALs noticed fresh tracks in the snow from recent human activity. No one was supposed to be up there. NAIL 22, an AC-130, had told BOSSMAN there was no activity atop Takur Ghar. Moments later, an RPG round went through RAZOR 03 as it hovered over the LZ, and machine-gun fire punctured the helicopter's skin. RAZOR 03's pilot team went to full throttle in an attempt to get off the peak. In the sudden jolt of getting airborne, a member of MAKO 31, Navy SEAL petty officer Neil Roberts, fell off the back ramp and landed in the knee-deep snow. RAZOR 03 attempted to return for Roberts but was forced to land on the valley floor due to battle damage suffered in their first attempt. A Predator flying overhead projected on the CAOC's white forty-foot-tall wall screen SEAL Roberts fighting for his life.

Gramps began the conversation. "Remember how we were told

A-10s would not participate? Anaconda's going to hell. They need CAS assets bad, and guess who just got tagged for the show? Hawgs from the Jab are going downrange. Someone said something about people on the Hill in DC asking why Hawgs weren't participating after they'd spent all this money to keep them in the fleet. That's the political rumor going around. The best part, Sluggo, is that the Hawg guys don't know where they're going to land yet. We have five hours to figure that out. Five hours, Sluggo."

"Five hours? When do they take off?!"

"Wheels up at oh-nine-hundred."

Opportunity knocks only once. There were a lot of planning brushstrokes to consider in moving armed Hawgs forward. It was 0153, about seven hours before wheels up. Plan A had to be ready by 0700, so Face, the 332nd Air Expeditionary Wing commander; El Cid, the 332nd Expeditionary Operations Group commander; and their planning staff would have time to digest the details. The A-10s would be heavy, carrying Mavericks, five-hundred-pound bombs, rocket pods, and a full gun while flying at 210 knots. Two hundred ten knots meant a five-hour transit from the Jab to the Shah-i-Kot Valley. We didn't have a place near the Shah-i-Kot to refuel the Hawgs down low either. Where were the tankers going to do that?

The good news was that only two Hawgs were moving that morning. Additional Hawgs would follow in pairs over the next few days. Gramps, the Tims, and I began sketching out a plan. Sheik Isa was the closest tanker base to the Jab. I told Timmay to get Sheik Isa on the phone. They needed to pump up a jet to 220,000 pounds gross weight; the heaviest KC-135s could refuel A-10s because the tanker pilots had to extend the flaps at a 210-knot refueling speed. Timmay and I agreed that ripping off one of Sheik Isa's sorties to dedicate it to the first hookup and dragging the Hawgs to Pakistan should be the first action. But where to hook up?

Fortunately for us, previous tanker planners had kept everything they created in a big black safe. Dewey's operational navigation chart (ONC) remained in a folder in the safe. Gramps and I pulled out Dewey's ONC and looked for old refueling areas near Bahrain. There was a critical opportunity here, because tankers had to refuel A-10s low, within range of shoulder-fired heat-seeking missiles. All we needed was a point over water, an altitude, a hookup time, and a radio frequency for the Hawgs' first join-up in the northern Arabian Gulf. Maybe a closed refueling area was already in the system? No luck. I called the frequency management folks in the comm cave for a discrete UHF radio frequency the Hawgs and the tanker could talk on. Comm cave gave us a standard CAOC answer: "We'll call you back." Gramps and I picked a random point over water north of Bahrain and southeast of Al Jubail, Saudi Arabia, for joining up, away from all the Persian Gulf airline traffic. If either Hawg could not take gas, they would return to the Jab or divert to Bahrain. Gramps and I followed the Employment School airspace construction checklist from memory, building a long, low track toward Afghanistan.

KC-135 Combat Employment School had a phrase for times like this. When a student made things up as he or she went along, it was called "Monkeys flying out your ass," a play on the *Wizard of Oz* scene in which the Wicked Witch of the West stands in the castle window releasing her Flying Monkeys of Doom to find Dorothy, Toto, and her merry band of misfits. A hand signal created by the initial cadre indicated this egregious phrase: a cupped hand motioning inward and outward behind your butt. Just after the comm cave called to give us our radio frequency, Gramps made the hand signal as we continued planning. None of the planners knew why Gramps and I were laughing.

In time-constrained planning situations like this, I would rather be lucky than good. The Hawgs needed one more refueling location near the Strait of Hormuz, and we got a really lucky break when we looked over Dewey's ONC chart. Gramps found an old straight refueling track created for Enduring Freedom's opening night in October 2001. The Bold Tigers of the 391st Fighter Squadron, an F-15E unit from Mountain Home Air Force Base in Idaho, had created an extended refueling track just north of the Strait of Hormuz using the 366th Fighter Wing's nickname, GUNFIGHTER. GUNFIGHTER had a low track from nine thousand to eleven thousand feet and a high track from twenty-one thousand to twenty-four thousand feet. GUNFIGHTER was perfect for the Hawgs and gave us our first big break of the night.

By activating GUNFIGHTER LOW in the airspace control order (ACO), all Coalition nations understood that it was back in use. Aircraft exiting GUNFIGHTER LOW had overflight clearance across the United Arab Emirates, a straight line into the Gulf of Oman and around the corner of Iran into Pakistan. Once a tanker and the Hawgs got to Afghanistan, they would have access to two refueling areas located side by side over the flat desert plains northwest of Karachi, perfect for low-altitude A-10 refueling. During the initial air campaign, all refueling anchors had been named after Greek mythological characters. MERCURY and APOLLO anchor areas sat next to each other over the Balochistan Province of Pakistan, just south of Afghanistan's Registan Desert plains. A KC-135 from Al Udeid, added to the schedule, would meet the two Hawgs in APOLLO and drag them to the Shah-i-Kot Valley. One issue remained: How would the Hawgs refuel high over the mountains in RUSH, O'REILLY, or HANNITY? We agreed to let the aircrews work those issues out during refueling.

Last, we had to figure out where the Hawgs would land. Flight-planning math revealed that they had to land somewhere in Afghanistan or Pakistan, not having enough crew duty hours to fly back to the Jab. Both Hawgs departed not knowing where they would land after an eight- to nine-hour mission. Recovery was El Cid and his Hawg planner's problem, but tankers might be required to fulfill their recovery plan. El Cid had faced this same situation in October 2001 when Baltimore Guard A-10s alerted in preparation for moving to Afghanistan. Leadership canceled their movement at the last minute. El Cid had kept all the planning paperwork in a briefcase behind his desk, which was another great break for us. Gramps and I briefed General Scott for his approval around 0545 Monday morning. I e-mailed the information to El Cid's staff at 0612.

Moose took over the director of operations chair in the CAOC's crow's nest Monday morning at 0600. From this elevated position, he could see across the CAOC floor. During the changeover brief with Moose's night director counterpart, the movie *Black Hawk Down* streamed as a screensaver on one of his nine computer monitors. Approximately twelve minutes after his changeover, Moose began living his own Black Hawk Down disaster. A 160th SOAR MH-47 Chinook, call sign RAZOR 01, approached Takur Ghar carrying the quick reaction force (QRF) to rescue SEAL Neil Roberts. RAZOR 01's pilot team did not know the satellite communications frequencies had changed, so they did not hear the warnings about Takur Ghar's hot LZ. As RAZOR 01 flared for landing, everyone on the CAOC floor saw an RPG round enter from the Predator video's right-hand side, smashing into the helo broadside. RAZOR 01's rescue force ran off the back and spread out near some rocky outcroppings. Three Rangers dropped to the ground just a few feet from the ramp door. The MH-47 door gunner and the three Rangers died immediately, and the rescue force was fighting for their lives—all on Predator video projected on the CAOC wall.

All eyes on the CAOC floor watched the firefight on the huge wall screen and then turned to Moose, who stood in the crow's nest. BOSS-MAN was broadcasting on command net in the background. The question on everyone's silent faces was "What are you going to do now, Mr. Director?" Radio chatter from BOSSMAN and STILETTO were the only situational-awareness tools Moose had at the moment. None of the directors had air-battle-management training for situations like this. Moose's ops floor mates used their years of battlefield experience to build a plan and began executing it. RAZOR 01's demise created another ripple in the refueling plan but also an opportunity to save soldiers. When I approached the crow's nest at 0800, Moose had his right foot up on the desk and was rocking back and forth. I'd learned his battlefield crisis tell from watching him over the last two days. When Moose put his right foot up on the desk and rocked back and forth, something was very wrong.

"Not now, Sluggo, we're in deep dog squeeze. Get your tankers ready, because we're going to need a buttload of gas."

"My team anticipated this, Moose. Yesterday we planned on stacking KC-135s two high in RUSH, O'REILLY, and HANNITY with a KC-10 overhead everybody in RUSH."

His comeback kind of stunned me. "That may not be enough, Sluggo."

"Moose, they're carrying six hundred thousand pounds of available gas!"

"It may not be enough."

"Okay, you tell the ops desk folks when you want to launch a strip alert bird from Al Udeid. Remember, it's a two-hour drive to Afghanistan. Anticipate events two hours ahead."

"Thanks, Sluggo" was Moose's way of saying the conversation was over.

The attack on RAZOR 01 played over and over on computer monitors as intel analysts tried to determine where the Al Qaeda fighters were hiding, finally determining they lined a series of trenches along the mountaintop. I cannot think of that video to this day without getting a lump in my throat. I stopped by the tanker ops desk before going upstairs to the GAT cell, and the atmosphere was quiet and somber but very busy.

The two A-10 pilots call signs Soup and K-Nine walked out to their aircraft parked in the Kuwaiti sun with old Russian maps of Afghanistan folded in their flight saddlebags. The information drawn on the maps in Cyrillic was old and sketchy at best. Leaving the Jab for Afghanistan at 0900 as MISTY 11 and 12, both pilots used the five-hour flight to talk over a plan on the radio. The first interjection by Murphy's Laws of Armed Conflict happened early. Arriving at the Persian Gulf tanker rendezvous point, Soup and K-Nine looked around at empty air; no tanker was in sight. They called on the air refueling frequency and met with silence. Soup and K-Nine slowed to best endurance airspeed and waited.

Tailwinds had placed Soup and K-Nine at the tanker rendezvous point early. Five minutes later, the Bahrain KC-135 appeared in front of them, boom down. The formation turned south toward GUN-FIGHTER after making sure both Hawgs could take gas. As they came around the Iran corner, the Al Udeid tanker joined them for the last leg into Afghan airspace. By the time they arrived over the Shah-i-Kot Valley, the sun was setting, and their information was five hours old over a hot battlefield. Troops on the ground screamed over the radio for close air support once Soup and K-Nine found the right frequency. They immediately went to work.

Low on gas after their first of three vulnerable periods, Soup and K-Nine found a tanker in RUSH at twenty-one thousand, a high altitude for heavy Hawgs. Their load of antipersonnel weapons made refueling difficult over tall mountains. Descending in a three-hundred-foot-per-minute maneuver called a toboggan, Soup and K-Nine stayed connected to the boom, taking on fuel. Tobogganing was the only way MISTY 11 and 12 could maintain the speed needed to refuel. The KC-135 crew worried about the mountains and who might be hiding on the peaks. MISTY 11 and 12 plunged back into the battle with full tanks, and the chaos in the Shah-i-Kot Valley continued in the dark. After seven more refuelings and an eleven-hour mission, Soup and K-Nine let their engines wind down after recovering at Jalalabad. Word got back to us that the Hawgs needed lower and slower airspace to refuel. I had no idea where we would find it.

The next day, Gramps and I got lucky again. Airspace used by Christine KC-135s and their AC-130 gunship receivers, called BIGFOOT, stretched across a broad valley in the federally administered tribal areas of Pakistan. Fifty miles southeast of the Shah-i-Kot, BIGFOOT's low-altitude anchor was perfect for the Hawgs. Finding BIGFOOT was a huge break, because getting new airspace clearances from Pakistan took at least five days. The high, mountainous terrain surrounding BIGFOOT put tankers in possible shoulder-fired SAM range, though.

I doubted anyone would shoot, but I asked the Defense Intelligence Agency's Missile and Space Intelligence Center (MSIC) in Alabama to give us their threat analysis for RUSH, O'REILLY, and BIGFOOT. MSIC sent us their report a few hours later. Just as I had thought, over the tallest terrain the charts were colored yellow—SAM engagement potential medium. Not good. AMC headquarters' Threat Working Group reviewed our airspace and probably thought Gramps and I were nuts. If some moron shot at the Hawgs, though, he would not live to tell his story. Special Ops tanker planners gave us permission to use BIGFOOT as long as we did not interfere with Christine's operations.

The next day, two more Hawgs left the Jab for the Shah-i-Kot Valley and Jalalabad. BIGFOOT worked well, but it took the Hawgs some time to transit back and forth. A search for something closer to the Shah-i-Kot came up empty. Some of the mountains there reached up to twelve thousand feet.

All of this work moving the Hawgs turned out to be a great opportunity for airpower and the soldiers on the ground. Working with strike aircraft, the A-10s pinpointed targets for other CAS aircraft dropping tons of bombs on Al Qaeda and Taliban troops. Soup set the standard for A-10 employment in Anaconda, winning three Distinguished Flying Crosses in three days. The refueling schedule finally started settling down on day three of Anaconda, when we off-loaded over six million pounds. But another fuel crisis turned up late Monday afternoon. Colonel Geno Redmon, my old squadron commander, was the TACC vice commander at Scott Air Force Base near St. Louis. Realizing the 160th SOAR would replace the MH-47s lost on Takur Ghar, Geno put Dover's 436th Airlift Wing's C-5 Galaxys on alert Sunday morning. He got a lot of flak for the move, but was proven right a day later. C-5s delivered AH-64 Apache helicopter gunships to Bagram Airfield, replacing those that were shot up on day one. The increasing number of Apache helos operating from Bagram caused a critical fuel shortage. Bagram was running out of gas.

★ ★

LESSONS FROM THE COCKPIT:
INSPIRATION

Val often hears me say, "No prior amount of planning can compensate for pure dumb luck." I don't believe in pure dumb luck anymore. I believe that 99 percent of the time, dumb luck is more inspiration than luck. We had to come up with a plan to move Soup and K-Nine's Hawgs, and do it fast. Finding airspace and getting country clearance to fly armed attack airplanes would have put us well beyond the Hawgs' timing for meeting their vulnerable period over the Shah-i-Kot Valley. I believe inspiration drove us to pull those old charts out and find GUN-FIGHTER. Once we found GUNFIGHTER, putting the plan together was easy. The rest of the route of flight was over international waters.

I never went into work without praying for inspiration first. Our gut feelings are sometimes the truest inspiration we get when facing difficult situations. Have the courage to implement those inspired feelings in your life. Your inspiration will allow your team to be successful. GUNFIGHTER gave the Hawgs the opportunity to save lives in the Shah-i-Kot Valley. The following evenings, we sent four more Hawgs down in pairs, using the same route each time with no issues. The lesson from this is to have the courage to listen to your inspiration and gut feelings and to implement those ideas, even when you feel they are the craziest things to pass through your head.

★ ★

Fuel Elevator

1630 Tuesday 5 March 2002
Combined Air Operations Center
Prince Sultan Air Base
Kingdom of Saudi Arabia

It doesn't matter how brilliant your vision and strategy are if you can't get the soldiers, the weapons, the vehicles, the gasoline, the chow—the boots, for God's sake!—to the right people, at the right place, at the right time.

—Tom Peters, author of "Rule #3:
Leadership Is Confusing as Hell," Fast Company

If it's stupid but it works, it's not stupid.

—Murphy's Laws of Armed Conflict

A constant stream of VIPs arrived in the Middle East to visit the troops and meet with Coalition dignitaries. It was no different with Anaconda in March 2002. Vice President Dick Cheney met with General Tommy Franks and the Qatari government in Doha, then continued flying around the theater in a Doha-based armored-up C-17. His security detail traveled on a second, similarly armored Globemaster II. Many were looking at a future war in Iraq: War Plan 1003 Victor, code-named Polo Step. I had recently been allowed to see Polo Step, and Gramps and I began working on refueling issues. Basing support in the Gulf Coast countries was critical for Polo Step. Geno's TACC controlled the Doha-based C-17s, performing special air or channel missions. As long as Vice President Cheney remained in theater, Doha's C-17s were going to stay busy flying vice presidential support missions. General Scott's airlift control team, or ALCT, couldn't use the C-17s without TACC's permission. General Scott talked with TACC several times, asking if we could use one of them. He got the same answer every time: "They're flying other high-priority missions right now."

General Scott came into the GAT shop looking for me at about 1630 Tuesday afternoon. My day had started at 0115 that morning after two hours of sleep, so I was really tired, but the adrenaline kept me awake. General Scott wanted to meet in the Air Mobility Division office. Rocco, the ALCT chief and a C-130 Weapons School grad, was already downstairs waiting for us. A message from 10th Mountain had come in seeking more help. Apache attack helicopters flying into and out of Bagram had made the fuel situation there critical. Though the number of Apache attack helicopters on Bagram's ramp had increased, no one had thought to increase fuel capacity at the same time. Bagram was running out of gas. I found out that Humvees used the same gas as Apaches—kerosene, of all things—which compounded the fuel-starvation problem. Both Rocco and I understood that AMD could not do this by ground transportation. Any ground convoy required force protection, since Al Qaeda and the Taliban owned the roads through the mountains. A long line of fuel trucks driving over roads planted with IEDs would give Al Qaeda plenty of propaganda videos. All of us agreed that a ground convoy option was a no-go. General Scott told us to figure it out. Great, another science project . . .

While Rocco and I continued to work on the Bagram problem, General Scott came to us at around 2000 that evening. He had a message in hand from AMC headquarters with a suggestion for how to fill Bagram back up.

Geno's staff had read the same 10th Mountain message we received, and his tanker planners were also working on the Bagram issue. TACC asked if landing a KC-10 at Kabul's airport would work, airmailing gas to Bagram.

Handing me AMC's message, General Scott said, "Sluggo, I need to know why this is a bad idea. I know it's a bad idea, but I don't know enough about your business to write a quick letter back to AMC."

I counted off the issues to General Scott. Number one was sending Gucci, the second-largest aircraft in the Air Force inventory, to an Afghan base. There was no way to force-protect Gucci while in the air or on the ground. Second, fixing a broken jet at Kabul meant that the jet would be on the ramp for days, a prime mortar target. The third issue was landing weight. After talking to the Tims, I realized there wouldn't be enough gas coming out of a KC-10. The KC-10's maximum landing weight would not give us much gas from its fuel tanks—only eighty-five thousand pounds. Eighty-five thousand seemed like a bunch, but divide that figure by 6.5 pounds per gallon and you get 13,077 gallons—not enough to gain for the risks involved.

The fourth issue was departing Kabul. Intelligence reported that Al Qaeda and Taliban fighters had man-portable air defense systems, or MANPADS. Tankers were most vulnerable during takeoff and landing—perfect for an easy-to-launch Russian-made heat-seeking missile. Last, we didn't know the conditions at Kabul airfield. Kabul's runways and taxiways had been bombed in October but were recently repaired. One blown tire, though, and Gucci would have to stay until a maintenance team could arrive, providing a nice big stationary mortar target. I didn't know whether Kabul could bear Gucci's maximum landing weight, anyway. General Scott told me these were all great reasons and asked me to put them in an e-mail he could send to AMC's commander, General Handy, and the TACC.

The airmail option kept banging around in my head. It was the only way to do this, but how remained a mystery. Rocco told me that the C-17s regularly carried large rubber fuel bladders to austere locations, which perfectly described Bagram. Bladders on Bagram might work, but could the Army fill them? Airlift was stretched to the max trying to keep 10th Mountain's requirements filled, so there were not enough tactical airlift airplanes to carry fuel. Maybe this was the exact mission we needed to rip off TACC's four Doha-based C-17s. Once TACC handed them over, however, how would AMD do this? Rocco looked up and said, "I know, Sluggo—a fuel elevator!"

He explained. First, we had to rip off all four of TACC's C-17s. We would then load the first one up with bladders and enough fuel to touch down at Bagram at maximum landing weight using the defensive assault landing technique. Once the C-17 was on the ground at Bagram, Army fuel specialists would unload the bladders and lay them out for filling. The bladders could hold two hundred thousand gallons, looking like the world's largest water beds. The C-17s would pump gas into the bladders from their gas tanks via the refueling panel on the fuselage. After downloading fuel, each Globemaster would take off and hook up with a KC-135 over Bagram, filling up again to maximum landing weight. After spiraling back down in an assault landing, the C-17s would taxi back to the Bagram bladders and pump more gas into them. Taking off for a third time, each C-17 would meet another tanker in ZEUS refueling area along the Afghanistan-Pakistan border, filling up for their return to Doha.

KC-135s could meet the C-17s near Bagram to make sure each one arrived at max landing weight. All I had to do was create a refueling anchor somewhere near Bagram, to refuel the C-17s. Crunching the numbers showed us that Bagram would need at least two C-17 sorties a day to fill up and maintain two bladders. The elevator might be a three-day ordeal or last until Bagram turned off the airmail spigot. After briefing General Scott, we stopped by the ops floor and showed CAOC Director for Operations call sign Stutz our plan. Everyone approved so far. It seemed like such a stupid idea, but Rocco and I figured it was simple enough to work. And it did.

TACC gave us the four C-17s as Vice President Cheney's visit came to a close. I talked to Geno on a secure phone and told him the elevator plan. He was ecstatic. Airpower was getting a bad rap from the Army due to our apparent lack of support, and the fuel elevator idea put C-17s in 10th Mountain's face. They would see Globemaster IIs filling up their fuel bladders and know Big Blue was making a max effort to keep their fight going. I was a little apprehensive during the first sortie. The new anchor in the ACO was nearby Bagram, because the airspace folks wouldn't let me put one directly overhead, but it was close enough—only fifty miles southwest. A Special Ops C-17 crew flew the first fuel elevator mission and followed our plan with exactness. I wanted to know when they left Bagram for the second fill-up so I could adjust the tanker timing. I received a call from Bagram saying they were on the ground for about an hour and a half, and told the Tims to readjust the afternoon's mission based on actual timing. The second C-17 arrived flawlessly—until shutting down engines. Apparently, the auxiliary power unit used to start the engines was bad. The air start cart, or huffer, at Bagram did not have the power to turn the C-17's engine fan blades during the start process. Sir Murphy and his Laws of Armed Combat had struck again: *If anything can go wrong, it will.*

ALCT put a huffer on the second C-17, which stayed at Bagram until the fuel elevator was called off three days later. Bagram's wing commander did not like having such a big airplane sitting dormant on his ramp. "Get that piece of crap off my ramp," he told the crew. Both C-17s left that evening for Doha. Two days later, 10th Mountain asked us to stop flights, Bagram now loaded to the gills with two two-hundred-thousand-gallon fuel bladders lying under the sun.

All the CAS sorties continued to stress the tankers flying over the Shah-i-Kot Valley. Stutz told Vinnie, one of the ops directors, to not let the strike aircraft stay past their vulnerable periods. It was just taking too much gas for the fighters and bombers to stay longer. He said in a meeting, "Fly the ATO! There are plenty of bombs coming and going, so no one needs to stay past their vul time." Stutz's edict was a huge relief for the tankers. My team made sure there was plenty of airborne gas for all receiver types, boom and drogue. Air Wing 7 flew their first combat sortie on 11 March, with F-14s and F-18s supporting XCAS and TSTs off the USS *John F. Kennedy*. We almost got bin Laden that same week—or at least we thought it was him.

Intel had a good location for bin Laden, in a camp in the Shah-i-Kot area. A Predator immediately parked overhead to establish patterns of life and to see if it was him. Bin Laden's bodyguards dressed in a certain way, making them very distinguishable on Predator video. Those bodyguards were in the camp. One morning, two groups of people lined up in single file leading to two white Datsun King Cab trucks. Moments later the bodyguards walked out, and a tall man in white robes passed between the lines, climbing in through the passenger door of the first truck. Watching this made the hair on the back of all our necks stand up. The convoy took off and headed for the Afghanistan-Pakistan border in an attempt to escape. And Moose could not get CENTCOM approval to drop bombs on them.

They weaved and bobbed through mountain passes heading for Pakistan, knowing the Coalition could not do anything if they got there. Moose couldn't stand it any longer and directed a Bone refueling nearby to drop two GBU-31 JDAMS to seal off the pass in front of the convoy. Walls of shale crashed down on impact, closing off the escape route. You could see each truck come to a screeching halt, turn around on the narrow mountain road, and dash off back the way it had come in. In a formation position change, one became two and two became one as they headed back down the canyon road at very high speed. These drivers were good. Knowing we had them on Predator video, the trucks unexpectedly split up. Truck number two, carrying bin Laden, raced off at around fifty miles an hour, and suddenly stopped on the side of a mountain. Four men got out and ran up the mountainside. What were they doing? Approval to drop finally came from Tampa while these four men raced for the mountaintops. An intel analyst finally figured out why they had stopped: they were *lost!* A CAG 7 Hornet then refueling in RUSH got the nod to drop a single GBU-12 laser-guided bomb on bin Laden's King Cab truck.

A bright flash momentarily washed out the Predator video feed. In the fireball, the truck backflipped into the air, making two complete revolutions before landing on what was left of its four wheels. A large crater about six feet to the right of the rear passenger-side wheel marked the spot where the GBU-12 had hit the ground. Some fluid poured off the rear cargo deck. It looked like blood, but I couldn't tell for sure from the infrared video. And then a really strange thing happened. Two Chinooks carrying Army Special Forces raced down the valley, the sound of their rotor blades echoing off the shale rock walls. Bin Laden's four guards heard their approach and ran down the mountainside. Opening the door, the four men grabbed bin Laden from the front passenger seat and ripped off his white robes while he lay on the ground. The people started running back up the mountainside as rotor wash from the Chinooks blew dirt and dust over the truck. After a short firefight, all four men were dead and the area was secured. All of us were anxious to hear what the Spec Ops team would find. After a long search and a lot of pictures, they determined that it wasn't bin Laden lying on the ground. To this day, I don't know who it was. The only thing one Army intel officer told me years later was that they thought it was some Al Qaeda fighter used as a decoy to cover bin Laden's escape into Pakistan via another route.

Tanker missions calmed down during the last week of Anaconda. After two weeks of operations, Anaconda closed. Air Force tankers had off-loaded eighty-four million pounds of gas in fourteen days, averaging six million pounds a day. The USS *John F. Kennedy* prepared to move into the NAG, and Southern Watch missions began again. I wrote down everything I could think of in a new composition book I kept at my desk. I wanted to capture all the lessons I had learned, so that the tanker community wouldn't make similar mistakes when the Coalition invaded Iraq. Polo Step benefited from the tragedies of Anaconda, and I wanted the KC-135 CES to know what the tankers had accomplished in fourteen days of intensive refueling operations. I felt it was a good time to visit the *John F. Kennedy* again to get their input on our Iraq plan. I sent a message to their chief of air wing plans before leaving for my room and a good night's sleep.

★ ★

LESSONS FROM THE COCKPIT: INITIATIVE

Murphy was inspired when he wrote his counter to the laws of armed conflict: "If it's stupid but it works, it's not stupid." Examples of crazy ideas implemented on the battlefield to overcome some obstacle litter the history of warfare. We never got the opportunity at the Combat Employment School to validate the concept of keeping fighters hooked to the tankers while waiting for close air support targets. No one thought air mobility planners were crazy enough to employ C-17s as elevators for refilling a base that was critically short on fuel. Operation Anaconda gave us an opportunity to try both techniques, and they both worked great. We were able to distribute fuel in the air *and* to the ground.

I learned to take the initiative and to try some of those crazy ideas. Air operations over Afghanistan and Iraq gave my team the opportunity to try concepts we knew would be successful, but there were still a lot of detractors. After we explained our fuel elevator concept to several people, they looked at us and asked: "Can you do that?" Sure, we could do it, and we felt it would work, but it had never been tried. A lot of people think a battlefield is not the place to try new ideas. The battlefield is a *great* place for initiative and new ideas. We didn't have any other way to get the fuel to Bagram, so General Scott told us to try it. In your role as leader, allow employees to take initiative. Yes, they might fail, but it's how they learn. Don't tell them their ideas are stupid, because you may be surprised when they work.

★ ★

16

Air Force Is Conning the Ship

0930 Monday 25 March 2002

On board a VRC-40 C-2 Greyhound

Flying to the USS *John F. Kennedy* in the Indian Ocean

I wish to have no connection with any ship that does not sail fast; for I intend to go in harm's way.

— JOHN PAUL JONES, AMERICAN REVOLUTIONARY WAR NAVY COMMANDER

The reward for work well done is the opportunity to do more.

— DR. JONAS SALK, DEVELOPER OF THE POLIO VACCINE

Training is everything. The peach was once a bitter almond; cauliflower is nothing but cabbage with a college education.

— MARK TWAIN, AMERICAN WRITER, HUMORIST, AND ENTREPRENEUR

Conan, a B-1 weapons system operator and member of General Moseley's Commander's Action Group, or CAG, was looking for me, said the sticky note on my desk. The rumor was that Conan and General Moseley's CAG were building a brief to answer the Army's noise about the lack of Air Force support in Anaconda, but no one had confirmed the brief's existence. The bigger rumor was that an interservice feud was brewing between the 10th Mountain and Air Force leadership. Big Army blasted the Air Force in the mainstream media for not giving 10th Mountain ground forces the air support they needed, which was pure bovine feces. I found Conan later that afternoon carrying a relatively large PowerPoint brief in his left hand. Its cover page stated: "Ninth Air Force Report on Operation Anaconda."

"Show me this brief I hear does not exist," I said as Conan and I leaned over the admin counter.

"You can see it, Sluggo, but I can't give you a copy. It's still rather sensitive."

"Oh, come on, Conan—there's no bad blood in the media between Big Army and Big Blue!"

Conan chuckled and laid the brief on the desk between us. The rivalry rumor was true, because the Air Force's answer to the 10th Mountain complaints lay before me.

Conan asked for my air refueling input. The old business adage is true in combat and defined air refueling support to Anaconda: you can have it quick, cheap, or easy—but you can have only two. If you want it quick and easy, the product will never be cheap. Air Mobility Division and my air refueling team received late notification of the 10th Mountain's support requirements. Anaconda's big spike in fuel consumption was not cheap and was directly related to our receiving tanker requirements only five days before Anaconda's kickoff. Understating requirements drove fuel costs through the roof after the increase in airborne artillery needed for Petty Officer Neil Roberts and RAZOR 03's rescue. Acts of God, such as Neil Roberts's falling off RAZOR 03, are never anticipated. A rescue operation looking for and fighting over downed troops always drives refueling and gas requirements higher.

Once Anaconda began, shifting battlefield objectives and a poor command and control setup caused delays on the battlefield, again driving fuel costs higher as fighters and bombers waited over targets. Our one-hundred-thousand-pound fuel reserve in Snooze's KC-10 orbiting near the Shah-i-Kot evaporated in the afternoon of the first day. A quar-

ter of the refueling events required drogues for Navy fighters, and there
were not enough in the theater if we were to go to war in Iraq. Strike aircraft returning with retained weapons needed more gas, because heavy
attack aircraft consume ridiculous amounts of fuel. Bringing fighters
from the Jab in Kuwait several times a day on nine-hour-plus sorties
threw every refueling plan off when they stayed past their three-hour
station times. The approval process for clearing US aircraft to refuel
from international tankers took too long, and the matrix used to schedule receivers to tankers was not up-to-date. I handed my notes to Conan
and asked where the brief went from there.

"First stop is COMACC, General Hornburg. He'll have to fight Big
Army over this one."

"Well, if you need any more input, see Gramps. I'm leaving for a
couple of days."

"Where are you going, and who approved this trip, Sluggo?" Conan
asked, smiling.

"Bahrain, and then on a COD to the USS *John F. Kennedy* in the
Indian Ocean. I'm discussing their move up into the NAG and getting
their Anaconda lessons learned so we don't make the same mistakes over
Iraq."

Conan told me to have a great trip, gathered up the brief, and stepped
off to his next appointments.

The USS *John F. Kennedy* was about to transit from the Indian Ocean
through the Strait of Hormuz and into the Northern Arabian Gulf to
begin Operation Southern Watch no-fly zone support. My team needed
to gather Carrier Air Wing 7's lessons learned while they were still fresh
in their minds and to brief them on current and future Iraq refueling
operations. Rolls, one of the Navy folks in San Diego I worked with at
the KC-135 Employment School, was now the Carrier Air Wing 7 chief
of plans. Even in combat, it's not always what you know but who you
know. Two days after I sent Rolls an e-mail about my travel plans, he
e-mailed back that the air wing had approved the visit. I do not know

of any aviation-related event on the face of this planet that compares to blue water Navy aircraft carrier operations in combat conditions. Every jet catapults at max gross weight carrying live weapons. General Scott said Afghanistan schedules were relatively static at the moment, so it was a good time to go see Rolls. Chunks, a good friend of mine in the States, sent me a new lunch bag filled with sixty rolls of Fujichrome Velvia 50 film just for this trip. I packed a light carry-on bag and my new Minolta camera.

A loadmaster escorted me to the C-130's cockpit for the hour-long flight to Bahrain. I talked with the flight crew for the entire hour about their airlift operations and their thoughts on going into Iraq. Folks working in the CAOC's Naval Air Liaison Element, or NALE, said that the only hotel to stay at in Manama, Bahrain, was the Ritz-Carlton, right on the beach. Being a very light sleeper from my SAC nuclear alert days, I just wanted one good night's sleep without jet noise waking me up. As I walked into the Ritz-Carlton lobby, I saw the NALE folks had not steered me wrong. My room on the sixth floor was silent—no planes departing nearby in afterburner. I was in bed by 2000 and slept for eleven hours. A taxi dropped me off at Manama's Navy Air Traffic Office the next morning. Four Grumman C-2 Greyhounds were parked behind the fence, all with red-and-orange sunset tails with a silhouette of a cowboy on a horse, the insignia of the VRC-40 Rawhides.

Leaving Manama at 0900, I settled in for the three-hour flight to the USS *John F. Kennedy*'s flight deck. Somehow my Navy counterparts could sleep in the back of the noisy COD, but I could not. As we approached the *John F. Kennedy*, the loadmaster began giving the same instructions I'd heard multiple times when approaching carriers for trap landings: feet and knees together, arms crossed and hands grabbing each shoulder harness firmly, chin down on my chest. We broke at 3 g's over the bow, and I could see Big John's wake under us. My grip on the shoulder harness tightened. After another loud *SCREECH—BANG— HALT*, I was back aboard the *Kennedy*, which was steaming in combat conditions. As we taxied out of the wires, the loadmaster dropped the cargo ramp. Hornets and Prowlers lined both sides of the bow. Two Hornets taxied behind us toward the waist catapults. Burning jet fuel is like crack in the nostrils of a military pilot, and the *Kennedy*'s deck reeked of it. When we reached the hummer hole, the COD's props reversed thrust and backed us into a parking space in front of the conning tower. Rolls stood behind the COD's cargo ramp, waiting for me. A few moments later, the engines shut down.

Over the loudspeaker, I heard "Lieutenant Colonel, United States Air Force, arriving!" Field-grade officers with ranks of O-5 and above are rendered honors when coming aboard a Navy vessel. I thanked Rolls for the Navy's formal greeting.

"Captain Bill Gortney and Air Wing Seven welcome you aboard, Sluggo."

"Rolls, thanks so much for letting me come down. We have a lot to talk about."

As we walked down the catwalks belowdecks, Rolls and I discussed what was going on in Afghanistan. After signing in at the *Kennedy*'s ATO office, Rolls walked me to the carrier's billeting manager's office. Lieutenant colonels got their own staterooms, which cost $35 a day for meals and incidentals. Anyone would pay ten times that amount to be where I was and to see the activity on the flight deck. Carrier air wing operations were the Valhalla aviation photographers dreamed about. After we dropped my bags in my room, Rolls walked me down to the CVIC. He introduced me to his staff, and I shook hands with Rolls's planners and intel analysts.

If you're on a carrier, the CVIC is the place to hang out. It's the nerve center for air operations, intelligence on enemy forces, analyses of targets and future operations, and the air wing schedule. Everyone had questions about air refueling during Anaconda, and Rolls scheduled a meeting for me to talk with his staff later that day. Our next stop was a short introduction to the commander of Carrier Air Wing 7. Captain

Bill Gortney, the air wing commander, call sign Shortney, discussed refueling over Afghanistan and answered my questions about his move to the NAG. His air wing pilots had great praise for the tanker operations in Anaconda; they were "the best we have ever seen," he said.

Rolls had strike plans to create, so he left me to my own devices, handing me his phone and bulkhead numbers if I got lost between decks. Fortunately, having been on carriers before, I knew my way around. Bulkheads and their numbers were something most Air Force people just smacked their heads on. But bulkhead numbers are a map to the carrier belowdecks, and I understood what to do when someone told me to find him or her at a particular number.

I walked aft, headed for the air wing ready rooms. Aircraft recovered one deck above my head, with the same *SCREECH—BANG—HALT* of my COD arrival. The sound of the arresting cables reeling out filled my ears as I walked through the door into the VF-143 Pukin' Dogs' ready room. A few F-14 Tomcat aircrew members stopped what they were doing and looked up at me; not a lot of Air Force lieutenant colonels visited the ready rooms.

The duty officer sitting behind a desk asked, "May I help you . . . sir?"

Every head turned to see who the "sir" was. I introduced myself as chief of the ARCT from the Prince Sultan CAOC, the guy who designed Anaconda's refueling plan. Everyone gathered around me at the duty desk. Some related how refueling had gone well, and a few others told me some things ARCT needed to change. Softer drogue baskets was a common theme, and I told them wing pods were coming soon. Others had questions about how big-wing tankers operated. In every business, the best learning tool has always been a long talk with your customers, and there I was surrounded by them. Pukin' Dogs Tomcats could not do their job unless they were refueled by Air Force or RAF tankers. Very few Pukin' Dog aircrews understood tanker planning and the math used to build a schedule. Ollie, the Pukin' Dogs' commander, asked if I could come back and talk to his junior officers and discuss tanker capabilities. All of his JOs' first hookups behind Stratobladders and Gucci Birds had been under combat conditions over Afghanistan, a terrible way to learn the Iron Maiden's foibles.

My next stop was the VFA-11 Red Rippers ready room. Lungs, the Red Rippers' skipper, asked if I would give his new Tomcat crews a briefing on tanker capabilities and limitations. I was beginning to notice a trend here. Lungs told me the same thing Ollie had, that most of his JOs refueled off Air Force tankers for the first time over Afghanistan in combat. What would happen if a Coalition air force went into Iraq? Trim, skipper of the VFA-131 Wildcats, and his executive officer, Satan, had a lengthy discussion with me about tanking over Afghanistan. I took notes as fast as my right hand could fly in a black-and-white composition book I'd bought for this occasion. I still have that composition book. I wanted to find out how the Lockheed S-3 Vikings of the VS-31 Topcats accomplished air refueling at sea. When I walked into their ready room, everyone noticed the Air Force lieutenant colonel and wondered how I got there. Pecker, the Topcats' skipper, had a meeting to run to but assured me he would hook me up with one of his pilots later on.

I met Rolls back in the CVIC, and his planners walked me through their goods and not-so-goods of Anaconda. I laid out the initial Anaconda refueling plan and explained how it had been overcome by events on the ground. They all understood the strain put on us by Petty Officer Neil Roberts's falling off RAZOR 03. This discussion evolved into refueling operations for Southern Watch and what would happen if we went into Iraq again. Knowing SPEAR probably had good reports on Iraq's Air Force and integrated air defense network, I asked to read their latest. It was a gold mine of information. After a quick swing by the Dirty Shirt Mess for a couple of sliders and some auto dawg, I slipped into bed at 2330, tired and pleased. Our Navy customers were really happy with how my refueling team had supported them, but the lack of drogues in theater was detrimental to Carrier Air Wing 7's ability to get gas and stay up longer, particularly if the US went into Iraq soon. I dropped my composition book on the floor beside me and rolled over to get some sleep. The clock said 0017. I always sleep well aboard a carrier at sea. Big John rocked me to sleep, and continued rolling all night long. Best night's sleep I'd had in a long time.

The next morning I was back in Lung's Red Rippers ready room drawing my tanker capabilities and limitations briefing on his presentation whiteboards. I drew a big picture of the Iron Maiden basket, with big teeth in the center and beady red eyes. A sliding whiteboard covered the Iron Maiden picture with training objectives and an outline. I asked the Ripper crews what they thought of the Iron Maiden, and most of their answers I cannot write here in a family-oriented book. I then slid back the panel covering my toothy Iron Maiden picture, and the whole room erupted in laughter. One training point I wanted to stick in their minds, even if they forgot everything else I told them, was that the airflow from the KC-135's big CFM56 turbofan engines calmed down markedly while plugged in the basket if they asked the tanker pilot to pull the inboard engines back. Every KC-135 pilot knew what that meant. Putting the outboard throttles up to compensate for the inboard-engine throttle reduction and loss of inboard thrust meant that the CFM56 engines' hot exhaust gases were not beating on the Tomcats' twin vertical tails. It was the same for the Hornet pilots. Every head in the room went down as they scribbled "pull the inboards back" on their notepads.

One pilot asked when the KC-135 fleet would get soft-basket wing pods like the KC-10's WARPs. A company in the United States called Cobham expected to test pods in the summer for release in the fall. The Air Force had bought only thirty-three pod sets for the forty-five aircraft retrofitted for MPRS pods. Everyone liked refueling off the Gucci Bird's WARPs, with their soft, collapsible baskets. One pilot called the Gucci drogue "the Nerf Basket" because of its soft contact. Note to self: find out from AMC Requirements when the MPRS pods were fielding and the health of the WARPs and Iron Maidens in case Iraq's air campaign loomed soon. I sent a message back to Gramps and AMC that night.

Rolls met me in one of the ready rooms and asked if I would like to attend the admiral's battle group staff meeting. Captain Gortney introduced me to the carrier battle group admiral and the entire O-6 staff. The admiral went around the room, speaking with each captain about their responsibilities. Their discussion was a fascinating look at carrier operations at sea. Captain Gunner, in charge of weapons, mentioned that the *Kennedy* would replenish its bomb lockers in a few days, during UNREP. The admiral told Captain Gortney that he wanted me to fly before leaving the *John F. Kennedy*. Shortney said he would see to it. I was elated at the possibility of an S-3 Viking hop before leaving. The next day, in his staff meeting, Shortney told Pecker I was cleared to fly.

The Rawhides' C-2 COD broke the next day. I was stuck haze gray and under way for at least three more days. When I met Rolls in the CVIC, he told me the *Kennedy* was scheduled for UNREP that afternoon from the USS *Seattle*. Pulling a ball cap over my head at the appointed time, I walked up several flights of stairs to the bridge. The officer of the deck announced my arrival—"Lieutenant Colonel, US Air Force, on the bridge"—and everyone turned to see me walk in. The same look appeared on everyone's face: "What are you doing here, Colonel?" Beyond the control desk and wheel, the auxiliary conning tower was full of people. The aux con is made up of wings off each side of the bridge, about fourteen stories above the water rushing beneath you. Navy officers controlled rendezvous and UNREP with the *Seattle* from the aux con via computer monitors and radios. The USS *Seattle* steamed along half a mile in front of us as the *Kennedy* closed to a position along *Seattle*'s left side. A US Coast Guard cutter approached *Seattle* from the right side to fill their tanks with fuel also. Three additional rolls of film jingled in the calf pocket of my flight suit with every step I took.

Half an hour later, the *Kennedy* and the *Seattle* were steaming side by side on a glass sea. Men on the *Seattle*'s decks shot rope lines across to fuel specialists standing in the *Kennedy*'s refueling areas on the right side. Big steel cables stretched across the open ocean between the ships, followed by black fuel hoses. Forty minutes after pulling alongside each other, the ships were hooked together and passing fuel, mail, and food. This was refueling of a very different sort. The *Kennedy* took on 1.2 million pounds of jet fuel over the next few hours through six hoses stretching between it and the *Seattle*. A young ammo shop lieutenant steered or "conned" the carrier through hooking up. All three ships—the *Kennedy*, the *Seattle*, and the cutter—glided through the water on a southeasterly heading.

The captain in command of the ship, call sign Harv, sat in his chair behind the lieutenant. Harv asked what an Air Force tanker pilot was doing aboard. I explained that I had come aboard for a few days to visit with each squadron to learn how Anaconda went for them and to teach the JOs about big-wing tanking.

The next lieutenant assigned to conn the ship failed to show up at his appointed time. The officer of the deck called his department to find out his whereabouts. He wasn't coming because of something that was happening in his department. Harv, in a moment of insanity, looked at me and said, "Hop in there, Sluggo, and conn the ship."

"Sir . . . with all due respect, are you nuts?!" I said.

Harv's UNREP staff chuckled quizzically, as if to say, "Yes, boss—you are joking, right?"

Harv wasn't joking.

"Sluggo, it's just like flying formation in your tanker. The only difference is anticipating rudder and screw inputs. Make one-degree heading changes at the helm, and only one-percent RPM changes on the inboard screws. Keep the two outboard screws at seventy percent RPM. Maintain eighteen knots speed and a two-hundred-twenty-five-degree heading on the computer monitor. The one-eighty stick on the Christmas tree there outside the window stays on *Seattle*'s waterline. Piece of cake, Sluggo."

I thought, *Sure, why not*. Outside the window below me, I could see the Christmas tree Harv was referring to; it was made of PVC pipe and stuck outward toward the *Seattle*'s waterline. Branches started at 130, climbing in increments of one hundred up to 230 feet. Harv had told me to keep *Seattle*'s waterline on the 180 limb, maintaining 180 feet of separation between ships. Yes, America, the largest Navy ship—one hundred thousand tons of steel aircraft carrier—maintains formation and separation with PVC pipe. A stripe on Seattle's side helped me keep position fore and aft. A single CH-46 Sea Knight helicopter used a sling to carry food and palletized bombs onto the *Kennedy*'s deck. The Sea Knight appeared motionless above the *Seattle*'s rear deck, even though the ship was moving at eighteen knots, while merchant seamen attached bundles to the hooks under the fuselage. Two SH-60s from Carrier Air Wing 7's Helicopter Sea Combat Squadron 5 Nightdippers slung smaller bundles from the *Seattle* to the *Kennedy* beneath their fuselages. Harv's crew in the aux con coordinated with *Seattle*'s crew in their aux con ahead of us.

Harv, in another temporary loss of situational awareness, radioed *Seattle*'s captain. Through my headset, I heard Harv ask, "Hey, Iggy, are you sitting down?"

Iggy replied, "Why, should I be?"

Harv shot back, "Air Force is conning the ship!"

All seven heads in *Seattle*'s aux con turned in unison. One officer held binoculars up to his eyes and pointed at me with his right hand. So I waved back. I don't know of another Air Force pilot who can say that he conned an aircraft carrier taking on fuel. In the fifty minutes the *Kennedy* spent next to the *Seattle*, 420,000 pounds of jet fuel passed into the *Kennedy*'s tanks. How's that for a big gulp?

The *Kennedy* slowly crept aft, getting heavier as the *Seattle* became lighter from pumping its gas through the hoses. Standard refueling technique as receivers gained weight was to push the throttles up to maintain speed. Over my headset, I told the young helmswoman, "Helm, make your RPMs seventy-one percent."

A young African-American woman from Alabama reported back, "Aye, aye, sir, making my RPMs seventy-one percent."

Iggy called over, "Hey, Sluggo, what do you do in the Air Force?"

"Sir, I'm a KC-135 pilot and currently chief of the air refueling control team at the Prince Sultan Air Base CAOC. My team manages air refueling for all four Coalition countries' tankers."

After a lengthy pause, Iggy said, "We love tanker guys!"

Harv's entire crew busted out laughing.

Iggy was an F-18 Hornet pilot, so of course he loved tanker guys and gals. Hornets were the fuel-critical fighter in every carrier air wing, holding little and burning a lot. Legacy Hornets held nine thousand pounds of internal fuel and burned it at the same rate Eagles do, eight thousand pounds an hour at tactical speeds. Understand the problem? Most Hornets flew with two external tanks, one on the centerline and another on a wing pylon, in a configuration nicknamed "goofy gas." Hornets had to use Air Force big-wing tankers on every strike mission Afghanistan support called for. The VFA-131 Wildcats and VFA-136 Knighthawks on the *Kennedy* consumed a lot of gas, so Iggy's "We love tanker guys" reply did not surprise me.

Fifty minutes later, another Navy lieutenant reported to the aux con to drive. Conning the ship was a training item junior officers needed to accomplish for mission certification at sea. I did not want to leave, because the *Seattle* and the *Kennedy* would remain tied together for another three hours. I handed the lieutenant the neck mic and stood next to Harv in his aux con captain's chair, discussing events in Afghanistan and Iraq and watching the sun set and all the ship lights come on. A big half-moon reflected off the ocean behind the *Seattle*. Who would want to leave a picture like this?

Friday 29 March was my last day haze gray and under way. I walked into the VS-31 ready room to see that Pecker's Topcat schedulers had my name on their flying board. My Viking ride would last about two and a half hours, followed by a trap landing back on Big John, running to the Topcats' personal equipment room, getting out of all my flight gear, running upstairs to the ATO office to sign out, and hopping onto a COD back to Bahrain. Friday would be a long day, and I had eighteen rolls of film out of the original sixty left. Another cat shot—the first of two in one day, and my tenth overall—happened just before official sunrise at 0633. By regulation, I could not sit in the copilot/tactical coordinator, or COTAC, seat during a cat shot before official sunrise for safety reasons. TOPCAT 706's takeoff time was ten minutes before official sunrise. With three of us on board, I would switch places with the COTAC once we were airborne.

A survival equipment specialist in the Topcats' PE room fitted me with flight gear: a survival vest, an oxygen mask, and a helmet. Petty Officer Reynolds briefed me on arming and disarming the ejection seat. Stick, the S-3 instructor pilot I was flying with, met me in the PE room. He reviewed all the mission specifics with me and a tactical coordinator, or TACCO, call sign Red Man. TOPCAT 706 would launch with TOPCAT 702, refueling the surface CAP above the *Kennedy* and then descending to 1,500 feet to tag ships in the carrier's vicinity. JFK's surface combat air patrol (SUCAP) orbited near the carrier at eighteen thousand feet, an additional protective cover for the battle group. Orbiting above recovering aircraft, or "hawking," TOPCAT 706 would act as a tanker for aircraft with emergencies during recovery. Stick briefed me on his ejection criteria. The most common reason for ejecting was a weak catapult stroke. He warned me not to get run over by the carrier after landing in the water, so I would need to steer away from the ship's forward movement.

Stick emphasized that I shouldn't touch the big yellow ejection ring between my knees unless we talked about it first or he told me to eject.

I didn't want to blast through Plexiglas at 1,500 feet, watch a parachute canopy bloom above me, and splash down into the Indian Ocean to wait for someone to pick me up, hopefully a friendly. The last items Stick briefed me on were the defensive maneuvers we would undertake if we came under fire from an enemy ship. Fortunately, he had never been fired at while tagging ships around the carrier.

Crouching down to get through the Viking's small entry hatch, I moved to the TACCO's ejection seat in the back of the jet. I buckled my survival gear to the ejection seat pan and fastened my lap and shoulder harnesses. Starting the engines and taxiing to the catapult took about five minutes. Red Man hollered over the interphone to get ready as I felt the catapult shuttle engage the nose tow bar and the engines spool up to 100 percent. Then came a big jerk forward, followed by a loud *bang*. A cloth curtain separating the cockpit from the TACCO's area angled backward about thirty degrees during the cat stroke. In three and a half seconds, TOPCAT 706 reached the end of the deck and was airborne at 160 knots.

Red Man and I switched seats during the climb to eighteen thousand feet, where we tanked the SUCAP Hornets. I wanted to get into the seat as fast as I could as Stick trailed the buddy store drogue. Two Hornets joined off our right wing, taking four thousand pounds each. It was a perfect morning for snapping pictures. Done with refueling, Stick rolled the Viking onto its back and pulled straight down toward the Indian Ocean. We leveled off at 1,500 feet, and Red Man called out our first ship contact at two o'clock for eight miles. Stick then gave me control of the aircraft. Banking right, I looked for the ship on the forward-looking infrared (FLIR) projected on the multifunction display in front of me. As we passed aft of a large gray-green cargo ship, Stick passed the ship's name and registry to Red Man. We flew from ship to ship, Red Man logging names, courses, speeds, and national registry. No one on the ships seemed to care as we buzzed them. One fellow on a ship came out of the bridge and waved at us as we passed aft.

We headed back to the *Kennedy* and the recovery stack, our wingman TOPCAT 702 radioing for us to join him, too heavy for an arrested landing. We were going to "swap spit," as Viking crews called it: we would take on some of 702's gas. Our Viking was lighter after giving a lot of gas to the SUCAP Hornets. As we pulled up behind it, I noticed TOPCAT 702's FLIR turret pointing at us. Stick said they always watched receivers behind them on the FLIR. The Viking's refueling probe extended above our heads as we pulled in behind TOPCAT 702. 702's drogue reeled out of the buddy store on their left wing and dangled in front of us. I was captivated watching probe refueling from the receiver's perspective. The basket hovered in front of us, barely moving. Stick mentioned that it was easier to refuel in the morning because of the calmer air. We plugged in on the first try, and the gas gauge needle climbed as fuel passed from 702.

Five thousand pounds off-loaded decreased TOPCAT 702 to trap weight. Stick let me fly in formation off TOPCAT 702's right wing back to the recovery stack, retaking control ten miles from the *John F. Kennedy*. Both Vikings orbited overhead during recovery, waiting for anyone who needed gas. The Hornets trapped first, because they were all low on fuel. The Prowlers landed next, and the four Tomcats last. Each time a group of Tomcats, Hornets, or Prowlers approached the ship for landing, Stick or TOPCAT 702 followed a thousand feet above and behind them. If a pilot needed gas because of missing the wires, or bolter, as they call it, or had an emergency requiring them to stay airborne longer, a Viking would pass above them for a "trick or treat." Recovery tanker Vikings always landed last for this reason.

We rejoined behind the carrier, and 702 led us down the right side at eight hundred feet and 350 knots. 702 broke hard left above the bow, and Stick rolled into a left break at a shallower bank angle. Watching this as a spectator provided another one of those mental pictures I'll take to my grave. The pattern from breaking overhead to landing took about two and a half minutes. I cannot describe in words what it looked like to roll out half a mile behind the carrier, come over the fantail, and then catch a three wire that pulled us to a stop in about two hundred feet. Stick folded up the wings and moved TOMCAT 706 out of the landing area. As we taxied past the island, a tug hooked up to our nose wheel strut and pushed us back into a parking spot.

I had to safe the ejection seat first before doing anything else. Stick and Red Man stayed in their ejection seats so I could get off the plane first. Thanking them profusely for a great flight, I ran down to the PE room to shed my flight gear. It was 0835, and RAWHIDE 42 would launch at 0900. Sweaty and smelly from cooking under TOPCAT 706's wide greenhouse Plexiglas canopy, I ran back to the ATO office and signed my name on the passenger manifest. Then I walked upstairs with my bags and threw them onto RAWHIDE 42's ramp, its engines already running, ready to taxi to the bow cats. I shook hands with Rolls and thanked him for a great week, and asked if he would please thank Shortney and Pecker for the S-3 ride. Two minutes later the COD's engines spooled up, and we taxied to catapult one on the bow's right side. A loadmaster told us to assume the position as I felt the launch bar go under tension and the engines wind up to 100 percent.

"GET READY! GET READY! GET READY!"

We were facing backward again. The cat shot started with its loud *bang*. My body rose half an inch out of my seat after a vigorous jerk forward. Three hundred seven feet—a hundred-yard dash—is the length of a cat shot, and it's over in three and a half seconds. I saw out my COD window that the blue Indian Ocean was still pretty calm as we climbed away from the deck.

During the three-hour flight back to Bahrain, I read through the notes I had taken over the week, which I still have. Everything the aircrews told me concerning tanking over Afghanistan was covered in the Employment School's Joint Maritime Operations syllabus. That gave me great satisfaction. I slept for the last hour and a half of the flight.

After landing at Manama, a taxi dropped me off in front of the Ritz-Carlton. I got another great night's sleep in a cold room and comfortable bed. At 1030 the next day, a C-130 delivered me and a bunch of cargo pallets back to Prince Sultan Air Base.

★ ★

LESSONS FROM THE COCKPIT: OPPORTUNITY

I saw a quote in a fighter squadron ready room a long time ago stating: "Every shot not taken is a shot missed." We tend to pass up learning opportunities that place us well outside our comfort zones. I didn't have any idea how to conn the carrier. I was frankly amazed that Harv even asked me to try. After some fear and trepidation, I thought, *Why not.* What a great opportunity to learn and build some confidence. Pilots never pass up the chance to fly in another airplane. Even if I wasn't touching the stick during the cat shot and trap landing, I was still going up in the S-3 to enjoy the ride. Both were incredible opportunities to learn.

From what I've determined, I'm the only KC-135 pilot to have driven an aircraft carrier while it refueled. It was a fantastic opportunity to operate outside my comfort zone. I'm thankful Harv had the courage to mic me up and let me drive his multibillion-dollar yacht for fifty minutes. When Stick rolled inverted and pulled from eighteen thousand feet, I felt some queasiness and told myself not to throw up. The Viking was a fully aerobatic airplane, way out of my comfort zone. But this opportunity gave me a firsthand look at how the Viking refueled and performed its sea-control duties. This experience was valuable when it came time to plan refueling operations during the Shock and Awe campaign, because I knew how the S-3s operated. Every missed opportunity to learn and gain experience outside comfort zones is a missed shot. Learn how to work outside of your comfort zone, and never miss a chance to gain valuable knowledge from customers and clients.

★ ★

On 4 November 1962, during the Cuban Missile Crisis, seventy-six B-52s armed with two to four nuclear weapons each flew CHROME DOME sorties near Soviet Russia's borders, waiting for the code words telling them to attack their targets. One hundred thirty-eight KC-135s from Europe and Alaska transferred more than 105,000 pounds of fuel each time the CHROME DOME Stratofortresses hooked up to their mated tankers, for a total of 14.5 million pounds on that day alone. *Courtesy of the author*

KC-135R tail number 63-8874 was my jet while I was stationed at Kadena Air Base in Okinawa, Japan, although I rarely got to fly it. The big CFM56 engines increased the fuel transfer capability of the KC-135 by 40 percent. We took off on training missions with 180,000 pounds of internal fuel, more gas than an American family will use in twenty-seven years. *Photo courtesy of Chief Master Sergeant Al Winzerling, 909th Air Refueling Squadron maintenance NCOIC*

KC-135s support national military goals at the strategic, operational, and tactical levels of warfare. One strategic support mission KC-135s perform is the refueling of all three versions of the RC-135 intelligence and reconnaissance plane, such as this RC-135U Combat Sent. The Combat Sent collects technical intelligence on enemy radar systems that is used to develop new or upgraded radar warning receivers, jammers, HARMs, and training threat simulators like those employed at the Nellis Air Force Base Test and Training Range. *Courtesy of the author*

18th Wing commander Brigadier General Jeffrey Cliver opened all cockpits to any aircrew wanting to fly in the Shogun Wing's aircraft. "Cruiser" Wilsbach and I are approaching a KC-135 in MOBILE 8 for refueling on a local Okinawa training mission. Lieutenant General Ken Wilsbach is the current Alaskan North American Aerospace Defense Command Region and Eleventh Air Force commander. *Courtesy of the author*

In July 1994, the 18 Wing supported the defense of South Korea when Kim il Sung died. This F-15 pilot call sign "Trike" wore a red bandana around his neck only on combat missions, like the KIM CAPs. Each of Trike's four flight mates took more than 15,000 pounds of fuel on each hookup during these tense two weeks in July 1994. *Courtesy of the author*

Three F-16CG Vipers rejoin on my crew's wing over Turkey's Cilo-Sat Mountain Range during an Operation Northern Watch vulnerability, or vul, period. The jets are armed for emergency defense suppression, carrying two GBU-12 laser-guided bombs used to kill antiaircraft guns or SAM sites. *Courtesy of the author*

This F-15C Eagle waits for gas on my wing over Turkey's Cilo-Sat Mountain Range during an Operation Northern Watch vul period. The jet is armed, as all Defensive Counter-Air (DCA) Eagles are, with AMRAAMs, Sparrows, and Sidewinders, in what Eagle drivers call "the Load of Justice." Eagle pilots can engage any air threats with this load. These missions were some of the most photogenic sorties I've flown, with aircraft armed live and backgrounds of snow-covered mountains. *Courtesy of the author*

I took this picture from the cockpit of an EC-130E during Operation Allied Force, the air war over Kosovo. We're approaching a Royal Dutch Air Force KDC-10's boom over the refugee camps of Montenegro. This is the same tanker the E-8 JSTARS was not cleared to take gas from during Operation Anaconda, a mistake I failed to catch on the schedule. *Courtesy of the author*

The Boeing B-1B bomber, or "Bone," has been a workhorse during the Global War on Terror, carrying twenty-four weapons in three bomb bays. The Bone typically took sixty thousand to eighty thousand pounds of gas from a tanker while performing on-call attack (XATK) sorties during the Shock and Awe campaign of 2003. Bones departed from Ellsworth Air Force Base in South Dakota for targets in Libya and then returned, refueling from tankers twelve to fifteen times as they transited across the US, the Atlantic Ocean, and Europe. *Courtesy of the author*

During my visit to the USS *John F. Kennedy* after Operation Anaconda, then Captain Bill Gortney, call sign "Shortney," commander of Carrier Air Wing 7, approved my flight in a Lockheed S-3B Viking from the VS-31 Topcats Sea Control Squadron. We refueled two F-18 Hornets flying surface combat air patrol (SUCAP) above the *Kennedy*. I logged a catapult takeoff and an arrested landing during this sortie, one of the great events of my career. Thanks, Admiral! *Courtesy of the author*

Our wingman during my S-3 sortie was too heavy for an arrested landing, so my pilot, Stick, took some of his gas to reduce his gross weight. Here, Stick is about to plug into their buddy store, the Cobham pod the Navy uses to refuel air wing aircraft. Our refueling probe, in the left of the picture, plugs into the basket trailing in front of us to transfer gas from one airplane to another. *Courtesy of the author*

I don't know of any other Air Force officers who can say they conned an aircraft carrier during at-sea refueling. During its underway replenishment (UNREP), the USS *John F. Kennedy* took on bombs, mail, food, and more than a million pounds of jet fuel. Navy aircraft carriers typically UNREP every three to four days, replenishing the items needed to keep the carrier, its air wing, and its crew of five thousand sailors going during operations at sea. *Courtesy of the author*

The boom extension is thirty-six inches away from my left shoulder as we refuel in an F-15. The extension pipe is painted with bands and arrows that correspond to the pilot director indicator (PDI) lights on the underside of the KC-135 and the KC-10 to help pilots stay in position. Cruiser Wilsbach is flying our F-15 at near-perfect extension, keeping the yellow ball we call the "apple" inches away from disappearing inside the boom's ice shield. *Courtesy of the author*

A USAF Weapons School A-10 Thunderbolt II, or "Hawg," comes off the boom after refueling during the Mission Employment phase of Weapons School training. All eighteen Weapons School divisions come together at Nellis Air Force Base every June and December for two-week training exercises known as Advanced Integration. My team had seven hours to plan the movement of two 74th Fighter Squadron Flying Tigers Hawgs from Kuwait to Afghanistan during Operation Anaconda in March 2002. *Courtesy of the author*

A 36th Tactical Fighter Squadron Flying Fiends F-4E Phantom II from Osan Air Base in Korea approaches our boom during their Operational Readiness Inspection in the summer of 1986. Osan was not an ideal place for KC-135s to operate from, as the tankers' big wings and tails extended over the small concrete parking ramp called "the Patio." Our engines blew freshly cut grass through the doors and windows of the 36th Squadron building as we taxied out of the Patio on one mission. *Courtesy of the author*

I've been on ten aircraft carriers during operations at sea, planning strike missions and learning how a refueling customer functions. Lieutenant Commander "Hey Joe" Parsons and Lieutenant "Dog" Kuhn are about to launch in an F-14A Tomcat, call sign GYPSY 212, on a Desert Shield mission in December 1990. Watching flight operations from Vulture's Row on the carrier's tower was another one of those great moments from my tanker pilot career. I could never be so lucky again. *Courtesy of the author*

17

Six Weeks in Hell

2030 Wednesday 19 March 2003
Combined Air Operations Center
Prince Sultan Air Base
Kingdom of Saudi Arabia

Never give up. Today is hard, tomorrow will be worse, but the day after tomorrow will be sunshine.

   —JACK MA, CHINESE BUSINESSMAN AND FOUNDER OF ALIBABA GROUP

There are no right and wrong ways to work in this business, but there are some basic commonsense practices. Work very, very hard and always be prepared; never give up; and once you get the job, give them more than they ever expected.

             —JIMMY SMITS, ACTOR

If you're going through hell, keep going.

     —WINSTON CHURCHILL, BRITISH PRIME MINISTER

Before I left the CAOC in December 2002, General Moseley told me my stay at home would not be long. I would be there just long enough to kiss Val, play with the kids, and enjoy Christmas before joining his Ninth Air Force staff at Shaw Air Force Base to work on the air campaign plan. My stay at home lasted twenty-six days. Once again, I left on Val's birthday for Sumter, South Carolina, and Ninth Air Force headquarters. There was a lot of work to do reviewing the refueling plan and the large number of receivers on the air campaign's opening night. Shaw was not the best place to tighten the plan, though. On the night of Saturday 1 February, the Ninth Air Force staff and I all walked out to a chartered Continental Airlines 777, departing at midnight for a flight back to Prince Sultan. I was walking much faster than everyone else out to the jet, and someone asked from behind, "Sluggo, why are you in such a hurry to get on the airplane?"

"This is a Triple Seven airliner. Continental didn't have time to change the configuration. It still has first-class seating."

Everyone rushed up the stairway and inside the jet after hearing that first-class seating was available. From seat 4J in first class, I watched Shaw Air Force Base pass by while we took off on runway 22 right for Saudi Arabia. After a short stop at Ramstein Air Base in Germany, we arrived on Monday morning at Prince Sultan. My review of operations and plans with the ARCT staff there didn't go well. Murphy's dictum "Plan early, plan twice" struck again—not because the Ninth Air Force planners did anything wrong, but because the nations in the Coalition of the Unwilling refused to allow access to their bases, and so the tanker plan was trash. None of what we'd planned at Shaw was going to work, and air operations continued to be increasingly short of tankers. My gut feeling was that we had to start over again because of several key factors that hadn't gone in our favor. The aerial refueling portion of the Polo Step invasion plan was not executable. The next six weeks, from the beginning of February to the night of Friday 21 March, was pure hell for the ARCT.

Everything we had planned hinged on a couple of countries approving Coalition forces locating within their borders, what we call dip clearances. Being denied access to prime tanker locations was driving everything to hell. Two sites in the Kingdom of Saudi Arabia would always be top tanker locations: Dhahran on the east coast and Jeddah on the Red Sea coast. Jeddah was such a great tanker location in Desert Storm because of its large parking areas, three runways, and, most important, unlimited fuel. King Abdulaziz International Airport had a refinery to produce the gas needed for all the airplanes coming and going during the Muslim pilgrimage. Prince Khalid made it very clear in a meeting with General Moseley that Jeddah was out of the question due to the upcoming hajj. During one tense meeting, someone asked General Moseley to request Jeddah one more time, which would solve all our tanker issues. His stern reply was, "The next one who asks for Jeddah puts five dollars in the can"; the can was an infraction slush fund used to buy pizza for everyone in the MAAP cell. Jeddah became the new $5 dirty word, which Peaches, one of my guys working in Plans Shop, promptly labeled "the Devil Speak."

Prince Khalid said there was only one place the US could locate in the Kingdom: Prince Sultan Air Base, which became the new tanker placeholder. Tankers coming to the Middle East would use Prince Sultan as a temporary lily pad until better places opened up after dip clearances were approved.

And then there was Turkey.

We all watched on flat plasma screens with great anticipation the Turkish Parliament's no vote against locating Coalition forces inside their borders. The offer of several billion dollars in aid did not affect their vote, and it impacted air operations. Incirlik was supposed to be one of our primary bases for tankers, fighters, and reconnaissance aircraft. All the planes flying in Operation Northern Watch had to leave by 17 March. Gramps, along with two other ARCT planners, Sexy Fred and Oscar, created a new tanker location plan, which Sexy Fred gave a unique name. When they came to review the PowerPoint brief about the new locations with me before going in to see General Nick Williams and then General Moseley, Sexy Fred had written in big bold letters across the first slide:

ROAST BEEF / NO TURKEY

General Moseley loved the name, but Roast Beef/No Turkey didn't even last twenty-four hours. Upon further inspection, we found that three of the bases involved could not support tanker operations as we'd initially thought. The Turks also denied overflying rights to any Coalition aircraft, rescinding approval to fly across their country. We had hoped to use the Northern Watch corridor to the eastern ROZ so planes could easily transit to northern Iraq. Nope; denied. The Turkish no vote left the two Mediterranean Sea carriers, the USS *Theodore Roosevelt* and the USS *Harry S. Truman*, with no avenue of approach to Iraq. Hell kept getting hotter for us.

The Operation Enduring Freedom Status of Forces Agreement with two of the Gulf Coast countries focused on the war in Afghanistan. The SOFA restricted all military airplanes located in these two nations to operations in Afghanistan. These two deals put tanker operations at a huge disadvantage as air operations increased prior to Operation Iraqi Freedom. One morning I called the air attaché in a Gulf Coast country embassy. I wanted to know if anyone had asked the Qatari minister of interior if US planes based there could fly operations supporting Iraq. The air attaché's answer surprised me: no one had asked the question. After I talked with General Buchanan, he instructed me to write a military white paper explaining the difficulties of refueling ever-increasing numbers of receivers with a shortage of tankers. The white paper went to the State Department and then to the US ambassador to Qatar. Two days later, General Buchanan walked down the row of desks with a smile on his face. His greeting to me was, "Sluggo! You silver-tongued devil!"

Everyone in the MAAP cell turned to see who the devil was. When the US ambassador took the white paper in to the Qatari minister of interior, the minister asked only one question: "Will the aircraft fly in Saudi airspace?"

The bad blood between Saudi Arabia and Qatar went back a long way. The ambassador assured him they would not, and the minister granted approval to support both Afghanistan and Iraq. I told General Buchanan to change the white paper's addressee to Bahrain and send it to the embassy. The ambassador walked it in to the Bahraini minister of interior, and he approved tanker support to both operations without any questions. We could finally use all the tankers in the Middle East for operations in Iraq or Afghanistan, which resolved a massive scheduling headache for refueling aircraft.

The next problem was that the Air Force did not have enough tanker airframes in the fleet for everything that was going on around the world. We could put millions of pounds of gas in the air, but if it was going through only one pipe, there would be a problem. Aerial refueling is all about the number of contact points receivers can plug into to get gas. Colonel Geno Redmon, the vice commander at the TACC, faced competing priorities for air refueling assets, and those of the AMC were at a premium. Tankers are called low-density/high-demand aircraft; every operation or contingency needs them, but there are not enough to go around. As Homeland Security threat levels rose in the US with the impending war in Iraq, so did the need for tankers on alert to support defensive combat air patrols over the major cities. Noticing that the Americans were busy in the Middle East, Kim Jong-il, the leader of North Korea, thought it was a good time to start rattling sabers on the Korean peninsula. Pacific Air Forces implemented Flexible Deterrent Option Bravo to keep him bottled up, but it required another twenty-six tankers to be deployed to Andersen Air Force Base in Guam.

During our weekly Thursday-night coordination phone call with TACC, Mac told me the bad news.

"Sluggo, I just sent you the last two tankers Air Mobility Command has."

"What do you mean, the last two AMC has, Mac?"

"There are no more tankers. AMC's tanker barrel is empty of aircraft. You'll have to go to war with the army you got, not the army you want."

Air Mobility Command was maxed out for tankers. My team would have to execute the air campaign plan with about half the number of KC-135s and KC-10s used in Desert Storm.

On Tuesday afternoon 17 March, my south MAAPer Bart received the air tasking order to build his refueling schedule for ATO Oscar, the opening night of Shock and Awe. He was forty-two tanker missions short, equaling a fuel deficit of approximately one and a half million pounds. By Wednesday evening Bart had negotiated the deficit down to around twenty-five missions. We flew the opening night of Shock and Awe seventeen tanker missions short, knowing there would be receivers falling off the schedule for many reasons, which helped make up the difference. All the fighter, bomber, and intelligence planners were quick to point out that we'd never backed an air campaign into the gas available in any exercise or training event back home. Iraqi Freedom was the first time in Air Force history that a shortage of tanker airframes limited options. Every night MAAP cell liaison officers beat up my planners because of the lack of gas. The finite amount of fuel and the prioritization of its use just agitated everybody.

Three weeks before the opening night of Shock and Awe, I received an e-mail from Captain KC Albright, the air wing commander on the USS *Abraham Lincoln*. He was not a happy customer. Freddy's tankers at Prince Sultan were the first ones to use the brand-new Cobham MPRS drogue pods in combat conditions. The drogues were breaking off KC's Tomcats' and Hornets' refueling probe doors or nozzles. Our spanking-new MPRS pods were doing "basket slaps" caused by whipping hoses that made the drogues into wrecking balls. I compared the Navy's air refueling manual with Cobham's operations manual and found the problem. Navy regulations stated that aircraft must approach the drogues with at least ten knots in speed overtake. Cobham's instructions said the take-up reel springs that compensated for overtake were set for only five knots of overtake. When the Navy aircraft plugged into the basket with a higher forward rate of motion, the drums could not reel in the hose fast enough. The ensuing sine wave traveled up to the pod and bounced back down toward the receiver with enough force to snap off the probe or door. Basket slaps were one reason many Tomcats and Hornets flew with missing refueling probe doors. I sent an e-mail out to all Navy units telling them to slow down when approaching the MPRS pods. Cobham, to their credit, sent a team of technicians over to the region to adjust the take-up reel springs to handle at least ten knots of overtake. Once the Navy slowed down and the springs were adjusted, the basket slaps stopped.

Air operations ran a Gulf Coast country out of gas! The UAE was capable of producing only 1.2 million gallons of aviation fuel a day in its refineries, and our base was using 1.7 million gallons a day. I had known, from reading a logistics chapter in Desert Storm's *Gulf War Air Power Survey*, that two Gulf Coast countries became oil *importers* instead of exporters because of intense flight operations. Colonel Jones, the head of Ninth Air Force logistics, had a cool solution. He brought in a massive supertanker loaded to the gills with jet fuel and parked it in Dubai's port. Fuel was pumped directly into storage facilities at the airfield. If the air campaign had lasted three more days, the base would have drained the supertanker.

Saudi Arabia, however, had no gas problems. Prince Khalid told General Moseley he was in the Kingdom of Saudi Arabia, and fuel would not be an issue. The only issue was storage at Prince Sultan. Engineers cleaned out three fifteen-thousand-gallon storage tanks that had lain unused for over a decade. One afternoon while driving back to work, I noticed a four-kilometer-long line of trucks waiting to get on base. These 8,500-gallon fuel trucks filled up all three storage facilities in a single day, but the storage tanks needed refilling every three days because of the intense air operations. I told one of the security policemen that he needed to have somebody from law enforcement go out to the truck drivers and tell them not to cook their lamb and brew their chai tea on open flame pits next to their trucks. Imagine the explosion and fire had fuel vapors ignited next to 264 8,500-gallon fuel trucks parked nose-to-tail waiting to get on base.

One last issue gave all of us a real fright. A week before the air campaign began, one of Saddam's very experienced MiG-25 Foxbat pilots took off from Al Asad Air Base west of Baghdad and flew across the country just a few miles from the BART and WYBO refueling areas. The pilot, call sign ROCKET 01, spiraled up over Baghdad to forty-five thousand feet and took off like a bullet for the Saudi border. LUGER, the call sign of the US AWACS, clocked his ground speed at 1,245 knots, faster than a .30-06 bullet. All the tanker, intelligence, and reconnaissance planners took notice: Would ROCKET 01 go on a one-way suicide trip to shoot down a big airplane flying inside Saudi Arabia?

Moose left Prince Sultan's CAOC shortly after Anaconda for his next assignment as deputy commander of USS *Theodore Roosevelt*'s Carrier Air Wing 8. I asked an Air Wing 8 Tomcat pilot if he had Moose's office number aboard ship, and he took a piece of paper out of his wallet that contained all relevant phone numbers. Dialing Moose's number, I worried the government classified phone wouldn't make a connection to a ship at sea. After a couple of rings, Moose picked up.

"Captain Laukaitis, may I help you, sir or ma'am?"

"Hey, Moose, it's Sluggo at the CAOC. How are you doing?"

"Slug-Meister! Please tell me you're running tankers for the Big Show."

"Yes, I am. I didn't screw up enough working for you, so leadership brought me back for Shock and Awe."

"Sluggo, you don't know how good it is to hear that. Have you talked to Shortney yet?"

"We see each other every day. I'm within thirty feet of his desk."

Captain "Shortney" Gortney, who let me fly with his Topcat S-3 squadron after Anaconda, had left his Carrier Air Wing 7 command position on the USS *John F. Kennedy* to command the CAOC's Naval Air Liaison Element, and would run the NALE through Shock and Awe. Shortney and I discussed the Navy's refueling headaches daily. I wanted Moose to know what our refueling problems were.

"Moose, a couple of things you need to know. First, keep this phone number; it rings right at my desk. If there's anything you need, don't hesitate to call. Wayno is your MAAPer, and he's a graduate of our tanker school."

"Okay, got it. Where are you going to locate the Incirlik tankers?"

"There is the North War Plan, but it's like Jell-O right now. Thirty-eight Incirlik tankers are going to RAF Akrotiri, compliments of Prime Minister Tony Blair and our British partners. It's going to take a while for the tankers to show up, but AMC turned the spigot on when the Brits approved. They'll begin arriving later tonight. The Bulgarians are new NATO partners, and six to eight KC-10 Gucci Birds are locating to an airfield north of Burgas on the Black Sea coast. A handful of March Reserve KC-135s leaves Southern California for Souda Bay tomorrow. Carrier Air Wing Eight has plenty of gas."

"Great, Sluggo. Tell me about the MPRS drogue pods."

"Here's what I've done for you, Moose. My planners felt that the best option was to put all the KC-135 MPRS jets at Akrotiri. Twenty-six of the thirty-three MPRS-configured KC-135s the Air Force owns will locate to Akrotiri, Cyprus. There's no getting around using the Iron Maiden, though. You'll plug into them too."

"My air wing owes your team a round, Sluggo!"

"One more thing about the MPRS pods: I discovered what's causing the basket slaps. The MPRS hose take-up reels are factory-set for five knots of overtake, not ten like your NATOPS manual states. Cobham knows the issue, and maintenance teams are at Prince Sultan adjusting the take-up springs. Those jets will move to Cyprus in the next forty-eight hours. Tell your fliers to use some finesse approaching the pods, and you shouldn't have any basket slaps."

"I'll get the word out to the ready rooms."

"Can you let the *Truman*'s air wing know about the MPRS pods also?"

"We talk to Cyrus every day. I'll let him know."

"Last issue: Shortney and my team are working on the dip clearance issue, which takes a while. Otter in J5 Engagements collaborates with the

State Department daily to get approvals, but it's taking longer because governments want more money now that it looks like we're going to war. The air attaché in Egypt is a brigadier general and remains engaged on the issue. All of us are trying to invent ways to keep your air wing in the war, but dip clearances are still moving at the speed of government."

"So what you're telling me is, both carriers don't have overfly rights yet."

"Jordan said no, Israel is out of the question, and Turkey is a maybe."

"Okay, Sluggo, I got it all. I have to run to a meeting. Thanks for your help."

"Wish I had better news on dip clearances, because your air wing has nowhere to go."

"Keep working your magic, Sluggo. Thanks for the call." Moose hung up.

I didn't know what SOF forces found in Iraq's western Anbar Province on the night of Wednesday 19 March, but Coalition aircraft dropped tons of bombs on it. One hundred airplanes supported Spec Ops forces in western Iraq, attacking the H-2 and H-3 airfield complexes. Special Forces on the ground used laser designators to call out targets to armed aircraft overhead. Bones, F-15Es, RAF GR4 Tornados, F-16CJ Weasels, and EA-6B jamming aircraft rotated on and off US and British tankers and returned to additional targets or to their bases. The ops desk managed gas from twenty tankers flying in BART, WYBO, and ZAM over a three-hour period. Hundreds of other armed aircraft, intelligence and reconnaissance platforms, and Navy aircraft trailed tanker icons in the FISK military operations area (MOA), which now zoomed into northwestern Saudi Arabia to watch the SOF-directed airfield attacks. The Air Force tanker fleet transferred eleven million pounds of fuel on Wednesday, a good indication of invasion off-loads.

While flipping through BART's fuel shortage numbers, Q, the F-117 stealth fighter planner, approached my desk at about 2030 time. He stood in front of me with a sense of urgency on his face.

"What's up, Q?"

"Sluggo, I need gas. A lot of gas."

"Q, everybody needs gas. What makes your need so unique?"

"Sluggo, I'm waiting for the president to approve the target. I need the gas tonight!"

There was only one target requiring presidential approval.

"What's going on tonight, Q?"

"We know where Saddam and his sons are this evening. I'm building a Black Jet strike package to bomb his ass at a place called Dora Farms."

The importance of Q's statement was evident to all my planners, who were listening in. The attack—a time-sensitive target, or TST in military terms—was potentially the perfect decapitation strike on a leadership target, which would nullify the reason to invade. Q explained that the target location was on a big bend of the Euphrates River, easy for the F-117's infrared and laser targeting system to acquire.

Q's Black Jet mission was very high-risk. General Moseley asked Q if it was doable, based on a question President Bush had asked him from Washington, DC. Q's answer surprised no one: "We can accomplish the mission by reducing risk." Dora Farms lay in the heart of Baghdad's air defenses, a precarious target to attack even for a low-observable fighter. Both F-117s would have to cross downtown Baghdad, the most heavily defended city in the Middle East, to drop laser-guided bombs on Dora Farms. So many SAMs protected the city that the overlapping missile-range rings created a big black blob over Baghdad on all our maps and charts. Two Black Jets flying through the dark blob would be exposed to antiaircraft guns and missiles.

Ideally, the tanker ops desk would meet Q's strike package's fuel needs using a Reliability KC-10 in SKITTER or TWITCH, directly south of Baghdad. But we couldn't afford Reliability tankers; Iraqi Freedom didn't have the luxury of Reliability tankers because there weren't enough aircraft. Q's top priority TST mission meant Cerb's night tanker crew at the ops desk would have to steal fuel from other aircraft and missions. The shortchanged fighters and bombers wouldn't have the gas to attack lower-priority targets, so LUGER would cancel their sorties and send them home. If the air strike delayed for presidential approval, any extra gas would go into the KC-10, keeping it full. A full KC-10 would give Coalition leadership additional time and options for short-notice target attacks, but it would burn twenty thousand pounds an hour to stay on station—more fuel consumed than the F-117s would take.

Q accompanied me downstairs to the ops desk. Cerb's crew was working the desk tonight, and Struks was part of this great group. She was one of the Air Force's best refueling experts.

"Struks, this is Q, the F-117 planner in the MAAP cell. He needs help tonight."

"What's going on, Sluggo?"

"Q's F-117 strike package has priority over everything."

"What do you mean, everything?"

"Intelligence sources located Saddam and his sons in Baghdad. The F-117s are going in sometime tonight; we just don't know when. The strike package is a mix of boom and drogue receivers. Q is waiting for presidential approval, so we don't know what time this is going to happen. It must take place before sunrise. But when the green light comes from Washington for launch, Q's package happens fast and takes priority over everything."

"Okay, sir, I'll take a look through the plan tonight and see where we can steal gas. We'll have to cancel sorties to make it up."

"Do whatever it takes for Q's F-117 package to get the gas going in and coming out."

I turned to Q. "You'll have the gas when needed."

"Thanks, Sluggo. I'll be upstairs waiting for approval and working on attack timing."

Q handed Struks his phone number before leaving the ops desk.

Everyone waited for President Bush to give the F-117s cross-border clearance for the attack; the forty-eight-hour ultimatum window would close at 0400 in the morning. An additional risk for the F-117s was sunrise at 0607. Backing up their time on target, the F-117s would have to take off before 0315 Baghdad time to pass over Dora Farms in darkness. President Bush gave the green light to attack at 1912 in Washington, 0312 in Baghdad. RAM 01 and RAM 02 departed minutes later, leaving Qatar for the TWITCH refueling anchor. RAM 01 and RAM 02 took on twelve thousand pounds of pre-strike gas apiece and turned north. One LUGER airborne battle manager tasked two F-16CJ Prince Sultan Weasels and three EA-6B Prowlers to support RAM 01 and 02 on their mission, two Marine EA-6Bs already airborne and patrolling over Iraq and another launched from the USS *Constellation* in the Persian Gulf. LUGER rotated the Weasels and Prowlers on and off a tanker as we waited for presidential approval. Q's attackers consisted of seven boom and drogue receivers.

President Bush addressed the world from the Oval Office.

"My fellow citizens, at this hour, American and Coalition forces are in the early stages of military operations to disarm Iraq, to free its people, and to defend the world from grave danger.

On my orders, Coalition forces have begun striking selected targets of military importance to undermine Saddam Hussein's ability to wage war. These are the opening stages of what will be a broad and concerted campaign."

Later that day, Saddam appeared on Al Arabiya and Al Jazeera. Looking pale behind thick reading glasses, he addressed the media wearing a military uniform and a dark beret. He looked hideous as he stumbled through a prepared speech. Later, the world learned that Saddam and his sons were nowhere near Dora Farms that night. The short-notice decapitation strike against Iraqi leadership didn't produce the effect we had hoped it would. As we watched the news broadcast, someone in the MAAP cell said, "Well, ladies and gentlemen, strap in, because it looks like we're going to war."

★ ★

LESSONS FROM THE COCKPIT:
MOTIVATION

The tanker team faced numerous critical issues during those six weeks. Coalition airpower success hinged on tanker gas, and I was the Daddy Rabbit for all refueling. Every day brought a new series of problems. Leaders of agencies around the CAOC stood at my desk pressuring my team and me to solve complex refueling problems faster. Twice I worked thirty-six hours straight to resolve issues in a constantly changing environment. It was difficult to stay motivated under so much stress to perform. But my team of planners and executors couldn't quit, because so much was riding on what we did.

Winston Churchill said it best: "When you are going through hell, keep going." I couldn't quit, and I didn't have a safe space in which to retrograde. I stayed motivated because when we did solve some of those problems, job satisfaction was high. By not quitting and curling up in the fetal position under my desk, I learned a lot about myself. Those six weeks in hell made me feel bulletproof through the rest of the air campaign. I felt I could deal with anything. All of us face difficult health issues, financial hardships, and even the loss of a loved one that put us in our own private hell. Keep moving and don't quit. Believe in yourself and don't get discouraged, because the financial security you've been seeking or the job you've always wanted may be on the other side of your six weeks in hell.

★ ★

18

Release the Hounds

2100 Friday 21 March 2003
Combined Air Operations Center
Prince Sultan Air Base
Kingdom of Saudi Arabia

In-flight refueling converts the tactical fighter into a strategic, long-range participant. It sustains combat air patrols, enables indirect routing, extends interdiction and strategic penetration depth, and increasingly is an integral component of front-line strength.

—ANTHONY MASON, ROYAL AIR FORCE AIR VICE MARSHAL

Tonight you are going to the big city [Berlin]. You have the opportunity to light a fire in the belly of the enemy that will burn his black heart out.

—ARTHUR HARRIS, ROYAL AIR FORCE AIR CHIEF MARSHAL

I Marine Expeditionary Force captured the Rumaila oil field and its pumping station, nicknamed "Crown Jewels," and turned west toward the town of Nasiriyah. The Army's 3rd Infantry Division continued their march toward the same objective. Coalition aircraft kept attacking strategic targets and providing close air support for troops in contact with Iraqi Army and irregular fighting units. Fighter and bomber aircraft refueled in the FISK MOA, a short two hundred miles from the battle. Refueling so close to the action kept fighters and bombers over the troops longer; the only factor limiting troop support was the number of bombs each aircraft could carry. Lack of additional tanker sorties nagged at me. Several MAAP cell planners voiced their displeasure at having to tell squadron mates scheduled to fly that they could not go that night because there weren't enough tankers; their sortie wasn't first-string worthy.

Carl von Clausewitz's fog of war would continue to insert itself throughout the night, and Murphy's Laws of Armed Conflict were sure to take over once the Shock and Awe portion of the campaign started in earnest. A lot of strike, attack, and other nonessential sorties got cut out of the ATO to make it executable. None of us liked having to cut sorties because of gas, but it was a fact in this war. There were 230 tanker sorties that day, with more tankers arriving over the next few days. The maximum number we could fly was 265 because of aircrews and aircraft. The shortage of tankers and our inability to put KC-135s on strip alert at Prince Sultan or Sheik Isa still bothered me. My concerns centered on effectiveness, emergencies popping up as they did in Desert Storm and Operation Anaconda, and sending strike or reconnaissance sorties home because the ops desk had to steal their gas.

I walked away from the tanker ops desk at 2015 to go back upstairs. I pondered where the best place to watch the opening of the Shock and Awe air campaign would be. The best place to watch the opening of any air campaign was standing next to its leader. I told Gramps I would be in the Battle Cab if he needed me. Gramps said he would take care of everything going on. The security guard outside the Battle Cab checked my badge for clearance and opened the door. I walked through the Battle Cab's glass door to see a long table with three folding chairs standing behind the press box–like desks. General Moseley, Admiral Nichols, and General Buchanan were sitting behind big windows and looking down on the CAOC floor. The long folding table was covered by Tactical Pilotage Charts, or TPCs, of Iraq, showing small details like power lines along roads and topography lines. Anytime anyone passed target coordinates over the command net AC-1 radio, General Moseley or his deputies could turn around to this folding table and find what was at those reference points. General Moseley turned around as I came in.

"Evening, Sluggo. What can I do for you?"

"Sir, I just wanted to go someplace and watch the big air schwacking of Baghdad."

"Well, Sluggo, I may have questions for you, so sit down right here at the TPC desk." He pointed to a chair.

"I figured this would be the best place to watch the start of an air campaign, sitting behind its leader."

He turned back to look down on the CAOC floor through the open windows. The linguist was listening to Baghdad's air defense commander on his radio net and translating the Arabic out loud.

AWACS and JSTARS data-linked their radar return picture to the CAOC, which showed up on one of General Moseley's four computer monitors. General Moseley took a picture of his screen about forty minutes before the first bombs impacted Baghdad. He wanted to capture a piece of history. The big opening-night strike packages refueled behind tankers spread across northern Saudi Arabia. F-15s orbited in five lanes below the 33rd parallel, waiting to jump on any Iraqi MiG stupid enough to take off. Radar return icons for CAS aircraft supporting the troops concentrated near Ramallah and Basra. B-52s from Diego Garcia roamed over Republican Guard units, dropping two-thousand-pound JDAMs on troop concentrations and vehicles, clearing the path for General McKiernan to achieve his ground war objectives as troops marched toward Baghdad. To my right, two UAV Predator intelligence analysts watched flat-screen TVs hung on the wall. These two Predators had one purpose: to stimulate Baghdad's air defense network so the Weasels and Prowlers could kill it. The Predators' call signs identified their purpose: CHUM 01 and CHUM 02. Antiaircraft shells and

SAMs shot at CHUM 01 and CHUM 02 passed through the broadcast picture on the two big plasma screens. Six Predator UAVs and four U-2 reconnaissance planes sent information via their datalinks to screens in the Battle Cab. At 2025, the captain of the Aegis destroyer USS *Laboon* radioed the start of Baghdad's pounding.

The Navy's Tomahawk Land Attack Missiles, or TLAMs, come from the factory painted two tones of gray. Their gray color scheme was why the Navy nicknamed them "Greyhounds." USS *Laboon*'s captain employed a unique way of telling the world that the first round of cruise missiles was on its way. In a perfect British accent, the captain said, "Sir! *We've released the hounds!*"

Everyone in the Battle Cab laughed. Moments later, all of us realized the seriousness of the radio call. Everyone went quiet in the Battle Cab for about five to eight seconds as the gravity of what was happening sank in. None of us knew what to say. AC-1 continued to blare in the background, and Arab voices on Saddam's command net transmitted orders to Baghdad's air defense network. General Moseley turned around with his arms folded.

"Well, gentlemen, strap in. Here we go. You can't recall those things."

Other US Navy ships started calling in to say they had released their hounds toward Baghdad. I looked at the clock: 2036. Three hundred cruise missiles left their vertical launch system boxes and headed toward Baghdad that night. Some cruise missiles were programmed to orbit south of Baghdad in a racetrack pattern, showing the Iraqi air defense radar operators they were there, and the radar operators couldn't do anything about it.

But now we waited.

CNN's Wolf Blitzer continued to broadcast from downtown Baghdad for at least an hour or more. He kept asking when it would start. General Moseley looked at the flat-screen TV and said to no one in particular, "All hell is going to break loose in twenty minutes, Wolf."

Blue radar return icons had left the tankers in the FISK MOA, and they now spread out across Iraq. My team had worked so hard and had done everything they could to satisfy the air refueling needs of all those blue icons. Hundreds of images moved north toward their targets in Baghdad, looking like a big blue airmailed fist. The intensity of antiaircraft fire over Baghdad increased dramatically at 2050, ten minutes to first bombs on target. As we approached 2100 local Baghdad time, several people in the Battle Cab began counting down the seconds.

Ten . . . nine . . . eight . . . seven . . .

Cruise missile engines have a very distinct whine, which we could hear in the background of the three news broadcasts.

Six . . . five . . . four . . .

The distinct sound of JDAMs falling at supersonic speeds after being released from B-2s passing high overhead now came through the news broadcasts. They sounded like a bedsheet ripping.

All of us gravitated toward the flat-screens, standing in front of them to witness the opening of Shock and Awe like NFL fans waiting for the Super Bowl kickoff.

Three . . . two . . . one . . .

Fiery explosions bloomed upward from the buildings as the red second hand of the clock swept past the straight-up nine o'clock position as the first wave of weapons impacted buildings in Saddam's version of the Washington Mall. Weapons impacted dead nuts on their time on targets, or TOTs. Several explosions bloomed from Saddam's capitol building, and cruise missiles would impact it in a few moments. The digital clock was two seconds ahead. All of us stood in silence, witnessing this fiery phenomenon. CHUM 01 broadcast excellent streaming video of impacts in the government district of Baghdad. CHUM 01's sensor operator moved the Predator's sensor ball to stare into two discrete sections of Baghdad as the bombs and cruise missiles exploded.

Someone suggested to General Moseley that Lieutenant General Bahadur, the Saudi CAOC liaison, should be a part of this opening.

He had done so much for the Coalition, fixing problems we faced with airspace and gas. A captain walked out to General Bahadur's office, ten steps behind the glass doors. Moments later, General Bahadur sat next to me at the table. I had been flipping through the MAAP cell brief that was lying on the table, looking at the strike packages and their targets on small maps of Baghdad. It was now four minutes after the first bombs had impacted the Baghdad area. I flipped through the MAAP cell brief pages to the 2105 time slice, preparing to watch the next series of weapons impact. Pointing to the page, I told General Bahadur which package was about to strike which targets in one minute. He could clearly see the buildings burning in the government section of Baghdad on the news channels. He also could see the video from CHUM 01 and CHUM 02 on the flat-screens just to his right. As he sat down next to me, one of the linguists listening to Saddam's air defense network began laughing. Baghdad's air defense commander had screamed at his SAM site troops, "We'll make them die like dogs!"

General Bahadur sat in silence. The MAAP cell brief showed strike packages in three-minute time slices, red triangles overlaid on a satellite picture illustrating the target; it also detailed the types of weapons to be used on the target set. It was obvious from the general's facial expression that he had never seen anything quite like this brief. After watching the bombs and cruise missiles from the next strike package hit their targets, General Bahadur leaned over to me and said, "Sluggo, this is the greatest display of firepower I've ever witnessed."

I thanked the general for his support and for getting us through a lot of the roadblocks and obstacles that had stood in the air campaign's way. Twenty minutes later, I said good-bye to General Moseley, Admiral Nichols, and General Buchanan and turned to walk out of the Battle Cab. General Bahadur followed me and went to his office. His words kept going through my mind: "The greatest display of firepower I've ever witnessed."

Imagine what the display would have been like if my team and the

ATO had had more tankers and gas. I swore that if I ever had the chance to talk to people in the Pentagon, they would know we had to cut lower-priority attack missions because the ATOs didn't have the gas.

The MAAP cell was busy finishing ATO Quebec for Sunday and had received initial planning documents for Monday's ATO Romeo at 2200. An electrical engineer on the MAAP cell staff figured out how to silence the fire escape door alarm and opened it so we could hear the jets leaving. The MAAP cell's fire escape door was located at the extreme northeast corner of the building, looking directly north. From the top landing area, MAAP cell personnel could see Prince Sultan's runway to the east of us. Ten of us stood on the landing and stairs watching fighters depart, long tongues of bright orange flame illuminating the tails of four F-16 Wild Weasels blasting off in afterburner. Approaching the edge of the airfield, each of the four Weasels pulled its nose upward at a forty-five-degree angle and zoomed up off the runway. Four RAF Air Defense Variant Tornados followed the Weasels, spiraling up to twelve thousand feet above our heads. Tornado ADVs are notoriously fuel inefficient; their afterburner tactical departures consumed three thousand to four thousand pounds of fuel. Each Tornado disappeared into the blackness, its blue afterburner flames and flashing collision lights visible through the climbing spiral it employed to stay over the protection of the airfield's security forces. Tornados needed ten thousand pounds of fuel after launching, but aggressive, spiral-up departures reduced the risk of Iraqi sympathizers shooting a jet down with a shoulder-fired heat-seeking missile. Yes, we knew there might be jihadis out there, waiting.

The next wave of tankers departed after the fighters for the FISK MOA to refuel the second wave of strike, attack, and reconnaissance aircraft going into Iraq. Three KC-135s, a KC-10, and a VC-10 followed the Tornadoes by spiraling up and leveling off to head north for the FISK MOA anchors. Every Air Force tanker departed with its lights out, disappearing a mile off the end of the runway. Fighter and bomber planners standing on the stairs could only follow the sound of the tanker engines climbing above our heads. This nighttime mass launch from one of Iraqi Freedom's largest and most populated air bases reminded me of nighttime mass launch at Nellis during the second week of Weapons School's Mission Employment phase. Prince Sultan Air Base launched three times as many airplanes in half the time. Prince Sultan had a runway event—an aircraft taking off or landing—every ninety seconds. The continuous launch of fighters in afterburner, white-top ISR aircraft, and dark gunship-gray KC-135s and KC-10s went on for hours. All of us were witnessing air warfare history from the fire escape.

Bart and Wayno continued negotiating with other MAAP cell planners to fulfill the ATO fuel requirements. All the KC-135 and KC-10 airframes in the region were flying in ATO Papa on Saturday 22 March. Each ATO averaged 260 tanker sorties per day for the next three and a half weeks, maximizing the gas. Freddy's double-turning KC-135 aircrews would burn through their monthly flying hours in twenty-six days. If everything went right, the tankers would transfer nine million pounds of fuel in the next twenty-four hours.

Deputy ARCT Chief Jerry and I changed over at midnight. I told him Bart and Wayno were backing all the ATOs into gas available, and the fighter guys were pretty upset. They didn't realize that, as it got hotter, available fuel would decrease even more. Robie, one of the F-16 planners, was the first fighter pilot to understand that when I showed him the tanker performance charts. No one else seemed to care.

The biggest news concerned the potential move of the *Roosevelt* and the *Truman* back north toward Turkey just before I left Friday at midnight. I fell asleep on the bus ride home. I dropped my flight suit and boots on the floor next to my bed, too tired for anything else. With all the fighters leaving in afterburner, it was a noisy night for sleeping.

On Saturday 22 March, General Moseley met me at the top of the stairs as I came into work at noon.

"Sluggo, I need you to find something out for me."

"What's that, sir?"

"Last night six F-117s didn't get gas and missed their target windows. The Black Jets bingoed out of TWITCH when the tankers didn't show up. Can you find out what happened?"

My heart sank. The air campaign was a day old, and tankers had already missed critical refueling control times. It put an unfortunate stain on the tanker community when the Combined Forces Air Component commander told me about missed refuelings as I was walking into work.

"The tankers didn't even show up?"

"From what I read in the after-action report, the tankers weren't there when they were supposed to be. Can you find out what happened?"

"I'll find out from Q what package they were in so I can track down which base the tankers came from. I'll call their squadron commander and see what happened."

"Okay, thanks, Sluggo. I just want to know what happened."

When I looked for the ATO, I found that the six F-117 Black Jets had been assigned three KC-135s in TWITCH from Al Udeid. I sat down at my desk and mentioned to Bart, Peaches, and Gramps that six Black Jets didn't make it to Baghdad because of gas last night, the opening night of the campaign. The six Black Jet pilots must have been really frustrated to fly all the way to TWITCH in central Saudi Arabia and find only empty sky for thirty minutes before going home. Peaches asked how I found out.

"General Moseley met me at the top of the stairs."

Peaches said, "Ain't no spankin' like a CFACC spankin'!"

I turned around in my chair to call Visch, the KC-135 squadron commander at Al Udeid, as everyone laughed at Peaches' comment. He was right, though. Visch picked up after two rings.

"Hey, Visch, it's Sluggo at the CAOC. General Moseley just met me at the top of the stairs with a question. He wants to know why six F-117s didn't get gas last night. The tankers were from your unit. What happened?"

"Sluggo, you won't believe this! The tankers taxied on time and reached the runway eight minutes before their scheduled departure time. Big fighter packages were blasting off right in front of them. The supervisor of flying in the tower, a fighter guy, held the tankers at the end of the runway for thirty minutes!"

"I'm sure cell lead was screaming at the SOF, correct?"

"Cell lead called the SOF constantly, telling him they had to leave. The fighter SOF repeatedly said, 'No, I'm letting all the fighters go first because they don't have gas.' Isn't that amazing, Sluggo? The six F-117s took off and left their tankers behind because the SOF said they didn't have the gas to wait for their tankers. The tankers took off thirty minutes late and couldn't make their ARCT. The six Black Jets bingoed out of TWITCH and came home."

"So what did the tankers do?"

"They left thirty late and went to TWITCH anyway. All three 135s probably passed their Black Jet receivers on their way to TWITCH. They stayed up for three hours refueling opportune receivers. Each plane off-loaded over eighty-five thousand pounds to unscheduled receivers."

"Good, Visch—that's exactly what they should've done. Thanks for letting me know."

"Sorry, Sluggo, but there was no way they could make up thirty minutes."

"Make sure in the next Wing King meeting that General Rosberg knows the SOF needs some additional refueling and integration training."

"Will do, Sluggo. I was sick when I found out what happened."

General Williams had to know what happened. He and General Cichowski sat in their office discussing other matters. Both asked what was up.

"Sir, three tankers at Al Udeid missed their A/R last night. General Cichowski isn't going to like who the receivers were either."

Ski asked, "Who?"

"Six Black Jets going downtown in the first package had to bingo out of TWITCH when the tankers were a no-show."

"What happened?" General Williams asked.

"The six F-117s didn't get their gas because the fighter SOF in the tower held the tankers at the end of the runway for thirty minutes, waiting for all the fighters to depart first. They watched their receivers leave right in front of them. Once they made it off, they couldn't make their ARCT thirty minutes late. Cell lead still took his three-ship to TWITCH for three hours, each jet off-loading eighty-five thousand pounds to unscheduled receivers. General Moseley asked me to find out why the 117s didn't get gas."

"Okay, Sluggo, thanks for letting me know."

General Moseley stood at his admin desk talking to Conan. I told him I had his answer to why the six Black Jets didn't get gas. I told General Moseley what happened. What he said next is a hallmark of great military leaders.

"Fog of war, Sluggo. These kinds of things are going to happen. There's nothing you can do about it. Calvin the chief of plans will re-MAAP the targets, because they're not going anywhere. We'll attack them in a couple of days. Don't you and your tanker team worry about this."

General Cichowski wanted to know what General Moseley said about the Black Jets not getting their gas. He was very keen on the 117 community because he knew everybody. Ski had been a Black Jet pilot himself. I told him Moseley had stood with his arms folded and said, "Fog of war, Sluggo. These kinds of things are going to happen." Ski smiled and said that was what he had expected him to say. The Black Jets missing their refueling was one of the reasons all of us loved working for General Buzz Moseley. Like all great military or business leaders, he didn't get wrapped around the axle over things he couldn't control from 250 miles away.

The tanker plans team faced one of its biggest challenges in keeping the *Roosevelt*'s and the *Truman*'s air wings active in the campaign. Shortney walked down from the NALE Wednesday afternoon to tell us the *Roosevelt* and the *Truman* were moving off the coast of Alexandria, Egypt, and overflight permission for the Sinai had come through. Wayno, my North Tanker MAAPer, and a few others needed to design the refueling scheme to bring Moose's Carrier Air Wing 8 and Cyrus's Carrier Air Wing 3 from the eastern Mediterranean to the BART and WYBO refueling areas before going into Iraq. Wayno, and Finn and Tatu, two Navy S-3 crewmembers working tanker plans, developed an ingenious plan for adding the *Roosevelt*'s and the *Truman*'s airpower to the ATOs. Air Force tankers made naval aviation history in one of the longest fighter missions performed off aircraft carriers. S-3 Vikings and Prince Sultan tankers would drag *Roosevelt* and *Truman* aircraft to their targets in Baghdad.

★ ★

LESSONS FROM THE COCKPIT: VISION

The bottom-line reason I was upset that the Black Jets didn't get their gas was that we broke a hard-won trust with our receivers. Tankers were always right where they were supposed to be—always. I was sick thinking that those six pilots waited for thirty minutes and the tanker didn't show, and they had no idea why. In an air campaign with thousands of moving parts, one decision by that tower SOF rippled across an entire war. It wasn't the SOF's fault, because he made a decision based on the information he possessed at the time. The fog of war had grabbed us by the throat, and the tankers were the first ones to get choked. General Moseley showed real leadership by brushing it off and telling us to keep moving.

All great leaders have the ability to see the bigger picture. I got lost in minutiae because the general asked a question. This incident involved nine airplanes out of eight hundred. I momentarily lost sight of the bigger picture. The fog of war had driven me to look beyond the mark at what we were trying to do. General Moseley's statement that we would hit the targets later brought my picture back into focus. The three tanker aircrews did what they should have done—they flew out to their assigned area and passed a buttload of gas. There are a lot of things you cannot control in your life. You'll get involved in big projects with lots of moving parts—but don't get lost in the small details and lose sight of the larger corporate picture.

★ ★

19

The Pig Pen

2115 Wednesday 26 March 2003
SHANIA refueling anchor
Above the An Najaf Province of Iraq

Innovation comes from people meeting up in the hallways or calling each other at 10:30 at night with a new idea, or because they realized something that shoots holes in how we've been thinking about a problem.

—STEVE JOBS, FORMER CEO OF APPLE

The operative assumption today is that someone, somewhere, has key information or a better idea; and the operative compulsion should be to find out who has that better idea, learn it, and put it into action—fast!

—JACK WELCH, FORMER CEO OF GENERAL ELECTRIC

A Scout is never taken by surprise; he knows exactly what to do when anything unexpected happens.

—SIR ROBERT BADEN-POWELL, CREATOR OF THE BOY SCOUT MOVEMENT

General Moseley met me walking back from dinner as I came up the stairs on the night of Monday 24 March.

"Sluggo, you got a few minutes? I need to talk to you."

"Yes, sir, what can I do for you?"

"Sluggo, the gas is in the wrong place. We need to move the tankers farther north."

Three days into the air campaign, I knew what the general was telling me. Tankers would be moving over Bad Guy territory, into Iraqi airspace.

"I can do that, sir, but there are a lot of things we need to figure out."

"Sluggo, I need it done now. There are nineteen-year-old kids getting shot at south of Nasiriyah. Your tanker bubbas are going to have to assume some of the risks. They cannot sit in safe airspace when fighters have too far to go to fill up and return to the target area. The tanker community is going to have to take some risks so we can protect these kids fighting on the ground."

"When do you want this by?"

"I want it as soon as possible, Sluggo. There are plenty of fighters out there protecting you guys. Come up with a tanker protection plan, but move them into Iraqi airspace by tomorrow night."

"We're on it, sir."

I relayed my conversation to Gramps, Peaches, Bart, and the Ninth Air Force tanker planner Burl. Gramps stated the obvious: it was too soon. I agreed, but the CFACC had said move, so we would move. We still didn't have a good idea where Saddam had placed his air defense science projects. Mobile SAMs and antiaircraft guns were running all over Iraq. My fear was mobile guns and SAMs operating beneath new refueling areas built inside Iraq's borders. A second concern was available fuel. The farther tankers had to fly to refueling areas, the more gas that would typically be transferred to receivers gets consumed to get there. Yes, we could operate near the target areas the fighters and bombers were attacking, but the cost would be that the tanker fleet had less gas to give. Many fighter and bomber pilots and WSOs in the MAAP cell didn't initially understand the trade-off, and got mad at us for even mentioning that there would be less fuel available. Plus, the temperatures at the tanker bases were getting hotter, so fuel loads had to decrease to allow the aircraft to get off the ground.

All of us were very hesitant to move tankers into Iraqi airspace on just the fourth night of the air campaign, thinking back to Desert Storm when the Black Hole moved tankers into Iraqi airspace. Their purpose was to refuel Eagles and Tomcats that were blocking Iraqi fighters from fleeing into Iran. F-15 Eagles patrolled the "Cindy CAPs" southeast of Baghdad, while the F-14s patrolled the "Bong CAPs" northeast of Baghdad. Two refueling anchor areas were set up in Iraqi airspace to keep the Eagles and Tomcats full of gas: one near Tallil Air Base called BEAR, and another near H-2 Air Base called STRAWBERRY. One night late in the war, a Jeddah-based KC-10 refueling F-15s that had rotated out of the Cindy CAPs in BEAR had a frightening moment. Remember, none of us had ever practiced retrogrades in the aircraft. BULLDOG, the eastern AWACS, called bandits south of BEAR, possibly making a run on the Gucci Bird and blocking its escape route out of Iraq. BULLDOG committed two Eagles holding on Gucci's wing to engage the Floggers. In a moment of total loss of situational awareness, BULLDOG told the KC-10 to turn south for Saudi Arabia, toward the engaging Floggers and Eagles. The Eagles found the offending Floggers first, blowing them to pieces. The SHAMU KC-10 from Jeddah landed safely and told everyone about BULLDOG's call to turn south. Their story unnerved every tanker crew, and none of us wanted to go to BEAR anymore after hearing about their experience. Our concerns were probably unfounded, since every Eagle and Tomcat crew wanted to pounce on a MiG and kill it. SHAMU's incident in BEAR made me realize that I had no idea how to protect tankers orbiting in Iraqi airspace when General Moseley asked us to move north.

Gramps, Bart, and I constructed two refueling anchors directly south of Baghdad, standard thirty-mile-wide by seventy-mile-long rectangles. I left it up to the aircrews how they used the airspace, but I still put a rendezvous control point near the northeast corner of each rectangle. Two more refueling rectangles lay directly south of Najaf and just northwest of the disputed diamond-shaped Saudi/Iraqi border area we called "the Klingon Neutral Zone." I e-mailed the anchor areas to the Army's MSIC to get their analysis of threats to the areas. Their report returned three hours later all yellow: SAMs could potentially engage tankers up to thirty-seven thousand feet. Both anchors' ceilings were set at twenty-eight thousand feet. Gramps, myself, and Scott, a navigator from McConnell Air Force Base working on all airspace issues, began poring over all of the Surface-to-Air Fire (SAFIRE) events, looking to see if anyone had fired at Coalition aircraft in the southern Najaf Province. Our two refueling anchors were perfect for close air support fighters because we'd put them near An Najaf and Karbala, two places ground forces were racing toward. Scott and I had some additional fun naming these Iraqi anchors. I decreed that all refueling anchors in Iraq must receive female country-and-western singer names. The first two Scott opened in the ACO were SHANIA and REBA, two of my favorite country singers.

When all the MAAP cell planners saw SHANIA and REBA in the ACO, every fighter and bomber piled into them. Gramps and I designed two elevations for refueling in both areas: SHANIA LOW, in the twelve-thousand- to eighteen-thousand-foot block, and SHANIA HIGH, in the twenty-two-thousand- to twenty-eight-thousand-foot block. REBA was designed the same way, low and high. Slow-moving A-10s and faster RAF Tornado GR4s would refuel in the low blocks, while fast-moving fighters and ISR aircraft would use the high blocks. The MAAP cell planners tried packing all the receivers into SHANIA and REBA that they could, but Calvin made some gut priority calls.

Calvin set priorities for which strike and attack missions used SHANIA and REBA first. Everyone else had to refuel in the FISK MOA anchors. Gramps and I knew that there would need to be more refueling anchors opening inside Iraq soon, but at least SHANIA and REBA were a good start. The things we learned from opening SHANIA and REBA helped us in designing newer Iraqi anchor areas, but also, more important, set the procedures for defensive tactics when Iraqi air defenses shot at tankers. SHANIA and REBA opened on the night of Tuesday 25 March and stayed open for the rest of the air campaign. I waited to hear how often tankers were engaged in both anchors before going back to my room that night. The biggest threat remained us, so I told all the units to keep their lights on and full up, even inside SHANIA and REBA. None of the units wrote about being shot at in those two anchors. I told my counterpart, Jerry, to keep a record of all the SAFIRE events involving tankers through the night and hopped onto the bus for my room at 0030.

Wednesday night I got a frantic call from Rubber, the Sheik Isa squadron commander. One of his KC-135s, call sign TOGA 33, had been engaged by Saddam's air defense systems seven times during its mission in SHANIA. Rubber very tersely told me, "Sluggo! You'll be the first guy to get a tanker crew killed!"

I explained the CFACC's story about the nineteen-year-old and his orders. Rubber wasn't buying it. He e-mailed TOGA 33's SAFIRE report over so we could take a look at events in SHANIA. As we read through TOGA 33's after-action report, we found a couple of things that didn't make sense. I understood antiaircraft fire coming from the north near Najaf—that's where Saddam's army lived. But some of the SAMs fired at TOGA 33 came from the south, near the Saudi border. TOGA 33 reported four missiles streaking over their heads while making a left turn at the north end of SHANIA. Could Saddam have SAMs installed close to the Saudi border, trying to cut us off? I grabbed the report and walked over to the Joint Intelligence Center, straight to Jennifer's cubicle. Jennifer was the intelligence analyst who pored over every SAFIRE event in Iraq.

"Evening, Jennifer. I have an interesting report for you."

"Evening, Colonel Hasara. What's it say?"

"I moved refueling anchors into Iraqi airspace last night on General Moseley's orders. Here's a really discouraging SAFIRE report from Isa. TOGA 33, orbiting in SHANIA, was engaged seven times tonight. Can you find out what types of SAMs or guns are under SHANIA and REBA for me?"

"Who's the country-and-western fan?"

I tapped my chest with my right index finger.

"Let me see what I can find out. I'm working on another project right now; can you come back in about an hour and a half?"

"Here's the number at my desk—just give me a call when you're ready."

I walked out of the JIC and went back to my desk, formulating plans to defend tankers flying inside the Iraqi anchors. About an hour later, Jennifer e-mailed me asking if I could come back over. As I entered the JIC, I saw that there was a lot of activity and background noise, as analysts discussed events and cable news played on three flat-screens. I asked Jennifer what she'd found out. Her answer to SHANIA's SAFIRE events sent a chill down my spine.

"Colonel Hasara, I have both good news and bad news for you."

"How can there be good news and bad news about a tanker engaged by ground fire, Jennifer?"

"Easy. Saddam's air defenses engaged TOGA 33 on only three occasions."

"What?"

"You need to go talk to the Army in the Battlefield Coordination Detachment about the other four."

"Jennifer, what are you talking about?"

"Sir, four of the SAFIRE events weren't Saddam."

"What do you mean they weren't Saddam?"

"I think you need to find out where the Army forces are in Iraq."

"Are you telling me there's a potential blue-on-blue situation here?"

"I think so, sir."

I held two different reports in my hand—TOGA 33's SAFIRE report and Jennifer's analysis, which I could not make sense of—both telling me SHANIA and REBA were dangerous places to refuel. I asked Bart, Wayno, Gramps, and Peaches to join me at my desk. I explained what Jennifer told me, and all of us were confused by her recommendation. Three Iraqi antiaircraft defenses engaged TOGA 33, but four events might be the US Army. We couldn't know whether friendly fire was involved with TOGA 33's flight until I talked to the BCD. I left for the BCD to find out what was going on. What I learned shocked not only me but also the U-2 spy plane community.

The Battlefield Coordination Detachment sat in a first-floor office just off the tanker ops desk. They were the Army's liaison element, co-ordinating the ground forces' efforts with all of us Airedales. An Army sergeant from an M109 Paladin 155-millimeter howitzer unit met me as I walked in. A few nights earlier I had given him a ride back to the compound and had learned a lot about artillery. His bros were all really happy because they were using the red bags of powder, the war bags. The Army destroyed many of their TSTs in front of the advancing troops with precision-guided 155mm rounds.

"Hey, Colonel Hasara, what can I do for you?"

"Sergeant Gonzalez, last night we moved two refueling anchors into Iraqi airspace. Tonight a tanker was engaged seven times—three by Saddam. Jennifer, the JIC's SAFIRE analyst, told me to come talk to you about the other four."

I showed him a printed chart indicating the locations of SHANIA and REBA. The look on his face was priceless—a look of "What the hell could she have told you?"

I handed him the chart. He studied their positions, and then looked up with an expression of horror on his face.

"What?!"

"Sergeant Gonzalez, tell me why this is a bad thing."

He walked over to his Blue Force Tracker screen. Taking the mouse in his left hand, he narrowed the Blue Force Tracker image to the Saudi border just south of SHANIA. The Falcon View computer planning system the Air Force used for mission planning didn't talk to the Army's Blue Force Tracker; do you see where this is going? He narrowed the area underneath SHANIA and showed me where Big Army was operating. Both of us stared at the screen as the view zoomed in. Sergeant Gonzalez looked at my chart and moved the Blue Force Tracker over to REBA and took a long look at the Army forces beneath the anchor point. I had never thought to coordinate opening the refueling area with Big Army. I would never make that mistake again.

Big Army's rocket forces were located at the south ends of SHANIA and REBA and fired through and over both anchor areas at targets south of Baghdad.

"Sir, our Multiple Launch Rocket Systems and Tactical Missile systems are located right here, here, and here," he said as he pointed to many icons on the Blue Force Tracker. MLRS and ATACM icons were dispersed below SHANIA and REBA. It was time for an education.

"Sergeant Gonzalez, what is Big Army using these things for right now?"

"Colonel, Multiple Launch Rocket Systems and Army Tactical Missile systems are used to attack TSTs near Najaf, Karbala, and even south Baghdad to support the march up. Our process is to open a restricted operating zone above us whenever firing ATACMs. By regulation, we are not required to open a ROZ when firing MLRS or even Paladin 155 howitzer guns at TSTs."

"Sergeant Gonzalez, how far and how high do these things shoot?"

"Paladins shoot about thirty-five miles, and the round tips over at twenty-seven thousand feet. MLRS fires fifty miles and tips over at around thirty-two thousand feet. ATACMs shoot over one fifty and tip over around one hundred twenty thousand feet, depending on how the crew aims it."

I gasped.

These three Army weapon systems were shooting *over* all of us flying in Iraq, including U-2s and the Global Hawk UAVs. I asked Sergeant Gonzalez to print out a screen shot so I could show the humble MAAP cell pilots and WSOs upstairs. He looked at the scale of my chart of SHANIA and REBA and printed out a similarly sized screen shot. Grabbing it as it rolled out of his printer, I laid my chart of SHANIA and REBA over his Blue Force Tracker map. Holding both up to a bright light, I saw that Army MLRS and ATACM systems stretched across the southern boundaries of SHANIA and REBA. Sergeant Gonzalez and I just laughed. Four of the missiles TOGA 33 encountered came from us! Sergeant Gonzalez and I were looking at another blue-on-blue engagement, just like the Patriot shooting down the RAF Tornado GR4 a day ago.

The first person I needed to show the charts to was Randy, the U-2 liaison officer. Randy had been a navigator in the Young Tiger tanker squadron at Kadena and now worked as the U-2 planner. I told him Big Army missile systems were shooting over us. His comeback was, "Well, we're a lot higher than you guys."

"They're shooting over *you* too, no pun intended."

Randy's eyes widened. He said the same thing Sergeant Gonzalez had: "What?!"

I showed him the two charts and held them up to the light. All of us learned a valuable lesson that night. MAAP cell had coordinated all our operations among the chest-beating egotistical air-breathing portion of the air campaign. None of us thought of talking with Big Army about how they prosecuted TSTs. When I told some MAAP cell folks that Army MLRS shot to thirty-two thousand feet and ATACMs up to 120,000 feet, everyone got really quiet.

My team opened four more anchor areas inside Iraqi airspace over the next week, each one coordinated with BCD before it went into the ACO. One sat in the center of Anbar Province and was named LEANN, after LeAnn Rimes; it allowed the Scud-hunting Guard and Reserve Vipers from Jordan to fill up on gas. A second anchor was located southwest of Al-Taqaddum and Al Asad Air Bases for F-15 Eagle CAPs; I named it FAITH, after Faith Hill, because you had to have a lot of faith in the Eagles to refuel forty miles south of both active Iraqi MiG airfields. The third anchor we opened near the Syrian border for strike aircraft supporting Task Force 20, a Special Operations group you will never hear of. TF 20's air support came via F-15Es and shore-based VF-154 Black Knight F-14A Tomcats at Al Udeid. TF 20's fighters refueled in an anchor near the border town of Al-Qa'im called MARTINA, after Martina McBride. Too many airplanes wanted to pack into SHANIA and REBA close to Baghdad, so we opened MILA east of REBA, named after Mila Mason. The Army moved their MLRS and ATACMs north of SHANIA and REBA a day later. If any tanker was shot at now, it was Saddam's guns and SAMs.

Two nights later, Gramps and I were commiserating about more SAFIRE events under SHANIA, REBA, and now LEANN. As we were reading through the SAFIRE event report rather loudly, Oatmeal, an A-10 pilot from the 190th Skullbanger Hawg unit at Boise, perked up. I saw his head rise in my peripheral vision five desks down. As I read another SAFIRE event aloud, Oatmeal stopped me mid-sentence.

"Sluggo, are those SAFIRE events under the Iraqi refueling areas?"

"Why, yes they are, my good friend Oatmeal! Tankers are being engaged almost every night now. Some of the tanker guys are pretty discouraged about going into these areas."

Oatmeal hollered at me, "Sluggo! Those are targets!"

He got up from his desk and walked toward me, holding a list of A-10 operating locations.

"What do you mean, Oatmeal?"

"Sluggo, tell all your tanker dudes and dudettes when they're getting shot at to dial in WHITE ONE, the Hawg VHF threat frequency, and call it in. Tell my Hawg bubbas the location of the piece firing at them off the Baghdad bull's-eye. Once we have their location, all the Hawgs will punch their lights out. These are the lucrative targets Hawg guys live for, Sluggo!"

"Sit down next to me here, Oatmeal . . ."

One mental checklist I learned at the KC-135 Employment School concerned the creation of new defensive tactics and procedures. I believe it was Mojo who taught us all this valuable lesson, that creating new tactics must follow a logical process. First, ask yourself what the objectives of the new tactic or process you are creating are. Second, figure out how you will know those objectives have been met; some measure of performance needs to be included. Third, are the new tactics or processes trainable? Can you teach the masses how to do it? Last—and most important—is the cure worse than the disease? There's no reason to teach and train new tactical procedures if it kills the crews trying to accomplish them in the airplane, or if they're so complicated that no one can understand them.

With these four steps in my mind, I asked Oatmeal to help me understand better ways to protect the tankers. He mentioned a group I hadn't thought of who could help protect us on the ground. The plan we worked out launched search-and-rescue alert A-10s from the austere base at Arar into the deserts of southern Iraq. If a pilot was shot down, the Joint Recovery Center would launch two Sandy Hawgs to go hunt for him or her. Oatmeal and I coordinated the Sandy Hawgs patrolling under SHANIA, REBA, MILA, and LEANN with the JRC. If Oatmeal's Hawgs needed to go cover the pickup of a downed pilot, one of the tankers would fill them back up on their way to search for the pilot and WSO or RIO. Sandy Hawgs roamed underneath the tankers twenty-four-seven, killing anything shooting through REBA, SHANIA, MILA, and LEANN. The new procedures gave Oatmeal's Hawgs an advantage too. Rescue forces would have a head start on searching for downed pilots when they were already airborne in Iraqi airspace. I assured Oatmeal that RESCAPing Sandy Hawgs would get all the gas they needed. I e-mailed every unit that night with the new procedures.

After Oatmeal had made a secure call to his Hawg counterparts at Arar, they devised a name for the area underneath SHANIA, REBA, MILA, and LEANN: the "Pig Pen," named after the Warthogs who were now hunting under the anchors. A-10 Warthogs roamed the Pig Pen, killing anything that moved. Based on Oatmeal's additional tip, I took a walk over to the Special Operations Liaison Element, or SOLE. I told the SOLE's commanding colonel about the tankers' guns and SAMs problem and asked if his operators running around underneath the refueling anchors looked for Saddam's air defense pieces firing at us in their spare time. The SOLE's staff all smiled at me—oh good, more things to shoot and kill. I also gave the colonel Oatmeal's WHITE ONE VHF threat frequency for immediate air support if Spec Ops needed their help.

The third method we implemented to sweep the Pig Pen concerned our receivers. Fighters came up in groups of two, while the second element loitered beneath the tankers looking for SAMs and guns with their infrared targeting pods or the moving-target indicator modes of their radar. When the first element had filled up, they would switch with the second behind the tanker. JSTARS began looking for SAMs and artillery pieces moving under the anchors with their long-range ground-mapping and moving-target indicator mode.

I authored special instructions changes for the next ATO distribution. The new tactics and procedures were pretty easy to understand, and asked tankers only to climb and get out of the Hawgs' and fighters' way. All the defense measures for protecting the tankers flying in the Iraqi anchors were implemented and sent out to the units. Everyone seemed happy with the new procedures, which needed only one small refinement to the process of climbing to the higher-block altitudes. Not one group complained about having to fly in Iraqi airspace after I told them about my conversation with General Moseley and related the story of the nineteen-year-old kids getting shot at. But the tankers remained unnerved by Saddam's SAMs shooting at them. None were happy when I told them about the possible blue-on-blue TOGA 33 had lived through. But the plan worked better than we could have imagined. Not one SAFIRE event crossed my desk after implementation. Two reports from the Spec Ops guys did, though.

Over the weekend, a Green Beret in the SOLE asked me to come see him. One of his Spec Ops teams out in the west deserts of Iraq doing strategic reconnaissance along the main highway looking for Scuds heard a vehicle approaching their position. A Russian-made SA-8 Gecko SAM system drove down the Amman-Baghdad Highway and pulled off right in front of them. One team member carried a British Javelin antitank missile on his back, perfect for blowing up mobile SAM vehicles. They had gotten word to find, fix, and finish any antiaircraft system they saw. The soldier took the Javelin off his back, sighted in the Gecko vehicle, and squeezed the trigger. The Javelin shot from the tube and began its ascent profile so as to come down on top of the vehicle. His teammates became alarmed as he started laughing and running toward the Gecko. He screamed back over his shoulder to his brothers, *"Take a picture when the missile hits! Take a picture when the missile hits!"*

Just as the Javelin impacted the vehicle, one of the soldier's teammates snapped a picture. The unshaven and unwashed man had a big smile on his face as Gecko parts flew through the air behind him. They uploaded this picture via satellite link and sent it to the SOLE to show the tanker community that Spec Ops had our back. I asked the SOLE to make copies of the picture or, better yet, to send it to me on a PowerPoint slide. I slipped the slide into my morning staff meeting brief. Later that night, another Spec Ops team found a French mobile SAM vehicle coming down a road. After shooting a thousand holes in the vehicle and flattening its tires, the team took a picture for the SOLE. Across the bottom, the team had written "SOF 2 / Iraqi SAMs 0." Everyone in the Air Mobility Division meeting laughed uproariously when the two slides went up on the screen. I told them that this should be a lesson for all of us. We needed to be joint warfighters. All of us needed to use all the resources available to solve the complex problems we faced every day. I also told them that the person they did not coordinate with was probably the person shooting at them. I told them the MLRS and ATACM story, and everyone's head went down as they scribbled in their notepads.

I sent a long e-mail to the KC-135 Employment School with our lessons learned for the week. In combat, just like in business, there are customers with whom we don't coordinate, and those actions affect revenue and the bottom line. Don't overlook resources that can help you accomplish your mission or solve a complex problem. Initially, my vision included only the fliers. We could not have survived some of these engagements, in my opinion, if we hadn't changed the way we operated. By the beginning of the war's second week, all Iraqi anchors were stacked high with tankers. Everyone became pretty comfortable with flying into the Iraqi anchors, and no additional SAFIRE events crossed my desk. Ground troops closed on the outskirts of Baghdad, but a typical Middle Eastern weather phenomenon was about to bring the war to a halt.

★ ★

LESSONS FROM THE COCKPIT: INNOVATION

All commanders on the battlefield or CEOs in boardrooms must deal with risk and resources. We were constantly asking what resources were available to reduce the risk to tanker operations. Tankers and refueling operations were never designed to go into enemy airspace. We had to create very innovative methods of protecting tankers while operating in the Pig Pen, something that had never been done before.

I learned from developing the Pig Pen procedures that innovative ideas needed to involve agencies I had never previ-

ously thought to coordinate with. Each one of those agencies—
Oatmeal the A-10 planner, Sergeant Gonzalez in the BCD—had
meaningful input that refined our innovative approach to protecting the tankers. Each of the fighter planners gave me good
gouge on how they employed their sensor systems to find, fix,
and finish antiaircraft guns and SAMs shooting up through the
Iraq anchors. Implementing these defensive procedures allowed
the fighters and bombers to remain above ground troops longer, protecting them while also fighting the enemy. My team's
quick, innovative approach to defending the tankers was new
and untested, like many innovations on the battlefield or in the
marketplace.

★ ★

20

The Jump into Bashur

2000 Wednesday 26 March 2003
Overhead Bashur Airfield
Erbil Province in northern Iraq

An organization's ability to learn, and translate that learning into action rapidly, is the ultimate competitive advantage.

—Jack Welch, former CEO of General Electric

First comes thought; then organization of that thought, into ideas and plans; then transformation of those plans into reality. The beginning, as you will observe, is in your imagination.

—Napoleon Hill, American self-help author

I was just beginning to stir at around eight o'clock in the morning when my roommate, Fred, walked in. Fred was a bodybuilder: big legs, big chest, big arms, and little head, just like in the muscle magazines. His call sign was Fred Head.

"Morning, Sluggo. You need to get out your sand gear."

"Why's that, Fred Head?"

"We're about to get a royal butt whooping from the weather. Another one of those shamals is coming through tonight and tomorrow."

"What does that mean to the air war, and how will it affect flying operations?"

"By tonight Prince Sultan's weather will be seventy-five-knot winds with blowing sand and dust. The worst thing about this storm is that it rains mud. The mud droplets feel like a thousand needles on exposed skin."

Dragging out an equipment bag from under my bed, I pulled out goggles, a scarf, and gloves. Later, as I walked up to my desk, Jerry asked if I had heard about the weather. He showed me the satellite picture of the low-pressure system moving across the Middle East.

Fortunately, Prince Sultan's runway 35 pointed northwest into the shamal. At least Prince Sultan could launch and land sorties. My plans team looked at every tanker base runway heading to see how the shamal would affect refueling operations. All the tanker base runways in the Saudi peninsula and Gulf Coast countries were within twenty degrees of the shamal's northwesterly winds. The only remaining problem was low visibility. Tankers could take off with a runway visual range of 1,200 feet on operational missions. The weather forecast stated runway visual range would probably be above the minimum. I felt the plans team needed to remind crews about adjusting their takeoff and landing speeds based on gusty winds.

The shamal was howling later in the evening. Thunderstorms crossed through the Persian Gulf, limiting carrier operations. Aircraft landing on the carriers had some really sporty wind conditions to deal with, plus low visibility because of the blowing sand and dust. Regardless, tankers launched from every base in this sandstorm to keep the pressure on Saddam's forces.

By the afternoon, I couldn't see the mess hall less than two hundred meters away when I stepped off the CAOC bus. Shamals were depicted very well in the movies *The Mummy* and *Hidalgo*. That wall of approaching sand in the film is what a shamal looks like—a wall of sand, followed by brownout. As I rode on the bus back to my room, I watched a KC-135 disappear after departing from Prince Sultan's single usable runway. Where the tankers would divert to remained a question in all our minds. Today was going to be a long two days.

Saddam's Republican Guard miscalculated the Coalition forces' capabilities on their playing field, and American forces struck hard in the sandstorm. Coalition Air Forces continued to support troops through the blowing sand and mud. Tankers launched and recovered from several bases throughout the Gulf Coast and the Saudi peninsula, but in smaller numbers because of the storm. Above six thousand feet visibility cleared out, except for a few thunderstorms. The US and RAF tankers stacked into refueling anchors in Iraqi airspace and refueled the fighters, bombers, and ISR aircraft supporting ground troops. But every takeoff and landing was dicey. When they made their preflight walks around their airplanes, tanker pilots would be stung by the flying mud, wondering all the while where they were going to land after the mission. Engine and pitot-static system covers were removed just before getting on the airplane. By the time the pilot had accomplished the exterior checks, all the engine inlets would be full of sand and mud again. The only place that was safe from the storm was inside the aircraft with the hatches closed. The big tankers bounced around a lot as they climbed away from the runways and as they landed. Shamal windstorms contained a lot of static electricity, and St. Elmo's Fire danced in purple waves of light across tanker windscreens in the mud-brown clouds. The tankers still had a good off-load day, around ten million pounds, but the second day of the storm required a bigger effort because we had caught Saddam's elite Republican Guard out in the open.

The shamal gave us an opportunity no one had expected. We knew Saddam and his leadership received most of their intelligence from the news networks, like CNN, Al Jazeera, and Al Arabiya. Several MAAP cell planners saw the windstorm as an opportunity to punch Saddam in the face. All the news networks were broadcasting shots of Army and Marine soldiers hunkering down in their foxholes, covering up to wait out the storm. This information led Saddam to believe that it was the perfect time to strike. A JSTARS reconnaissance aircraft tracking Iraqi movement with its long-range ground-mapping radar noticed a large convoy leaving Baghdad and heading south on Highway 8. Moving Target Indication systems in the Bone and Strike Eagle radars confirmed the convoy's southward movement. Many people gathered around the JSTARS ops desk on the CAOC floor that night, watching the data-linked ground-mapping radar picture on a computer screen. Hundreds of yellow triangles followed the convoy like lemmings down Highway 8. Special Forces teams on and around the highway sent their strategic reconnaissance information via radio. They positively identified Medina division vehicles as they moved south.

Infrared imagery and laser-guided bombs were useless in shamals. But JDAMs didn't care about blowing sand, dust, and mud. Once the target's latitude, longitude, and elevation filled the JDAM guidance brain, the bomb would go to whatever point on Earth's surface you told it to go. All strike aircraft attacking this column carried GPS-guided two-thousand-pound GBU-31 JDAMs. Heavy Strike Eagles and Bones pulled up to tankers in SHANIA, REBA, and LEANN for gas while they waited for target coordinates to show up in their weapons computers. One Strike Eagle four-ship carrying four two-thousand-pound JDAMs on each aircraft flew over the column of vehicles on Highway 8 and released weapons. In one pass, sixteen two-thousand-pound JDAMs destroyed or disabled approximately seventy tanks and vehicles. Satellite-guided JDAMs continued to rain down on the Republican Guard forces in this convoy moving down Highway 8 in the middle of the sandstorm. JDAMs decimated the division.

General Ra-ad al-Hamdani, the lieutenant general in charge of Baghdad's defense, would surrender later in the war. During his interview with Joint Forces Command interrogators, he spoke of this sandstorm bombing. He could not understand how the Americans were able to do it. Joint Forces Command interviewers showed him the JSTARS video from that night. General al-Hamdani stated that he had fought along the Golan Heights during the Six-Day War in 1967 and against the Americans in Desert Storm. He had never seen a display of firepower like the one he witnessed during the shamal. One brigade decreased from over 70 percent combat capability rate to around 12 percent, annihilated by bombs that did not care about wind speed or surface visibility.

The shamal's lingering effects were a concern for us as we planned for another big event in northern Iraq. When Turkey denied the US permission to move the 4th Infantry Division by ground through their territory, leaders at European Command tasked the 173rd Airborne Brigade to plan for an airdrop into northern Iraq. The 173rd was acting as a stabilizing force with the Joint Special Operations Task Force–North soldiers, who were already working with Peshmerga forces on the Kurdish side of the UN-mandated Green Line. Saddam then had the dilemma of fighting in the north and defending Baghdad in the south. CENTCOM chose Bashur Airfield, just southwest of Harir, Iraq, in Erbil Province, for the 173rd's airdrop zone. Bashur was the barest of bases. The airfield was nothing more than a seven-thousand-foot runway in a green grassy valley. There was nothing there—no running water, no electricity, no paved roads. There wasn't a single building on the airfield; it was just a runway capable of handling C-17 traffic.

But it was a vital airfield to the Coalition. Dropping nine hundred troops would fix six Iraqi Army divisions in a defensive position along Saddam's northern flank, so they couldn't interfere with the capture of Baghdad in the south. The shamal covered the airfield with blowing sand and mud, however. Before the 173rd could jump into Bashur, an airdrop support team needed twenty-four hours to set up and assess airfield conditions before a go/no-go decision could be made. Turkey denied the support team overflight permission night after night, until finally an MC-130 was given overfly approval; it left the SOF base in Constanta, Romania, and flew at a very low level to Bashur Airfield.

Italian prime minister Silvio Berlusconi provided crucial diplomatic support to the 173rd's airdrop, despite intense opposition to US efforts in Iraq. Fifteen C-17 Globemaster cargo planes delayed their arrival at Aviano Air Base in Italy because the diplomatic clearances took longer to obtain. The C-17s carried heavy equipment in the first five aircraft and 995 paratroops from the 173rd Airborne Brigade in the last ten. The 173rd's jump was the largest airdrop of men and material since the Normandy invasion in 1944.

The five different US military services involved in the airdrop continued coordinating their efforts as they waited for the shamal to pass and for country overflight permissions to resolve. The Special Operations team tasked with surveying the airfield and directing the fifteen C-17s from the ground couldn't parachute into Bashur in seventy-five-mile-per-hour winds, pushing the airdrop schedule to the right. Air Force AWACS, Special Tactics teams, and Navy carrier air wing fighters and jammers would need to cover the entry, airdrop, and exit from Bashur. After the drop, Special Forces teams would work around the airfield to secure it, and CIA operatives would work with local Iraqi Peshmerga fighters once the 173rd established its foothold in the north. Planning and coordination during the airdrop delay remained intense for two days. The night of 26 March became the new airdrop target date.

Refueling support from tankers at Akrotiri, Burgas, and Souda Bay had to deal with a critical fuel-consuming hitch. Turkish leaders refused the Mediterranean-based tankers passage on a jet route over Ankara to meet the fifteen C-17s in the Black Sea north of Istanbul. Because of Turkish restrictions on the unit from March Air Reserve Base at Souda Bay, their KC-135s' route of flight was twice as long, decreasing fuel transfer capability because of an Air Force regulation. March Reserve KC-135s would have to leave Souda Bay for Adana, Turkey, near Incirlik, flying through an ONW corridor already packed with Moose's Carrier Air Wing 8 and Cyrus's Carrier Air Wing 3 fighters. Once in the ROZ, the refueling formation would turn north to the Black Sea and then back toward Istanbul to meet with the Strategic Brigade Airdrop C-17s. Rendezvousing with the Globemasters, each tanker would transfer sixty thousand pounds into the cargo planes. The March Reserve tankers would then reverse route back across the Black Sea toward the ROZ and recovery at Souda Bay. The Globemasters also needed to refuel on the return flight to Aviano, so the process would happen twice.

March Reserve called my desk that stormy shamal night. Their mission planning cell chief wanted to talk about their support to the upcoming airdrop. All the tankers would be recovering below a restriction level called Island Destination Fuel.

"Sluggo, we need to talk about regulations and the Black Sea refueling track."

"I'm assuming this is not a bodily function issue requiring the liberal distribution of ex-lax to all players involved, correct?"

"That's correct. We are not dealing with a lot of bovine feces on this one. I'm just crunching some numbers for reserve gas. Due to the route of flight to the Black Sea, every one of my jets lands below Island Destination Fuel."

"How much are you landing with?"

"Each jet lands at around fifteen thousand pounds, when they should have about thirty-two thousand. Here's why I'm not concerned and request your permission to execute as planned: 26 March is a CAVU day here at Souda Bay. The shamal will not affect us in Crete. Winds are straight down the runway at ten knots. If we can get DIRMOBFOR permission to waive the Island Destination Requirement, my wing will fly the missions as planned."

"I'll tell you it's approved, but will let the DIRMOBFOR know. I know what General Nick and Ski will say."

Regulations required KC-135s to have an hour and a half of fuel left when recovering into an island destination like Souda Bay in Crete. The March Reserve KC-135s would be landing with half that. March's MPC chief was all go, though—the March Reserve unit would do whatever it took to support this historic airdrop. When it comes time to support the troops on the ground, under fire, tankers do everything they can to keep soldiers safe and accomplish the mission. I felt waiving Island Destination was a risk they could comfortably take.

The shamal finally cleared out, and the jump into Bashur was a go on 26 March. An AWACS orbiting in the ROZ transmitted its radar picture over datalink, and it was projected on the CAOC wall to show the fifteen-aircraft C-17 train crossing into the Black Sea. Standing behind the tanker ops desk talking with Cerb's team members, the five of us watched the tanker icons roll out in front of the C-17s north of Istanbul. Cerb, Struks, and two other tanker executors working on the floor call signs, LT and Jeff, remained busy with another 130 sorties throughout the night. As the cell formation of Akrotiri KC-135s passed over the CYRUS carrier rejoin point, radar icons representing Moose's fighters and jammers converged on the tankers as they moved toward Incirlik and the ONW corridor. Carrier Air Wing 8 planners in the Prince Sultan MAAP cell told me the aerial refueling was almost as scary as a nighttime arrested landing back aboard ship because of the terrible weather in Turkey. Navy pilots use two methods to try to find dark-gray KC-135s at night in bad weather. Tomcat and Hornet pilots first lock the tankers up on air-to-air radar and drive to them based on steering cues on a cockpit display. As they close in on the tankers, the pilots switch to night-vision goggles to continue searching visually. Anticollision lights are first visible about a mile behind the KC-135s, and the tankers' shapes at a quarter mile. Trailing drogues appear within a few hundred feet of the tankers. Rendezvous like these take more time, and time was a diminishing commodity with the C-17s turning the corner near Hopa, Turkey, and heading south toward the ROZ.

Departing from RAF Fairford in England, two KC-135s transferred eighty thousand pounds into two BUFFs above the North Sea. The B-52 flight path crossed Germany and turned southeast over the former Warsaw Pact countries of Poland, Slovakia, Hungary, Romania, and Bulgaria and continued into the Black Sea. An interesting thought for both BUFFs was that they were flying over areas considered targets for nuclear weapons only twenty years ago. KC-10s departed from Burgas, Bulgaria, to rendezvous with the BUFFs on the Black Sea refueling track, with the C-17 train about twenty minutes behind the bombers. The B-52 icons approached the ROZ as the Carrier Air Wing 8 Tomcats, Hornets, and Prowlers completed refueling in the MAC and VANER areas and fanned out over northern Iraq. Strike aircraft contacted ground-based forward air controllers, who began radioing targets for Moose's pilots and RIOs to bomb in the Bashur killbox.

Brigadier General Danny "Dagwood" Darnell stood up in the crow's nest above the CAOC floor. Speaking loud enough so everyone could hear him, he said, "Okay, everybody, listen up. We're about thirty minutes out from another big event. The Strategic Brigade Airdrop's progress projected on the CAOC wall shows the fifteen C-17s on their way south to Bashur. Fighters and jamming EA-6Bs off the *Roosevelt* join with two Fairford BUFFs in a few minutes and push south to destroy anything threatening the airdrop in the killboxes around the airfield. Let's all pay attention to details and stay on our toes for changes in the target area."

Whoever controlled the CAOC wall projectors zoomed in on the airfield as the C-17 train closed on Bashur. Predator video showed movement at the airport as forces on the ground prepared to receive the men and equipment. With only a couple of miles left to fly, the projector zoomed the AWACS picture in again so that it covered a circle of approximately ten miles in diameter from the airfield's center point. The Special Forces support team radioed the C-17 formation leader that the drop zone was clear and ready to receive equipment and troops. The first five C-17s dropped the heavy equipment on large pallets, rolling out off the ramp behind under parachutes at exactly 2200. Ten minutes

later, ten C-17s dropped 963 paratroopers into Bashur in fifty-eight seconds. A note to all our enemies: Let that sink in. The US can drop a
thousand soldiers on your country in under a minute.

As the C-17s passed over the airfield, the Hornets, Tomcats, Prowlers, and BUFFs circled nearby, some aircraft dropping JDAMs on targets called out by the JTACs. Tomcats, Hornets, and Prowlers cycled in
and out of MAC and VANER for gas. The BUFFs rotated in and out of
the POPS anchor, located south of Turkey's Lake Van.

Moose told me in a phone call two days later that he rolled his Tomcat LANTIRN targeting pod cursor over the C-17s as troops came out
the doors. He said it was surreal watching the parachutes descend with
his night-vision goggles and LANTIRN targeting pod imagery. He
watched the parachutes blossom and pull the heavy equipment out the
back of the first five C-17s and sink onto the airfield. Moose could clearly
see each jumper come out the aft aircraft doors, their chutes unfurling
and descending into the airport environment. One great thing about
the LANTIRN and the F-18 Nighthawk targeting pods is their recording function, and a few pilots sent targeting pod video to their planning
buds in the NALE, which of course made it into our nightly MAAP
cell's Greatest Hits over Baghdad review. Except for the terrible weather
in the refueling areas and having to plug into drogues using night-vision
goggles, Moose said it was a great night for naval aviation.

Five minutes after the paratroops landed in Bashur, the embedded
CNN reporter began broadcasting from the airfield. He jumped with
the airborne troops so he could cover the 173rd Airborne's war in northern Iraq firsthand. His show confirmed that the troops were on the airfield and spreading out to hunt down the six northern Iraqi divisions.
Air mobility operations continued at Bashur for the next few days until
the runway began breaking up. Refueling support for the C-17s continued over the next ninety-six hours as twelve C-17s landed at Bashur each
day. The Air Force moved an additional 1,260 soldiers and 381 pieces of
heavy equipment over those four days.

Once the weather cleared up in the ROZ, refueling went smoothly in MAC, VANER, and POPS. One EA-6B ripped off an MPRS pod drogue because it was on a different radio frequency and didn't hear the warning about the bad hose.

Combat forces deep in Iraq changed the support requirements, affecting the refueling of Moose and Cyrus's air wing fighters and jammers. Hooking up with tankers in MAC, VANER, and POPS was not effective, because the fuel-critical Hornets had to fly farther to fill up off KC-135s and KC-10s. Wayno realized that the refueling tankers had to move out of the ROZ and into Iraqi airspace. Moose and Cyrus's air wings were using gas they needed to stay on station to run back and forth to the ROZ tanker areas. Looking over a detailed map of northern Iraq, Wayno and his Carrier Air Wing 3 and Carrier Air Wing 8 planning counterparts felt that two refueling anchors located side by side north of Mosul would work well. Every refueling area established in Iraqi airspace had to go through a very intense threat analysis process, which included sending area coordinates to the CAOC JIC, the MSIC in the States, and AMC headquarters' Threat Working Group. The JIC, MSIC, and AMC assessed the Mosul refueling areas as yellow, meaning potential threats to tankers still existed in the southern portions of both areas. Wayno moved MAC and VANER, originally located in Turkey, south into Iraq. Carrier Air Wing 3 and Carrier Air Wing 8 aircraft still needed another refueling area farther south. We had to find a place somewhere behind the Kurdish Green Line closer to Baghdad but still in protected airspace. Navy fighters and jammers could work on Baghdad's outskirts if they could refuel south of Lake Dukan.

But where?

Shortney's planners in the NALE wanted an aerial refueling area in Sulaymaniyah Province. I had never heard of the place. When Shortney pointed at the town on a TPC, it shocked me that they wanted this area. The city of Sulaymaniyah was twenty-five miles from Iran. The Islamic Republic of Iran Air Force Base at Hamadan was only 170 miles away; it was the base that launched the low-level attack on Saddam's H-3 Complex. Hamadan was protected by an SA-5 SAM site, so a Sulaymaniyah refueling area would be just on the outer edge of the Gammon missiles' range. Iranian MiG-29 and F-4s patrolled along the Iraqi-Iranian border. I e-mailed MSIC for their opinion, and their analysis came back all yellow: the entire anchor was potentially under threat of Iraqi SAMs and antiaircraft guns, and possibly Iranian interceptors. The NALE continued to emphasize how important opening this area was to their operations. I gave Moose another call to get his opinion. Maybe he was getting intelligence on threats in this area that I wasn't seeing.

Moose told me not to worry about any threats to tankers in Sulaymaniyah. He assured me that his fighter pilots would defend the tankers to their deaths. I asked him what kind of activity he saw on the other side of the border. Iranian Air Force fighters were flying air patrols, but there was no interference with Coalition flights. He assured me how critical moving his strike aircraft into the Sulaymaniyah area was, because his Carrier Air Wing 8 Hornets needed the tankers to be closer. Once again, the tankers had to assume some of the risk. I asked Wayno that night to design an anchor somewhere southwest of Sulaymaniyah to refuel Navy fighters and RAF Fairford's B-52s. I told him to have it in the ACO the following night. Wayno called the Sulaymaniyah area VALLEY. Several antiaircraft pieces shot at tankers refueling in VALLEY and were killed immediately. One lucky tanker crew observed the night launch of an Ababeel ballistic missile targeting the 173rd Airborne's area. Cyrus's fighters attacked the launcher, blowing it to smithereens.

I wondered what the Iranians thought upon seeing big, lumbering gas-filled tankers flying along their border in VALLEY with Tomcats or Hornets or B-52s on their radar. Iranian early warning radar operators did warn Coalition aircraft that flew close to the border, but none of the Akrotiri or Burgas tanker situation reports ever mentioned being threatened in VALLEY. One tanker had a close call when the Mosul air defense commander fired an SA-2 at a tanker making a left turn at the northern end of VANER. The tanker crew reported that the missile passed behind them and exploded, far enough away to not do any damage. This SA-2 site stayed hidden for several days before Coalition intelligence found it. Navy fighters attacked the site days later, blowing up several launchers hidden in palm groves. To my knowledge, tankers were never fired at again after that SA-2 site was destroyed.

★ ★

LESSONS FROM THE COCKPIT: ORGANIZATION

The 173rd Airborne Brigade airdrop into Bashur taxed my organizational skills. Numerous agencies across Europe and the Middle East had to coordinate around delays in departures and time over the target in order to ensure all the airdrop lights were green at the door on the night of 26 March. Coordination for this one event required us to talk with agencies in England, Poland, the Czech Republic, Bulgaria, Turkey, and Italy, and with nongovernmental organizations in Iraq and Washington, DC. Restrictions on routes of flight and the shamal reducing visibility to zero kept changing the airdrop schedule. I regularly talked with tanker planners in Cyprus, Crete, and England to update timing for all aerial refueling events.

What I learned from the jump into Bashur was that interactive organizations and processes have the highest freedom of movement and can react more quickly and effectively to change. I heard a Fortune 500 company vice president talk about how stovepiped his corporate culture was. He talked about organizing financial and market plans through what he called the "Titanium Cylinders of Excellence." Working in a very interactive environment like the CAOC taught me how important organization is. My team coordinated efforts with agencies on three continents. Numerous organizations actively worked together to support the success of the 173rd Airborne in the largest airdrop since the Normandy invasion. At exactly 2200 Baghdad time on 26 March, Moose watched paratroopers exit through the C-17s' doors on his cockpit multifunction display. This successful airdrop opened another front of the war, and within a week, Iraqi Army desertion rates skyrocketed.

★ ★

21

Cyrus Crosses the Sinai

2230 Thursday 20 March 2003
Aboard the USS *Harry S. Truman*
North of Alexandria, Egypt

Of these capabilities, the Air Force provides a very singular form of power: the ability to rapidly position and sustain forces at places and times of our choosing. This pivotal capability—air mobility—is the essential ingredient for modern US expeditionary operations and supports joint force commanders' desired effects to deter, dissuade, or destroy the enemy.

—General T. Michael Moseley,
Enduring and Iraqi Freedom air campaign commander

All the planning and the thousands of actions that go on in war depend on faith and trust. No single commander can know all that needs to be known, can be everywhere to make every decision that needs to be made, or can direct every action that is taken.

—Lieutenant General Chuck Horner, Desert Storm air commander

The ancient Achaemenid Empire was larger than any previous empire in history. Encompassing 3.4 million square miles of the ancient Near East, it stretched from the Mediterranean Sea to the Indus

River. Under one ruler, the Achaemenid Empire grew larger, liberating thousands from captivity and rebuilding the Jewish temple. One of the most revered kings reigned for thirty-one years from a city now lying in ruins near Shiraz, Iran; his name appears twenty-three times in the Old Testament. In October 539 BC, Cyrus the Great entered the Babylonian town of Opis, twenty miles southeast of modern Baghdad, not as a conqueror but as a liberator from the tyrant King Nabonidus, who'd ruled Babylon for seventeen years. Cyrus's empire expanded to the Sinai and Egypt after his son Cambyses II defeated Pharaoh Psamtik III in 525 BC, who had been ruler of Egypt for only six months. Over 2,500 years later, the Bush Coalition brought forces to Mesopotamia and the palaces of Babylon to unseat a tyrant and thug, and the name Cyrus was again heard throughout the Middle East.

Four days before the start of Operation Iraqi Freedom, Shortney visited my team with an e-mail from the vice chief of naval operations. The message stated that if the USS *Theodore Roosevelt* and USS *Harry S. Truman* could not fight in the war, their orders would be to come home. As long as Turkey kept its airspace closed, Carrier Air Wings 3 and 8 had no place to go. Shortney felt that at some point the Turks would open up, but no one knew when. Planners for Carrier Air Wings 3 and 8 leaned over an operational navigation chart in the NALE, trying to create an approved route from the Mediterranean Sea to Iraq. The first course attempt passed over Israel, through Jordan, and into Saudi Arabia. They were told the Israeli route would never work. The next proposed route, crossing Jordan, a Coalition partner, into Saudi Arabia, was also denied. Finally, NALE planners created a path across the Sinai into Saudi Arabia and Iraq, which Egypt and Saudi Arabia agreed to. All of us wondered why the embassies hadn't just told us to take this route in the first place! Carrier Air Wing 3's commander was Captain Mark Vance, call sign Cyrus. In an odd historical parallel, Cyrus would cross the Sinai to attack targets in the former Babylonian capital, destroying airfields and palaces.

On Wednesday 19 March, Cyrus ran a Sinai crossing dry rehearsal. The refueling plan worked, for the most part, but it required a lot of faith and trust in Air Force and British tankers waiting in BART and WYBO. The Sinai crossing required three S-3 Vikings to refuel the Tomcats and Hornets halfway across the desert. Turning east at Aqaba, the fighters would then drive north and hook up on KC-135s and British VC-10s in BART or WYBO on their way to Iraq. Cyrus's Tomcats and Hornets hooked up five times before returning to the USS *Harry S. Truman* steaming near Alexandria, Egypt. The Navy had good reason to trust the tankers.

During the early days of Enduring Freedom's air campaign, Carrier Air Wing 8 strike lead Mongo flew with the newest F-18 lieutenant in the War Party squadron. Their group launched off the USS *Enterprise* to Afghanistan, refueling from their prestrike tanker orbiting in Pakistan. Arriving in the APOLLO anchor, Mongo and his wingman were numbers seven and eight in line for the single drogue, low on fuel and running out of time. The KC-135 pilot told Mongo that there was a Stratobladder near Herat without receivers. Exercising good faith and trusting the Air Force tanker aircrews, Mongo and his wingman left APOLLO for the Herat tanker. He knew that if it wasn't there, he and his wingman would run out of fuel. Leading by example, Mongo set off on a 370-mile trip across the Registan and Dasht-e Margo deserts in darkness, using night-vision goggles. Both were sucking seat cushion as they closed on Herat with fuel tanks near empty, hoping the KC-135 was there as the tanker pilot said it would be. Mongo acquired an eighty-mile radar lock on a single airplane turning east over Herat, and, driving closer, he saw it was a KC-135 through his night-vision goggles. The only question remaining was, did it have an Iron Maiden? On approaching the tanker, he saw the boom down and trailing a drogue. The best part about their rejoin was that there was plenty of gas and no other receivers. Mongo accepted greater risk during his mission based on the precedent Air Force tankers had created: we were always right where we were supposed to be.

The Saudi government granted permission to cross their territory on the morning of 20 March. With Egypt's permission to cross the Sinai, Cyrus's air wing entered the war. Cyrus and Moose's air wings were tasked to fill an eight-hour DCA air patrol station south of Baghdad. The Tomcats, Hornets, and Prowlers had to cover 960 miles to reach the CAP station. Just before official sunset, four S-3 Vikings launched from the USS *Harry S. Truman* ahead of two Swordsmen Tomcats and two Gunslinger Hornets armed with air-to-air weapons. The four fighters joined on the S-3s for fuel, and the eight aircraft turned south toward the Gulf of Aqaba. The Vikings refueled the Hornets and Prowlers until they reached a predetermined point halfway across the Sinai. The Vikings then turned north to recover back aboard the *Truman*. Cyrus's DCA package continued south across the Sinai desert at night on night-vision goggles. When they reached the Gulf of Aqaba, the package headed northeast for the BART refueling area. BONDO, the British AWACS, relayed to Cyrus that their tankers were orbiting in BART and ready to refuel. Plugging into a KC-135, the six aircraft filled their tanks and moved off to their patrol station over Nasiriyah. Just before they were to leave Nasiriyah for the tankers, BONDO told Cyrus the tankers would be an hour late. All the fighters would be out of gas by then. A British VC-10 listening on BONDO's frequency said he had enough gas for Cyrus's package of planes. As Cyrus's planes cycled on and off the VC-10 drogue, another large group of airplanes approached BART from the north. In a moment of confusion, two Tomcats, three Hornets, and an EA-6B Prowler joined on the VC-10's wings. A familiar voice asked over the radio, "Cyrus, is that you?"

Cyrus recognized the voice. "Moose, is that you?"

Moose and Mongo led Carrier Air Wing 8's air patrol through their eight-hour vulnerable period. Moose and his flight mates had completed the long transit to the patrol area with one difference: his six S-3 Vikings hadn't escorted the package across the Sinai. Instead, Moose had chosen to refuel above the *Roosevelt* before pushing south. His Hornets and Prowlers reached the VC-10 very low on gas.

"Cyrus, get off the drogues and let my guys plug in. We're all at Divert Fuel!"

Cyrus's aircraft moved off the drogue, and Moose's six aircraft plugged in before heading to the Nasiriyah patrol station. Cyrus plugged back in after Moose moved north and took on enough gas to cross the Sinai and rendezvous with his Vikings. All Carrier Air Wing 3 aircraft landed on the *Truman* after a seven-hour mission. The refueling plan had worked well but needed some minor adjustments before 21 March. That would be the opening night of Shock and Awe, and Carrier Air Wing 3's strike package would contain twenty-six airplanes.

On Friday 21 March, four Tomcats led the attack, loaded with JDAMs and air-to-air missiles. Twenty Carrier Air Wing 3 Hornets carried three two-thousand-pound JDAMs each, bound for Saddam's airfields and palaces. Two EA-6B Prowlers protected the twenty-four strikers with HARMs. On a long trip like this, Hornets are always the critical-fuel aircraft. Just like the night before, Cyrus's strike package followed six Vikings halfway across the Sinai desert, taking on gas.

As they approached a cell formation of KC-10s in BART, timing became an issue. Two new Marine Hornet pilots couldn't plug into the drogues quickly. To meet his scheduled timing, Cyrus left the young pilots for their targets at Al-Taqaddum and palaces throughout Baghdad. Both Hornets took on enough fuel to cross the Sinai a second time, and recovered safely back on the *Truman*. After striking all their targets, Cyrus's strike package returned to BART and took on gas for their own return to the *Truman*. All Carrier Air Wing 3 airplanes plugged into the KC-10s' drogues and headed south for Aqaba. Right on cue, six S-3 Vikings that had been holding halfway down the Sinai turned north in front of the group. The Hornets plugged in first, as the Tomcats and Prowlers had plenty of fuel to reach the *Truman*. Twenty F-18s took turns plugging into the Vikings' drogues for fuel and landed back on the *Truman* after a seven-hour flight.

On Saturday 22 March, Cyrus's and Moose's air wings performed the same Sinai crossing to their targets in Iraq. Cyrus's air wing bombed more airfields and military targets, while Moose's air wing attacked targets near Fallujah. In analyzing the effectiveness of every Sinai crossing, we determined the twenty-six aircraft required more tankers than Persian Gulf air wings and consumed a lot more gas. General Cichowski brought a spreadsheet to General Moseley showing how fuel inefficient the Sinai crossing had become. General Cichowski said that the tankers couldn't continue this for much longer. General Moseley, however, had a bit of information General Cichowski didn't have: he told Ski that by the next day the Turks would let the *Truman* and *Roosevelt* air wings cross through their airspace. None of us knew how General Moseley had found this out, but just as he had told us, the Turks opened their airspace, and the *Truman* and the *Roosevelt* turned northeast from Alexandria and headed for Adana, Turkey. Three refueling areas in the old ONW ROZ, called MAC, VANER, and POPS, opened that Sunday to support the *Roosevelt* and *Truman* air wings. Mongo told me he had never felt the *Roosevelt* shake like it did moving at flank speed toward Adana. And it rained during the entire move.

On Sunday 23 March, Cyrus's and Moose's schedules were canceled due to inclement weather covering the entire southeastern portion of Turkey. All missions scheduled for 24 March were also canceled as the shamal windstorm moved across Iraq. Moose related how he had refueled one night at thirty thousand feet through night-vision goggles because of thunderstorms in MAC and VANER refueling areas. He said it was the scariest aerial refueling event he had ever flown.

After the shamal blew through, the tanker desk called me to say the Burgas KC-10s were all delayed because of the weather. I couldn't understand why. Burgas's weather in March remained cold, and snowstorms off the Black Sea dumped several inches of snow on the aircraft.

I hadn't factored Burgas's closing due to snowstorms into my planning as I sat in hot Saudi Arabia. KC-10 engines required inspection after it snowed, and Burgas didn't have the proper high-lift equipment to sweep out the engines.

On Sunday 23 March, the 507th Maintenance Company mistakenly entered the city of Najaf. While the convoy was backing up, Saddam's fedayeen forces attacked. In the firefight, several of Private Jessica Lynch's comrades were killed before she was captured. Within half an hour of her capture, the fedayeen were celebrating on cell phones. Because of those calls, we discovered that they had executed some of Private Lynch's comrades. All of us were concerned about her condition, and we knew they had her—but where?

★ ★

LESSONS FROM THE COCKPIT: TRUST

Air Force tanker crews had developed a reputation for being on time and on point from years of refueling operations. The Refueling Control Team exerted significant effort to ensure that our receivers' tanker crews never lost their trust in our capability to refuel Coalition receivers whenever they needed gas. Because of our impeccable reputation, Navy flyers accepted a higher degree of risk. Mongo took off across the most inhospitable desert in Afghanistan at night because he had faith that the KC-135 was orbiting over Herat. When Cyrus and Moose crossed the Sinai with their large strike packages, my team monitored their scheduled tankers very closely. We knew the fighters would be low on fuel, and there was only one divert base close enough for recovery. I never wanted to get a phone call from Moose asking, "What happened with the tankers last night?"

I have often been asked to accomplish more because I was told: "We've seen your best work." Some of the best work my tanker team performed during Operation Iraqi Freedom was in developing the plan to make sure that Cyrus's Carrier Air Wing 3 and Moose's Carrier Air Wing 8 never worried about fuel. They had great faith and trust that our tankers would be there waiting. Except for that one instance, KC-135s, KC-10s, and VC-10s were always waiting with enough gas to refuel the large Navy strike packages. Tanker aircrews trusted that the Navy fighters would protect them from Iraqi air defenses after we moved a refueling area as far south as Sulaymaniyah. Moose told me that the tanker fleet didn't need to worry about Iraqi or Iranian fighters intercepting us in VALLEY, that they would protect us. Clients' faith and trust in your abilities take time to develop but are very quickly broken. In business opportunities with customers and partners, develop good relationships, so when they call with a problem, they'll trust that you will be there waiting with impeccable and innovative solutions.

★ ★

22

Killbox 88

0150 Wednesday 2 April 2003
Aboard KC-135R TITUS 55
In LEANNE Anchor
Anbar Province of Iraq

I believe luck is preparation meeting opportunity. If you hadn't been prepared when the opportunity came along, you wouldn't have been lucky.

—Oprah Winfrey, American actress,
talk show host, and philanthropist

Give me six hours to chop down a tree and I will spend the first four sharpening the axe.

—President Abraham Lincoln

Working with limited resources is an excellent way to hone skills that will serve you well for the rest of your career. You will prioritize profitability from the start.

—Jon Oringer, CEO of Shutterstock

The preponderance of the Republican Guard divisions outside of Baghdad are now dead. I find it interesting when folks say we're softening them up. We're not softening them up, we're killing them.

—Lieutenant General T. Michael Moseley

Saddam's information minister Muhammad Saeed al-Sahhaf, better known as Baghdad Bob, bused media crews throughout Baghdad. World media kept wondering when Coalition ground forces would enter the city. Baghdad Bob assured the media that Coalition ground forces would pay a terrible price for invading Iraq. His statement "We will welcome them with bullets and shoes" had us all wondering about Middle Eastern sandal weaponization. As US and British ground forces approached Baghdad's outskirts, Coalition leadership increased air attacks on Saddam's forces protecting the city. Increasing air strikes severely overtaxed aerial refueling activities across the board. There were not enough booms and drogues in the air to pass gas. Tanker Plans created additional refueling areas throughout Iraq as ground forces moved north. As we watched Army and Marine Blue Force Tracker icons close in on Baghdad, many of us were concerned about what the Special Republican Guard and fedayeen forces had planned for the Coalition as we entered Saddam's capital. Maximum use of airpower destroyed entire brigades defending the city. Baghdad had another name in our battlefield language: Killbox 88.

Killboxes are just what the name implies: three-dimensional boxes superimposed across Iraq in which aircraft are allowed to engage and kill targets without cumbersome and time-consuming coordination with commanders. Our killboxes were thirty-mile-square cubes subdivided into nine smaller areas, called keypads—like the numbers on your phone—defining zones and boundaries. A former Army attack helicopter pilot who had become an Air Force officer created a new procedure for use inside Iraqi Freedom killboxes, which we called Killbox Interdiction/Close Air Support, or KI/CAS, pronounced Kick Ass. Using killbox grids, strike aircraft searched for and brutally destroyed Iraqi ground forces, vehicles, and pop-up targets that threatened Coalition troops.

As April Fool's Day approached, it seemed that Iraq had nothing that could stop the Coalition from entering the city. The day after the shamal cleared out, Coalition attack aircraft caught Iraqi Army divisions in the open. Al Udeid's forty-eight F-15E Strike Eagles flew ninety-eight sorties in one day, carrying heavy loads of nine five-hundred-pound laser-guided bombs each. All ninety-eight sorties recovered back at Al Udeid "clean," having dropped 1,176 GBU-12s on military targets across Iraq. Dead Iraqi vehicles littered the highways south of Baghdad. Killboxes opened and closed depending on the situation, and attacking aircraft ran back and forth to tankers in SHANIA, REBA, and FAITH southwest of Al-Taqadum Air Base for gas, so KI/CAS aircraft could support Coalition ground troops longer. Coalition tankers averaged fifteen-million-pound off-loads every day as troops marched to Baghdad. But the airborne tanker fleet had reached its physical limits.

The tanker fleet was completely maxed out as US and British ground forces approached Killbox 88. We'd reached the 265 tanker sortie wall. Tanker Plans could not schedule more refueling sorties because we didn't have enough aircraft in the theater for more sorties. More important, the KC-135 in-theater fleet didn't have enough aircrews for more. Freddy's KC-135 crews at Prince Sultan double-turned, flying two sorties every time they came into work. Double-turning Strato-bladder crews flew two five-and-a-half-hour sorties, exceeding the flying time limit imposed by regulation. In the next twenty-five days, a third of tanker crews would not be able to fly missions. What concerned me the most was that there were no spare or strip alert tankers available to launch in emergencies. Reliability KC-10s weren't available to wait in SHANIA, REBA, or FAITH if Saddam and his sons' location was suddenly discovered and attack aircraft needed gas, as RAM 01 and RAM 02 had for the attack on Dora Farms.

Kuwait's Ahmed Al Jaber Air Base became Iraqi Freedom's version of Desert Storm's King Khalid Military City, a rearming and refueling stop close to targets on the battlefield. To fly more missions, Strike Eagles landed at an intermediate stop to hang more bombs and fill up with gas. Strike Eagle refueling and bomb-loading crews were flown to the

Jab to accomplish Integrated Combat Turns, or ICTs. Good ICT crews could rearm and refuel planes in less than fifteen minutes. Intelligence analysts would plug into an external intercom panel and update the aircrews on the positions of Saddam's army and follow-up targets. US and British ground forces found themselves on the outskirts of Baghdad in fourteen days, not the 126 days the Iraqi Freedom plan had postulated. Coalition ground forces were knocking on the door of Saddam's capital in two weeks.

The historical precedent for the ICTs at the Jab goes back to the 1967 Six-Day War. Arab leaders could not understand how the Israelis were flying so many sorties. Israeli Air Force ground crews were turning the jets around for their next missions in seven to eight minutes! I watched an F-15 ground crew ICT four Eagles in less than ten minutes. ICTs at the Jab increased the Strike Eagles' ability to cover troops with more sorties and took pressure off the airborne tankers. Hustle works both on the battlefield and in the business world.

After the invasion, AMC praised the new MPRS and KC-10 WARPs. An AMC study stated, "The KC-135's multipoint refueling system and the KC-10's wing air refueling pods were indispensable force multipliers in supporting Navy, Marine Corps, and Allied aircraft using the probe-and-drogue in-flight refueling system." MPRS and WARPs were great, but they weren't enough. The lack of drogues for carrier-based fighters and jammers operating from the three Persian Gulf carriers limited Navy attack sorties. S-3 Viking crews had to be exhausted from all the refueling missions and from striking targets near Basra. The *Lincoln*'s VFA-115 Eagles maintained four Super Hornets as tankers, configured "five wet" with four external fuel tanks on the wings and a buddy store hose and drogue pod on the center weapons pylon, refueling Navy fighters and jammers leaving the *Lincoln* for targets in Iraq. But the USS *Abraham Lincoln* had been out for almost ten months, and the USS *Nimitz* was approaching the Strait of Malacca to swap steaming stations with the *Lincoln* in the Persian Gulf. The *Nimitz*'s Carrier Air Wing 9 operated two F-18 Super Hornet squadrons: the VF-14 Tophatters, in single-seat F-18Es, and the VFA-41 Black Aces, flying two-seat F-18Fs. Shortney came down one afternoon in late March to ask for tanker help. The Navy needed two KC-135 sorties scheduled out of Diego Garcia.

Diego Garcia?

I asked Shortney why.

In order to bring more drogues to the region, two Tophatter and two Black Aces Super Hornets launched five wet for Diego Garcia and then the USS *Abraham Lincoln*, a 2,700-mile transit. Carrier Air Wing 9 Vikings and Super Hornets refueled the four aircraft to their very range limits, disconnecting and returning to the USS *Nimitz* as it continued steaming west. The four Super Hornets crossed the Indian Ocean with nothing but blue water surrounding them. If either jet had had an emergency, there were no divert airfields. A Diego Garcia–based KC-135 joined the four Super Hornets east of the island, filling them up for the last leg of their Indian Ocean crossing. All four Super Hornets launched the following day behind another Diego tanker for the Persian Gulf. After the last top-off over the Arabian Sea, just south of the Gulf of Oman, all four Super Hornets continued to the USS *Abraham Lincoln*. After they landed, their refueling equipment was downloaded and placed on other Super Hornets. Increasing the number of five wet Super Hornets to eight, our sophisticated new hose multipliers transferred fuel into *Lincoln*, *Constellation*, and *Independence* strike fighters heading into Iraq. Moving tanker refueling areas into Iraq placed Air Force and British tankers beyond the reach of the older F-18C Hornet. By getting some gas off the five wet Super Hornets, the F-18Cs could make it to SHANIA, REBA, and MILA to refuel again before going on to their targets. The amount of gas needed to attack targets in Baghdad, even with refueling areas all over Iraq, still had its limitations, and Navy fighters based in the Persian Gulf welcomed the help of these four new tankers. I welcomed it too, because the five wet Super Hornets still carried air-to-air missiles to defend US and British tankers.

Early in the afternoon of Monday 31 March, an Army Green Beret from the SOLE stopped by my desk. Green Berets didn't generally talk with the ARCT chief.

"Sluggo, can you join us down in the SOLE?"

"Sure, what's going on?"

"The colonel would like to see you for a few minutes."

Peaches gave me one of his "you're in trouble now" looks as I left the MAAP cell. The SOLE commander, an Air Force colonel, started the conversation.

"Sorry for the cloak-and-dagger, Sluggo. We're going to need tanker help tonight."

"Cloak-and-dagger is your business, sir. How can the ARCT assist the Special Ops world this evening?"

"We found Jessica Lynch. Task Force 20 folks rescue her tonight."

"Can I tell my team about this?"

"The fewer who know, the better, but a Predator will cover the hospital rescue, so the raid will be on the CAOC wall."

"Hospital, sir?"

"The fedayeen are holding her in Nasiriyah's hospital."

In the Battle of Nasiriyah on 23 March, Private Jessica Lynch and her 507th Maintenance Company comrades got lost in the city streets. Realizing his mistake, the company commander turned the convoy around, and it became bogged down in the process. Fedayeen soldiers attacked with such ferocity that they killed eleven of Private Lynch's 507th comrades instantly and captured another six. Fedayeen killed two of the six prisoners and separated Private Lynch, holding her as a prisoner. An Iraqi lawyer whose wife worked in the hospital tipped off Special Forces operators to Jessica's location, and the planning cycle started. Task Force 20's SEALs would assault the hospital where Private Lynch was being held, based on detailed information the lawyer had gathered by walking through the hospital with a hidden video camera.

The SOLE colonel just needed some gas for the fighters supporting the helicopters, call signs PRINCE 41 through 43, and a ground convoy driving up onto the hospital grounds. Trip, my Special Ops tanker planning counterpart at Masirah Air Base, managed AFSOC's tanker schedule and used a random low-altitude refueling area for the AC-130 gunship covering Task Force 20's raid. The Spec Ops operators were so good at what they did that we figured Jessica would be on the helo in minutes.

The raid would be executed at 1:00 a.m. on April Fool's Day, less than eight hours away. Once again, the tanker ops desk stole gas from lower-priority strike missions and gave it to the F-15Es supporting the raid. Two refueling anchor areas that had recently been introduced in Iraqi airspace lay close to Task Force 20's target in Najaf. Another new anchor area, PATSY, was established southeast of Nasiriyah, its northern edge almost touching the outskirts of town. Both MILA and PATSY had high and low refueling areas for every type of fighter or bomber aircraft to use, so it didn't matter whether Task Force 20's support was A-10 Hawgs or F-15E Strike Eagles—they would all have a place to fill up and be back at the hospital in minutes. Assuring the SOLE commander he would have plenty of raid gas, my tanker ops folks at the desk scheduled two KC-135s for each anchor during the hospital raid.

Predator infrared video projected onto the CAOC wall gave us a good look at the hospital's patterns of life, showing people going in and out, oblivious to the staring eye overhead. During our quick midnight changeover discussion, I filled Jerry in on what was about to happen in an hour. The tanker ops desk was always the best place to watch operations, so I walked downstairs and sat in an extra chair near the desk. Cerb handed me a tanker ATO, and I flipped through the pages to find which tankers were in MILA and PATSY. The CAOC director, Brigadier General Darnell, announced what was about to go down on the CAOC wall screen, and told us all to be on top of our game. Announcing significant approaching events was General Darnell's way of motivating folks to be sharp and to prepare for a piece of military history. As

Task Force 20's time on target approached, everyone anxiously watched the streaming video for the helicopters' arrival.

A few moments before the raid TOT, four 160th SOAR Little Bird gunships entered the Predator's field of view over the hospital. Task Force 20 planners expected fierce fighting, since the local fedayeen headquarters was in the hospital's basement, but nothing happened. Two Little Birds landed in front of the hospital, and Task Force 20 operators rushed through the doors, guns up. A convoy of vehicles approached the hospital shortly after PRINCE 41 had landed in the courtyard. There were some tense moments as we waited for the SEAL operators to reappear. After what seemed like hours but was only minutes, SEAL operators reappeared at the hospital doors carrying a stretcher with someone wrapped in a blanket. The soldiers confirmed by code word that Jessica Lynch was on the stretcher. Watching the soldiers leave the building and scamper toward the helicopter, all of us on the CAOC floor began cheering loudly as operators loaded Jessica onto PRINCE 41 and left for Tallil Air Base, where a small cargo plane waited to make a short flight to Kuwait.

Most of you cannot imagine our feelings watching this young lady's rescue after what we had learned about her treatment through the fedayeen bragging on their cell phones. Battle-hardened men and women on the CAOC floor had tears in their eyes as Task Force 20 soldiers ran toward the helo and loaded her on. We later found those fedayeen soldiers one night, talking on their cell phones planning the next day's battle. An F-14 dropped two GBU-16 one-thousand-pound laser-guided bombs on the building as it was laser-spotted by British SAS soldiers. Job satisfaction that morning was immense.

SAFIRE reports continued flowing to my desk on Wednesday 2 April, none involving tankers. As I told Jerry the refueling high points for Wednesday, I had an idea: "Jerry, I just had a thought. I need to go out and see how this aerial fueling system works for myself."

Picking up an ATO folder, I scanned down Wednesday morning's KC-135 launches out of Prince Sultan. One mission, call sign TITUS— the call sign of Freddy's KC-135 squadron—was leaving in fifty minutes. I picked up the phone and let Freddy know I would be hopping on TITUS 55's mission. Freddy said G-Love and Monique from my Astra squadron were stepping to the jet in about twenty minutes. G-Love's flight would be in LEANN over Anbar Province, refueling Guard and Reserve Vipers from Prince Hassan Air Base in Jordan that were performing counter-Scud ballistic missile missions. G-Love's sortie would be five and a half hours long. I could fly the mission and get a few hours' sleep before returning to work at noon the next day. Perfect.

G-Love and his crew were scheduled to transfer about ninety thousand pounds into two four-ships of Alabama and Colorado Guard F-16C+ Vipers. Some things never change: as we flew by, I saw that the town of Gassim still had its name in lights on a hillside, just as it did in Desert Storm. After checking in with LUGER, G-Love continued northwest down the main highway paralleling the Saudi-Iraqi border. As he chatted with Monique in the right seat, TCAS gave an aural warning to the crew. A computerized female voice exclaimed, "Climb! Climb now!"

The resolution advisory told G-Love and Monique to move the jet upward to avoid a collision. As we watched the TCAS display, we saw a red box squawking 3725 and a red 3 next to it pass beneath us, missing us by three hundred feet. All of us heard the engine noise of the four Strike Eagles passing by outside Monique's window, heading to their killboxes. G-Love had followed highway procedures to the letter, keeping all his lights full up, so we assumed they had seen us. I asked G-Love how often they had near misses like that. Most crews experienced at least one a night, G-Love said; how could anyone not run into something with so many planes packed into a small space? Tanker Plans needed to look at the highway system in northern Saudi Arabia that was separated from the Iraqi areas by a freeway everyone used. Midair collisions remained the Coalition's biggest air hazard, just as they had been in Desert Storm and Allied Force.

Twenty-five minutes had passed as we traveled east on the highway when BONDO, the British AWACS controlling the western Iraqi deserts, told G-Love that he had a clear picture to the north and approved us for entry into LEANN. Once we were inside LEANN, BONDO told us our first two receivers were just coming out of their killbox to the northwest. A great thing about TCAS is that it's a situational-awareness tool for rendezvous. One Viper mode 3 squawk showed up on the TCAS display at our ten o'clock position, and G-Love began a lazy left turn toward the receivers. Unplugging my headset from the jump seat interphone panel, I grabbed an oxygen bottle from the galley and headed for the boom pod. G-Love's boom operator had just raised the sighting window as I lay down on the couch beside him. As we rolled out into a southerly heading, the Alabama Guard Vipers approached us from below. TOXIC 41 carried two GBU-12 five-hundred-pound laser-guided bombs on the right wing and a GBU-31 two-thousand-pound JDAM penetrator on the left. Once our nozzle made the connection, the boom interphone system came alive.

"TOXIC, TITUS 55, boom interphone check, how do you read?"

"Read you loud and clear, Boom. How me?"

"Read you loud and clear also, sir. How much you need tonight?"

"Boom, my wingman and I could use six thousand pounds if possible."

"Six thousand pounds it is, sir. How are you guys doing tonight?"

"This counter-Scud patrol is the most boring thing we do; it's eye-watering. We patrol out here for hours on end and don't see very much. I go home with my weapons still on the wings almost every day. When we do find something, it's pretty spectacular when we drop on it, though."

"Well, sir, our gas station will be open for the next three hours. I guess we'll be talking to each other numerous times tonight."

"Glad you guys are here, because this sortie burns up the gas. Boom, Scud patrol is a great advertisement for Preparation H!"

TOXIC 41 had a pressure disconnect at 6,100 pounds and waved to us on a half-moon night as he moved to the right wing. The conversation with TOXIC 42 was similar to that of TOXIC 41: Scud patrol is boring, and thanks for the gas. Once both Vipers were full, they departed high off the right wing into the night.

Weird radio calls came over the background of comm one, the command and control frequency, shortly after TOXIC left. Had I just heard the word *eject*? Soon after we made another radio call to BONDO, an emergency locator beacon buzzed over the guard frequency, coming from an open parachute. A Prince Sultan KC-10 radioed BONDO that they had just witnessed a double ejection low and to their right. BLACK KNIGHT 104 had developed a fuel system feeding problem and tried to reach TAINT 61 in SHANIA for gas. Before he reached TAINT 61's drogue, his engines flamed out due to fuel starvation, and BLACK KNIGHT 104's pilot and RIO ejected.

TAINT 61's boom, a reservist with the Travis Air Force Base squadron, carried a personal night-vision monocle with him in the boom pod. He observed the bright flashing lights of the Tomcat approaching and both engines flaming out. His night-vision monocle washed out when both seats left the stricken Tomcat's cockpit. Once each parachute blossomed, the Tomcat crewmembers turned on their IR strobe lights as they descended. TAINT gave BONDO an approximate location of the crewmembers. Two of Oatmeal's search-and-rescue A-10s flying in the Pig Pen asked BONDO for radar vectors to any tanker. A tanker in REBA LOW filled both Hawgs up before they turned toward the survivors. Two Air Force HH-60 Pave Hawk helicopters launched on orders from the CAOC's Joint Recovery Center, and picked up BLACK KNIGHT 104's pilot and RIO a few hours later.

BONDO's airborne battle manager consistently handled multiple receivers coming to TAINT 61 in SHANIA as they covered the downed Tomcat crew and their pickup. The controller made it seem like it was just another long Red Flag exercise over the Nellis range. He kept track of everyone's gas, vectoring people to and from the tankers when needed, and gave the SANDY Hawgs radar vectors to the Tomcat crew's positions based on information from the downed crew's radios. Another BONDO battle manager continued orchestrating with fighter and attack aircraft as they came and went from western Iraq, hunting for Scuds, on the same radio frequency. You could feel the confidence in each radio call BONDO made. If I ever went down in enemy territory, I hoped BONDO orbited overhead to control my rescue.

Discussions of effectiveness versus efficiency abound during air campaigns, particularly when airborne fuel is in short supply. Most of us will pick effectiveness over efficiency any day of the week. Effectiveness comes at the cost of efficiency in almost every case. With no shortage of targets, the MAAP cell included B-1 bombers from Oman in each schedule, holding them south of Baghdad tasked for on-call attack, or XATK, missions. XATK Bones carried twenty-four precision-guided munitions in three internal bomb bays. They held south of Baghdad, waiting for emerging targets, many of them time-sensitive and requiring quick destruction. XATK Bones usually refueled in BART, REBA, or SHANIA, filling up and returning to their hold points to wait for more targets. A bomb truck holding for target attack is very effective but not very fuel-efficient, because Bones carry 265,000 pounds of fuel and consume twenty thousand pounds an hour. XATK Bones were scheduled to take eighty thousand pounds each time they hooked up to a tanker. On 7 April, XATK proved why planners always take effectiveness over efficiency when Coalition leaders got another bead on Saddam and his sons' location.

Intelligence had gotten another juicy piece of information that Saddam would be visiting an internal security building near one of his favorite shawarma restaurants in the Al Mansour district of Baghdad. A

Marine special reconnaissance team hidden along a road saw Saddam's entourage pass down the main street toward the restaurant area. A Bone on XATK refueling in WYBO received BONDO's instructions to head at maximum speed to target coordinates in Baghdad. SLADE 72's offensive systems operator punched in the coordinates and saw that the target was in the center of Baghdad. SLADE 72's crew was told, "This is the big one" over the command net. Minutes later SLADE 72 released four two-thousand-pound JDAMs on those coordinates, two buildings known to be offices for Saddam's secret security police. The effect of eight thousand pounds of high explosives was spectacular, with masonry flying through the air as the penetrators went off under the buildings, followed by the GBU-31s milliseconds later.

I was in the Battle Cab talking with Admiral Dave Nichols just before the Al Mansour strike happened. SLADE 72 got thirty thousand pounds of gas and raced at almost mach speed to the target coordinates BONDO had passed to them. General Moseley walked through the Battle Cab's glass doors minutes after the four bombs had destroyed the suspected buildings. Junior, an F-15E Strike Eagle WSO, kept track of the high-value targets the Coalition tried to find and kill. General Moseley inquired how SLADE 72's attack had gone down, and Junior explained in detail how the air strike had unfolded, and now we were just waiting for the Global Hawk to arrive over the target area to transmit video pictures of the hole. General Moseley stood in front of Junior, arms folded, as he listened to the play-by-play. General Moseley said only one thing: "Junior, tell me you didn't blow up the restaurant."

"Sir, the Bone dropped two JDAM penetrators and two JDAM fat boys on the building's coordinates. Eight thousand pounds of explosives went off milliseconds apart."

"Junior . . . tell me you didn't blow up the restaurant."

"Sir, I'm pretty sure the restaurant's gone."

"Dammit, Junior!"

All of us straightened up in our chairs. None of us had ever seen General Moseley like this. He was as mad as when the Patriot had shot down the Navy Hornet pilot. Or so we thought.

"Junior, are you telling me you just blew up one of Saddam's favorite restaurants?"

"Sir, the Global Hawk will be overhead pretty soon, and then we'll know. But I'm pretty sure the restaurant is in the same hole as the internal security buildings."

"Junior, you just blew up the best chicken shawarma place in Baghdad! Where am I going to go when we take over Saddam's palaces to get chicken shawarma?" he said, smiling.

All of us saw the color beginning to return to Junior's face. Just to make sure, Junior asked General Moseley if he was in trouble, and General Moseley assured him he wasn't. But the Restaurant Strike made all the news channels for all the wrong reasons. Because we had been through this before, we waited to see if Saddam's body came from the rubble. The next day Al Jazeera broadcast video of him and his two sons mingling with the people somewhere in Baghdad. Saddam got up on top of a car and began his signature right-hand waving motion. He wasn't dead. And we had been so sure he and his sons were in the building.

Years later, driving onto Kirtland Air Force Base, I noticed a familiar name listed as the air base commander. I drove straight to the headquarters building and walked through the double glass doors. Standing in front of the secretary's desk, I asked her if Colonel Somminsby was in his office. A voice from inside the commander's office hollered who was asking.

I yelled, "Junior, tell me you didn't blow up the restaurant!"

I could hear Colonel Somminsby rising out of his chair and laughing. Approaching his office door, he said there were only a handful of people who knew that story. Turning the corner around his secretary's desk, he saw me standing there and just blurted out my call sign. "Sluggo!"

Everyone in headquarters wanted to hear this one. Junior recited the story of how he had participated in the destruction of Saddam's favorite shawarma restaurant. Who could believe such a tale unless told by the person involved?

Late in the evening of 7 April, LUGER vectored a KC-135 north of Baghdad, instructing it to hold in an east-west orbit south of a place no tanker had gone before. After landing, they explained to their squadron commander where they had been. Rubber gave me a phone call and e-mailed their ground track, which he had downloaded from the plane's flight management system. It showed TOGA 45 leaving SHANIA and heading straight north, skirting Baghdad's western city limits and making a slight right turn toward Tikrit. When the aircraft commander asked his nav what lights he was looking down upon from his cockpit window, she told him sharply that it was Tikrit. The pilot had a *Where's Waldo* moment and realized from his *Where in the World Is Carmen Sandiego?* knowledge that they were north of Baghdad near Saddam's hometown. Weasels and Strike Eagles rotated on and off TOGA 45's boom for forty minutes. Two Weasels remained on TOGA 45's wing until they returned south of Baghdad. TOGA 45 flew right over Killbox 88 on the outskirts of Baghdad without an air defense shot being fired at them.

I assured Rubber that my team had nothing to do with TOGA 45's northern Tikrit excursion. We didn't even have an area up there. "TOGA 45's venture north must be LUGER," I said, trying to calm him down. I walked down to the CAOC floor, but none of my ops desk folks knew that a tanker had orbited near Tikrit. The AWACS ops desk told me LUGER had vectored TOGA 45 north without telling them why. I was frustrated, because the AWACS ops desk was twenty feet away from Cerb and his night crew. I mentioned that they had flown through the heart of the Super MEZ, and asked that they please tell my ops folks the next time they wanted to do something like this. But LUGER had a good reason for sending TOGA north. During an attack on a target near Tikrit, a Strike Eagle hit the ground, killing the pilot and WSO. The remaining three Strike Eagles and four Viper Weasels rotated on and off TOGA 45's boom, protecting the KC-135 as they searched for the downed crew. All intelligence briefs the next day depicted the Super MEZ as completely green; Baghdad was no longer a threat to air operations.

Classic.

Intel analysts felt that if a tanker could lumber through the Super MEZ and Killbox 88 unscathed, then it wasn't a threat anymore. General Moseley hopped on his C-21 to Sheik Isa a few days later and pinned Distinguished Flying Crosses on TOGA 45's entire crew. Army Rangers found the crash site after the war, recovering both bodies, which were still strapped into their ejection seats.

Colonel David Perkins's Thunder Runs into objectives Woody East and West were so successful that it shocked all of us. We watched the tanks and Bradleys run down the highway toward the palace on Blue Force Tracker. Numerous tankers orbited in REBA, SHANIA, MILA, and PATSY and had a constant flow of fighters and bombers cycling on and off booms and drogues. Baghdad Bob showed up on cable news, screeching from a rooftop to a large number of media groups that there were no American troops in Baghdad. A couple of us walked out of the MAAP cell and went downstairs to the BCD for a quick look at what Blue Force Tracker showed. A blue line of M1 tanks and Bradley Fighting Vehicles were turning into Baghdad at Objective Mo, the spaghetti-like highway interchange just west of Saddam's palaces. The tank and Bradley icons began rolling down the main street toward Saddam's palace and parade grounds at Objective Mo. They didn't do this unopposed; numerous defenders were firing down on the Abrams and Bradleys moving into the heart of Baghdad. Fighters, bombers, and attack aircraft cycled off tankers as fast as possible, racing to cover Colonel Perkins's armored thrust into Baghdad. None of the Iraqis believed American forces were in the city because Baghdad Bob kept screaming to everyone that "There are no American forces in Baghdad. I will show you in ten minutes." Someone in the 64th Armored Regiment must have picked up on this news broadcast somehow, because an embedded Fox News reporter set up his camera equipment and interviewed M1 tanker crewmen on Saddam's parade grounds near the palace complex. These images from Fox News were broadcast all around the world. Baghdad Bob disappeared after that broadcast from the parade grounds.

Troops from the I Marine Expeditionary Force approached Firdos Square and the massive statue of Saddam Hussein in its center. A Marine Tank Recovery Vehicle backed up to the statue and threw cables around it.

I wondered what the best place to watch this would be, and decided that the best place to watch the fall of Baghdad was in General Bahadur's office. I poked my head inside to see him standing in front of his large flat-screen TV, which was broadcasting the Marines' attempts to pull down Saddam's statue. Both of us stood shoulder to shoulder and watched the Marines slip cables around the neck of Saddam and the Tank Recovery Vehicle move forward. The figure began bending at its feet while a Marine climbed the Tank Recovery Vehicle's forks with an American flag. Both of us cringed as he unfolded the flag and draped it over Saddam's head. Someone in his leadership must have given the Marine a big clue, because a few minutes later someone tossed an Iraqi flag up to him. He covered Saddam's head with that flag instead.

I momentarily looked over at General Bahadur standing next to me. Hundreds of Iraqi citizens begin swarming into Firdos Square, clutching a shoe or a sandal in one hand. The Tank Recovery Vehicle inched forward, and the statue toppled over. With one final push on the gas pedal, Saddam's statue detached from its base and crashed to the concrete. The camera crew zoomed in on Baghdad's population striking the metal statue with the bottom of the shoes and sandals they had brought. General Bahadur just watched intently. Finally I couldn't stand it any longer and asked him what he thought.

"Sluggo, the combined efforts of all the Arab nations could not do what you just did in twenty-three days."

I understood what he was saying. Many of his countrymen and Arabs throughout the region looked upon us as the Great Satan. I do not believe he felt we were the Great Satan. I had spent too much time with him to think otherwise. But everyone in the region understood that American military force applied effectively and efficiently was the greatest killing force on the face of the planet. He went on to say, "It's a good thing he and his sons are gone. They were a threat to everyone in the region. Hopefully, now things will stabilize, and the Iraqi people can enjoy the same freedoms you do, Sluggo, in the United States."

The question everybody asked now was, where were Saddam and his sons? Somehow, they had escaped the cordon around Baghdad and were now hiding somewhere in Iraq. Many believed he had returned to his familial home in Tikrit. Coalition forces continued focusing on the capture of Saddam and his sons, and anyone else in the deck of cards most of us carried in our pockets. The air campaign wound down, and it was time to start sending folks home. My team now had to create a redeployment plan for sending the tanker fleet back to bases across the US.

I was on one of the first planes to leave Price Sultan for home.

★ ★

LESSONS FROM THE COCKPIT: RELATIONSHIPS

I feel it's appropriate to discuss my last lesson from the cockpit by relating some observations about our Coalition partners and relationships. Throughout my career, I've met and worked with some of the finest international partners in extreme battlefield situations. Every one of them was extremely professional and willing to work with us to solve complex issues. I was frustrated during Anaconda that the only tanker the French Étendards could refuel from was a KC-10. KC-10s were at a premium in Anaconda. I sensed one day that the French Navy captain planning the *Charles de Gaulle* missions also felt my frustration. After the French Étendards' first successful mission, both the captain and the Air Force lieutenant general offered me their thanks for making French naval aviation history. Anaconda was the first time Étendards dropped bombs in Afghanistan. The captain from the *Charles de Gaulle* sent me a baseball cap from his carrier, compliments of the French Navy; the captain had found out that I collected ship ball caps. I've flown on RAF VC-10 tankers and ridden in the back of a NATO AWACS. All the Coalition personnel I've worked closely with have shown the utmost professionalism and offered support for many of the humanitarian relief efforts and combat operations American forces are involved with around the world. I've never been disappointed working with our allied friends and partners.

Captain Moose Laukaitis made a fascinating observation when I was talking with him on the phone, gathering his recollections on Anaconda and the Sinai crossing. He noted how all of us had had long relationships before working through the problems in Shock and Awe. Moose and I had worked together during Anaconda and knew each other's capabilities. I had met Admiral Bill Gortney aboard the USS *John F. Kennedy* when he approved my golden opportunity to fly in one of his S-3 Vikings. Our relationship continued when he ran the NALE during Shock and Awe. Trigger was a Navy strike lead and MAAP cell planner during Operation Iraqi Freedom. He and his wife, T, were our next-door neighbors at Kadena Air Base in the 1990s. As I talked with Wybo on the phone recently, now a successful lawyer in Spokane, he made a comment about "Water Cooler Relationships"; relationships fostered around the water cooler are usually your go-to people in bad situations. They are the first ones you call, which he did on 9/11. Wybo was invaluable to my CAOC planning team because he had a knack for seeing problems before they festered and would approach me with a solution ready to go. General Nick Williams asked me when I built my organization to put names in every slot. I got every name from my water cooler list but one. I chose people I had long relationships with from working in two CAOCs or who were graduates of the KC-135 Weapons School. You always go with the people you've developed relationships with in a crisis because they are a known quantity—you know how they'll react under pressure. Successful businessmen and businesswomen always surround themselves with people they know can get the job done when the floodgates open and others are running for higher ground.

★ ★

Epilogue

1645 Wednesday 23 November 2016

Marine Corps Base Camp Pendleton

Oceanside, California

Your big opportunity may be right where you are now.

—Napoleon Hill, American self-help author

When one man, for whatever reason, has the opportunity to lead an extraordinary life, he has no right to keep it to himself.

—Jacques Cousteau, French Navy officer, explorer,

and inventor of the Aqua-Lung

When I walked back into the MAAP cell, Peaches said Shortney wanted to see me. As I approached the NALE, I could see Shortney standing over two Navy planners at a computer screen. I asked what he needed.

"Sluggo, I just wanted to show you something."

He opened an Excel spreadsheet on the screen. It contained all the Navy air refueling numbers. Shortney and a couple of his staff members had gone through their historical data and compiled the amount of gas naval aviation took from Air Force tankers through the war.

"Look at this, Sluggo. The number you gave me from the Air Force

Studies and Analysis Agency and the number my staff guys came up with are within two hundred thousand pounds and some change of each other."

When talking hundreds of millions of pounds, a few hundred thousand is spitting in the ocean. Navy leadership in Washington, DC, had complained on numerous occasions that the carrier air wings were not getting their share of Air Force tanker gas. My team assured the Navy that, in fact, they were getting more, based on the number of F-18 Hornets deployed in the region. I was relieved that Shortney's number and that of the Air Force Studies and Analysis Agency were so close together. Shortney showed me a brief he had prepared for Vice Admiral Fallon, vice chief of naval operations. It had a number of bullet points on a refueling slide stating that the Navy had received just as much Air Force tanker love as everybody else, and in the case of the Hornets, more than all the Global Power bombers, ISR aircraft, and airlift aircraft combined.

While Shortney was discussing Admiral Fallon's PowerPoint slide, General Moseley walked by on his way to his office. He asked, "Sluggo, do you have a few minutes to see me now?"

We walked to his office, a few short steps from Shortney's NALE. Standing behind his desk, General Moseley opened the top drawer. Two stacks of military coins sat along the forward edge. He picked up two of them and held them in his open right hand.

"Sluggo, I just wanted to tell you that your team has performed magnificently. There is no way we could have done this war without you and your team. Tanker performance is a direct reflection on your team and its leadership. You had some very hard and complex problems to solve, and I could always count on your team to pull through. I never worried about tankers."

General Moseley had written in the air campaign Special Instructions that "fuel is my most precious commodity. We cannot afford to squander or misuse fuel because of the direct effect it will have on mission success." He reached out his right hand, the two coins wedged between his index and pinky fingers. I accepted the coins and shook his hand as he said to me, "If there is anything you ever need, don't hesitate to call me. When do you leave?"

"I leave with Freddy on one of his three tankers tomorrow morning. We stop at Lajes overnight, and then continue on to Spokane the next day. My report date to Norfolk is 1 June, so my family will be busy packing up the house and moving across the country."

Hopping on Freddy's tanker for Fairchild Air Force Base on 16 April seemed anticlimactic. All three jets just flew to Lajes and on to Spokane, like any airliner would. Freddy's jet wasn't tied to any CORONET move. All three crews sat around a long table at a good steak place that night in the Azores. I ordered the biggest piece of meat on the menu. Thank you, taxpayers, for a wonderful postwar steak dinner in Lajes. Flying north the next day, all three tankers crossed over Reykjavik, Iceland, and the southern tip of Greenland, then crossed Hudson Bay. I told the copilot to dial 15350 in the HF radio to see who would come up. Sure enough, a Canadian HAM radio operator answered, asking how he could help. I gave him my home number. After three rings, Val answered the phone—and a big lump formed in my throat.

"Hi, hon, I'm on my way home. How are you and the kids?"

"Where are you calling from? This sounds . . . scratchy."

"Before you say anything, remember that anyone on headset can hear you. I'm thirty-four thousand feet over Hudson Bay, talking through an HF phone patch. The Canadian HAM radio operator can hear you too. According to the flight management system, we'll arrive at about 3:35 this afternoon."

I'll omit Valerie's risqué comment.

Now everybody wanted an HF phone patch. Our Canadian HAM radio host remained very accommodating. Thank you, sir, whoever you are, for your expertise and for raising the morale of American troops returning home. When we landed at Fairchild, we were told to stay in a big group for the television news media.

After five deployments since 9/11 . . . nope, that wasn't happening.

Valerie and the kids stood to the left of the madding crowd holding up "Welcome Home" and "Hi, Dad!" signs. I didn't need a sign. As I walked directly toward Val, she and the kids couldn't stand it anymore and stepped over the yellow "DO NOT CROSS" tape and ran to me. These reunions are very emotional when you've been gone a long time. I hugged and kissed Val, saying, "Do I have a lot of stories to tell you."

The kids wouldn't let me go, afraid I would be home for only a short time and then have to leave again. During the drive to Spokane's South Hill, I told them we were moving to the beach, and Dad would be home every night. My last KC-135 flight took place on 20 May 2003.

I have not flown an airplane since.

As the Bible says, a hundredth part of what happened cannot be written in this book. There just isn't room for every story in and out of the cockpit. Looking back from the vantage point of fourteen years since my last flight, and six years in the corporate world, these lessons from the cockpit helped me survive the Goliaths of the boardroom and everyday life. I joked with my boss that I'd gone as far in engineering as my political science degree allowed, operating far outside my comfort zone. But I learned a lot and had terrific job satisfaction engineering airplane cockpits. I knew from working these cockpit projects that soccer moms and CEOs could learn from my military experience and these lessons, so I wrote *Tanker Pilot*.

My military experience and these lessons also helped me navigate the bumpy times of post-military life. Faith, joy, and relationships kept me going through my family's most painful trial. In 2009, we learned our fifteen-year-old son had contracted osteosarcoma, a form of bone cancer. Two days after surgery, Jeff moved only a few feet from his bed to a chair, but he moved. He was back on his skateboard seven days later, a testament to his faith and motivation. Many days I had to have faith that God meant him to live and look the other way as Jeff zoomed through the seven-story hospital parking garage on his skateboard, with only one arm. We found joy in the compassion that friends and family showered on him to lift his spirits after learning he was terminally ill. The miracles of friends opening doors from long relationships helped us cope with his death in August 2010.

Our greatest failures open doors to success if we recognize the vector check and pick ourselves up. I couldn't function after Jeff died, and was laid off in 2014. I soon realized being laid off was another open door, and walking through it, I began writing *Tanker Pilot*. It was a frightening open door at first. Some days I questioned my decision but *did the work*. I spent many days and nights in a university library, following a vision that friends and family thought I'd never complete. My new career as a writer began from resilience learned on the battlefield and following a passion for storytelling.

I'm watching the sun set late on Wednesday afternoon, writing the last few words of this book on my KC-135 career. As I sit on our patio at Camp Pendleton's Pacific Views Lodge, a United Airlines 777 passes overhead, leaving Los Angeles International Airport on the OSHNN SIX departure, the air traffic control procedure moving airplanes safely out of Los Angeles's airspace. Since I was a kid standing on Grandpa Andy's hood at the end of runway 26, I wanted to be a pilot and fly 707s. For twenty-four and a half years, my office was a KC-135 cockpit. Traveling all over the globe, I saw cool places, ate fantastic food, met great people, and took a lot of pictures.

No tanker pilot forgets the exhilaration of a heavyweight KC-135R model takeoff, the whine of four CFM56 engines in your ears. Light Grays carrying Slammers and Heaters looking for MiGs; Vipers and Prowlers armed with HARMs protect the strike force from SAMs;

Dark Grays and Tomcats loaded wall-to-wall with GBU-12s and GBU-31 JDAMs hang out in the observation position off my wings; all aircraft are cycling on and off the boom and the drogue as I lean over the cockpit fuel panel and activate fuel pump switches.

Nobody kicks ass without tanker gas.

Nobody!

Acknowledgments

Many people helped put this book together and kept it on track. First, I owe a debt of gratitude to Rush Limbaugh, who has encouraged me throughout this project to keep moving forward and who put me in contact with the right people. He and his wife, Kathryn, have been ministering angels through some very tough times in my family's life.

This book started around Colonel Geno Redmon's (ret) backyard fire pit. As my Young Tiger Squadron commander and mentor, Geno offered his advice on every story, and they are much better for it. Geno was the TACC vice commander at Scott Air Force Base in Illinois during Anaconda and Shock and Awe. I'm so glad whenever I picked up the phone, Geno's voice was on the other end.

Major General Nick Williams (ret), my boss and director of mobility forces, read through each story in the Iraqi Freedom chapters and offered his insights into mobility operations as the senior leader of AMC's operations in the region.

Lieutenant General Kurt Cichowski (ret) became a most trusted mentor after we met during Exercise Internal Look 2003. Ski was the Iraqi Freedom deputy DIRMOBFOR and sent me a number of Power-Point briefings he gave on mobility operations to senior leaders after the war.

Admiral Mark "Cyrus" Vance (ret) gave me his valuable time while

I wrote the Iraqi Freedom chapters. Cyrus's insights on Iraqi Freedom's North War as a customer were invaluable and are why a chapter bears his name.

Navy Captain Steve "Moose" Laukaitis (ret) and I met right before Operation Anaconda started. He has been gracious enough to read through the stories bearing his name and to give me vector checks on events in the two intense operations he and I were involved in.

Navy Captain Mike "Trigger" Saunders (ret) and I have known each other since his exchange tour with the Dirty Dozen F-15 squadron at Kadena Air Base in the early 1990s. Trigger was one of Cyrus's Iraqi Freedom strike leads and gave me one of his mission briefing books over tacos in Orlando. I used the book to re-create many of the refueling missions in the North War.

Navy Captain Dave "Mongo" Koss was Moose's strike lead on the USS *Theodore Roosevelt* in Iraqi Freedom. Mongo spent numerous hours with me on the phone and e-mailed tidbits to capture his Carrier Air Wing 8 missions over both Afghanistan and Iraq flying F-18 Hornets in VFA-87 War Party.

Colonel George "John Boy" Walton's (ret) story appears as the first chapter for a reason. It was my crew's first combat mission. John Boy spent many hours on the phone helping me capture the Desert Storm Wild Weasel story and used his lineup card, stored in his attic for twenty-five years, to re-create Drinks for PooBah's Party.

Colonel Doug "Disco" Dildy (ret) gave me advice and thrust vectors based on his journey through the publishing world. Disco spent hours mentoring me via e-mail and phone calls on how to focus the stories for a bigger audience.

Lieutenant Colonel Stu Pugh (ret) spent hours informing me how he ran the King Khalid International Airport MPC and planned tanker missions during Desert Storm. In Iraqi Freedom, it was Stu's group at the Air Force Studies and Analysis Agency that helped refine our refueling plans, making the tanker fleet almost as efficient as it was effective.

Major Dave Mason (ret) has been a motivating force throughout the writing of the manuscript. Dave spent numerous hours fine-tuning the stories while flying around the world as a United Airlines 767 captain.

Lieutenant Commander Dave "Hey Joe" Parsons (ret) escorted me during my first USS *John F. Kennedy* tour. Hey Joe offered his expertise while I navigated through writing this manuscript. A number of Hey Joe's pictures appear in the sixteen pages of photos, a testament to his photography skills.

Hey Joe introduced me to Peter Chilelli, who took time and exercised a lot of patience in reviewing pictures and restoring some of the twenty-five-year-old 35mm color negatives and slides to something usable. Peter's artwork can be found at peter-chilelli.pixels.com.

I spent many hours with my father, Robert Hasara, sitting in the carport and recounting all the stories you see here and many more that did not make it into *Tanker Pilot*'s pages. My dad has been my motivator, mentor, and cheerleader for this project ever since it was just a spark in my imagination.

My good friend Joe Medolo has called me every Thursday night for a decade to discuss stories and talk about what's happening in the plastic model airplane world, my "Weekly New Hampshire Morale Call." Thanks, Joe, for keeping me centered.

My wife, Valerie, is the reason this book takes combat experiences and finds motivational or moral lessons for success in them. I rewrote chapters to broaden the audience for *Tanker Pilot* by making each story applicable to everyday life.

Numerous others have been "Beta Readers" and given advice on how to improve my writing style and the *Tanker Pilot* stories. I thank all of you I haven't mentioned specifically for helping with this project.

Lastly, I raise a toast to the Initial Cadre and graduates of the 509th Weapons School, the tanker center of excellence, located at Fairchild Air Force Base in Washington State. In the post-9/11 world, the school's graduates' worth cannot be measured. Desert Storm and Allied Force refueling operations did not benefit from refueling planners and operators educated at the graduate level. 509th Weapons School graduates have been invaluable in employing Air Force tankers supporting everything the US does on the world stage. They embody the motto of the US Air Force Weapons School: BUILD—TEACH—LEAD!